Cyber-Diplomacy

Cyber-Diplomacy

Managing Foreign Policy in the Twenty-first Century

EDITED BY
EVAN H. POTTER

McGill-Queen's University Press
Montreal & Kingston · London · Ithaca

© McGill-Queen's University Press 2002
ISBN 0-7735-2398-7 (cloth)
ISBN 0-7735-2451-7 (paper)

Legal deposit fourth quarter 2002
Bibliothèque nationale du Québec

Printed in Canada on acid-free paper that is 100% ancient forest free (100% post-consumer recycled), processed chlorine free.

This book has been published with the help of a grant from the Humanities and Social Sciences Federation of Canada, using funds provided by the Social Sciences and Humanities Research Council of Canada. Publication of this book has also been made possible by a grant from the Canadian Centre for Foreign Policy Development.

McGill-Queen's University Press acknowledges the support of the Canada Council for the Arts for our publishing program. We also acknowledge the financial support of the Government of Canada through the Book Publishing Industry Development Program (BPIDP) for our publishing activities.

National Library of Canada Cataloguing in Publication Data

Main entry under title:
  Cyber-diplomacy: managing foreign policy in the twenty-first century
  Includes index.
  ISBN 0-7735-2398-7 (bound). – ISBN 0-7735-2451-7 (pbk.)
  1. Canada – Foreign relations – 1945– I. Potter, Evan H. (Evan Harold), 1964–
  FC602.C92 2002   327.71   C2002-900586-8
  F1034.2.C69 2002

This book was typeset by Dynagram Inc.
in 10.5/13 Sabon.

To Harold Herbert Potter

Contents

Contributors / ix

Acknowledgments / xi

Introduction / 3
EVAN H. POTTER

1 Hyper-Realities of World Politics: Theorizing the Communications Revolution / 27
RONALD J. DEIBERT

2 New Technologies and Networks of Resistance / 48
ELIZABETH SMYTHE AND PETER J. SMITH

3 Real-Time Diplomacy: Myth and Reality / 83
EYTAN GILBOA

4 The New Media and Transparency: What Are the Consequences for Diplomacy? / 110
STEVEN LIVINGSTON

5 Snapshots of an Emergent Cyber-Diplomacy: The Greenpeace Campaign against French Nuclear Testing and the Spain-Canada "Fish War" / 128
ANDREW F. COOPER

6 The New Diplomacy: Real-Time Implications and Applications / 151
GORDON SMITH AND ALLEN SUTHERLAND

7 Information Technology and Canada's
  Public Diplomacy / 177
  EVAN H. POTTER

  Index / 201

Contributors

ANDREW F. COOPER is a professor in the Department of Political Studies at the University of Waterloo, Ontario.

RONALD J. DEIBERT is an associate professor in the Department of Political Science at the University of Toronto. He is the director of the Citizen Lab, a University of Toronto–based laboratory for research at the intersection of digital media and civic activism.

EYTAN GILBOA is a professor of communication and government and chair of the Department of Social Sciences at the Holon Institute of Technology in Israel. He is also affiliated with the Department of Political Studies at Bar-Ilan University, Israel.

STEVEN LIVINGSTON is the director of the Political Communication Program of the School of Media and Public Affairs at the George Washington University, Washington, D.C. He also serves as the chairman of the board of the Public Diplomacy Institute at the George Washington University.

EVAN H. POTTER is the founding editor of the quarterly *Canadian Foreign Policy* and was a senior strategist in the Communications Bureau at the Canadian Department of Foreign Affairs and International Trade. He teaches in the Department of Communications at the University of Ottawa.

GORDON SMITH was deputy minister of foreign affairs (1993–97) at the Canadian Department of Foreign Affairs and International Trade. He is the director of the Centre for Global Studies at the University of Victoria, British Columbia.

PETER J. SMITH is a professor at Athabasca University, Alberta.

ELIZABETH SMYTHE is an associate professor at Concordia University College of Alberta.

ALLEN SUTHERLAND, at the time of writing, was on the Policy Planning Staff at the Canadian Department of Foreign Affairs and International Trade. He is now at the Privy Council Office, Government of Canada.

Acknowledgments

A number of people are owed a particular debt for their contribution to the completion of this book. Many colleagues in the Department of Foreign Affairs and International Trade (DFAIT) were extraordinarily generous with their time and thoughts. Colin Robertson, who recruited me into the Canadian public service, deserves special recognition. He encouraged me to continue to pursue my scholarly work while I was at the Treasury Board of Canada Secretariat and later at DFAIT, recognizing the urgent need to nurture policy-relevant research that "bridges the gap" between the worlds of government and academe.

Two organizations in particular made this book possible: the Canadian Centre for Foreign Policy Development (CCFPD) at DFAIT and the University of Ottawa. Quite simply, the project could not have been done without the generous support of the CCFPD and its executive director, Steve Lee. The CCFPD's mission is to strengthen non-governmental participation in the development of foreign policy. This book is a contribution to such policy development. The University of Ottawa's Department of Communications has provided me with a collegial environment in which to pursue my research. I would like to thank Professor Sherry Ferguson and Dean of Arts David Staines for their support.

This project was conceived while I held a post-doctoral fellowship at the University of Toronto. I would like to thank Professor Janice Gross Stein of the University of Toronto for her support and encouragement. Among those others to whom I owe a debt of gratitude I would mention Gaston Barban, Curtis Barlow, Robin Brown, Daryl Copeland, Randolph Mank, Maureen Molot, Leslie Pal, Hugh Stephens, Brian Tomlin, Rhianon Vickers, and Roman Waschuk.

Needless to say, although many people have been involved – directly and indirectly – in the preparation of this book, the responsibility for any defects in the book's organization must rest with me. I have appreciated the patience of the many contributing authors to this volume. I am also very grateful for the detailed reports prepared by the anonymous reviewers for the Aid to Scholarly Publications Program of the Humanities and Social Sciences Federation of Canada.

It has been my good fortune to work with Roger Martin at McGill-Queen's University Press, who has been with me every step of the way – encouraging and cajoling – in short, patiently steering me through every shoal in the book production process. His sound advice and encouragement kept this project on track, whatever the difficulty. A number of research assistants have helped in the preparation of the manuscript and I would like to thank Alexander Lofthouse and Darrel Houlihan for their efforts. Judith Turnbull's copy editing was outstanding. Jenny Strickland is to be thanked for her patience in developing the index.

To all the people who helped bring this project to fruition, I give my heartfelt thanks.

Evan H. Potter
Ottawa

Cyber-Diplomacy

Introduction

EVAN H. POTTER

Although Marshall McLuhan's global village has not entirely taken the place of the nation-state, today's villages are so thoroughly interconnected that the Westphalian world that gave rise to modern diplomacy is less and less recognizable.[1] Global mass communications and advances in new information and communication technologies (ICTs) are posing a fundamental challenge to the traditional conduct of international relations by dispersing authority to multiple terrains, increasing the activism of a global civil society, and driving the expansion of global finance and trade. If, as Canadian scholar Harold Innis observed a half century ago, "sudden extensions of communication are reflected in cultural disturbances," then we are facing a "cultural disturbance of global proportions," one that may rival the move from the oral tradition to printing.[2]

We stand on the threshold of an information revolution in which electronic forms of communication, largely immune to regulation, will be the primary means of communication. As reported in 1998 by the Washington-based Center for Strategic and International Studies (CSIS), "hierarchy is giving way to networking," "openness is crowding out secrecy," and "ideas and capital move swiftly and unimpeded across a global network of governments, corporations, and non-governmental organizations."[3] The advances in information technology will act as catalysts for the forces of both fragmentation and integration in the current international system.

Increased availability of, access to, and speed of delivery of large quantities of news and information to a global audience in real time are making the management of state affairs more complex than ever. Multidirectionality (redundancy and multiple paths) in communications is replacing the traditional, hierarchical one-to-many communications model, ensuring that governments no longer enjoy the extensive control over information they once did.

There has been an unprecedented explosion in information choices for individuals in most parts of the world since the early 1990s as a result of affordable telephone, facsimile, and electronic mail applications. The mass media have experienced similar dramatic changes thanks to digital, wireless, and satellite technologies. Many countries have seen the number of available television channels mushroom from one or two (often state financed and controlled) to hundreds. Global television networks have emerged, most of them private and U.S. based, but viewers in Sao Paulo and Mexico City do receive channels originating in the United Kingdom, Spain, the Middle East, Germany, France, and Japan.

Of all the communication technologies, the ones that are destined to be the most democratic and widespread are the new media led by the Internet and new digital technologies. It is instructive to recall that the Internet expanded exponentially from 500 hosts in 1983 to an estimated 109.6 million hosts in 2001. The Internet is operational in 214 countries, with the most rapid growth outside the United States and Canada (Russia, Hong Kong, and Poland lead in web adoption). The United Kingdom currently has 33 million users and Sweden 5.7 million. In Japan, the number of Internet users has grown from 5.3 million in 1996 to 49 million in 2001. In just one year (between 2000 and 2001), global Internet use grew from 377 million to 544 million. With a new website created every four seconds, it is not stretching credulity to estimate a billion by 2005, and half the world's population by 2010.[4]

However, the technological advances are not just being made in new media; they are also affecting old technology such as radio. Audio programs are being carried by cable, satellite, and now increasingly the Internet as well. In a few years the technology will allow for the easy convergence of data, audio, and video transmissions into a single communications pathway, to offer what will no doubt be a staggering choice of information and entertainment.

If we were to summarize the effects of the new information revolution, we would talk about *interconnectivity, decentralization, acceleration, amplification,* and *hypertextuality.*[5] Higher connectivity among individuals, institutions, and communities results from the exponential increases in contacts made possible by public and private telecommunications infrastructures. This connectivity in turn leads to decentralization and the possibility of bypassing traditional authorities, whether in the public or private domain. One consequence of reducing everything to its digital form, so that any content (video, text, still pictures) can be stored on any medium (tape, computer, disk, CD) or transmitted through any medium (wire, ether, infrared, optic fibre), while at the same time increasing the power of digital processors, is that decision making is being accelerated. This forces government to be a real-time actor. With increasingly greater processing power and bandwidth (amplification), unprecedented volumes of information can be accessed from anywhere at any time (e.g., the World Wide Web) at lower and lower cost, leading to a state of hypertextuality. The consequence of low cost in combination with vast content storage and acceleration is greater interactivity; seemingly isolated actions, which are often unpredictable, create greater global volatility.

The less obvious effects of this revolution are *dislocation* and *diminishing asymmetry.* Dislocation refers to the disconnecting of transactions from physical location. For example, interest groups can move constantly from one location to another without having a national "home." Asymmetry refers to the traditional advantage in information control enjoyed by states and corporations. A by-product of the advances in communication technology is that much smaller organizations – sometimes even individuals – can now compete as the larger ones once did or still do.

As can be seen, then, communication networks now entwine the entire globe, with many of these networks bypassing traditional gatekeepers of information, be they controlled by the state or private sector. The combination of more global media, less costly technology, and the exponential growth of the Internet means that the degree of global transparency is destined to increase by several orders of magnitude in the next decade. As networking overtakes hierarchy and bureaucracy as the primary mode of organization and communication, it will become progressively more difficult for governments to control, shape, and influence information and its distribution. This is especially so as we move from mass to customized media. And with more and more sources of information competing for increasingly fragmented domestic and non-traditional audiences, it will be more and more difficult (*a*) to attract others' attention to one's ideas[6] and (*b*) to hear distinct national "voices" as nation-state "brands" (e.g., the "Cool Britannia" campaign) vie with one another as well as with corporate brands for the mind spaces of people around the world. In the words of Peter van Ham, "Image and attention are thus becoming essential parts of the state's strategic equity."[7]

The above observations should not be overstated, however. While the state is certainly losing its monopoly of information, it nonetheless retains privileged access to information and has the capacity, with sufficient political will and investment, to project its image and voice into the emerging hypermedia.[8] Despite the emergence of a global civil society fuelled by communication technologies, the state still has the power to shape the contours of the international system.

One further point about the present "cultural disturbance" needs to be emphasized. Whereas the change from the age of the printing press to the telegraph should be considered one of degree alone, the leap from the telegraph to the Internet is a matter of both degree and substance, since the speed *and* channels of communications have increased exponentially.[9] In such a complex environment, small changes have distant and unpredictable consequences, much like the deleterious effect in 1998 of Thailand's currency devaluation on global financial markets and thus on international economic stability. Quoting political scientist James Rosenau, the CSIS report states that "the prevailing global turbulence is profoundly non-linear, uneven in its evolution, uneven in its intensity, uneven in its scope, and uneven in its direction."[10] The report goes on to say: "The Newtonian world of cause and effect [does] not suffice to explain changes that may occur in a richly connected network. This connectivity leads to both integration (stability) as more people know more and fragmentation (instability) as this stability is undermined if the flow of information through the system is erroneous, that is, if feedback loops exacerbate rather than dampen minor disturbances."[11] For this reason, the system must provide timely and accurate information to its numerous interacting parts. In short, the system must enjoy a high level of trust.

Diplomacy at its core is about how states exchange, seek, and target information. This book concerns itself with how diplomacy is adapting to the new global information order. It has been obvious for some time that a number of interrelated and mutually reinforcing forces are ensuring that the pursuit of classic diplomacy will no longer suffice. These forces of change include the globalization of business and finance, growth of new media, and more active and assertive civil societies. But the primary mover of change, that force which lies behind and accelerates these other forces of change, as described above, is information technology. Where nations were once connected through foreign ministries and traders, they are now linked "through millions of individuals by fibre optics, satellite, wireless, and cable in a complex network without central control."[12]

These trends have led to considerable speculation about the future of diplomacy. Some practitioners and scholars have suggested that the media is driving foreign policy and that interest groups are driving government agendas, making foreign ministries increasingly irrelevant. It is pointed out as well that current means of issue management are destabilizing, as journalists and the public expect governments to state positions and decisions almost as soon as issues arise. What governments do, decide, and say abroad is playing back rapidly into public debates at home, and what governments do, decide, and say at home is playing back rapidly into their operations abroad. At the same time, ordinary members of the public, through the use of information technology, are developing new competencies for global engagement and mobilization on a cross-section of economic and security issues. Together these conditions are making the public dimension a central element of diplomacy.

Paradoxically, as much as communication technologies are drawing the public into the foreign policy decision-making process, they are also fragmenting the public into smaller and smaller "national" constituencies. These constituencies will be expected to support government action on the dominant foreign policy issues of the next millennium: democracy and human rights, weapons of mass destruction, global crime, chemical and biological warfare, environmental concerns, refugees and migration, and disease and famine. However, with a fragmented citizenry it will be that much harder to generate a national consensus, as was the case during the Cold War, on the national foreign policy priorities of the day. What may replace these national constituencies are transnational coalitions of like-minded individuals bound together by information technology. The growth in influence of global social movements since the early 1980s and particularly since the end of the Cold War is a portent of the power of civil society and a major challenge for traditional diplomacy.

The purpose of this book is to analyse the implications of the aforementioned changes and to submit some of the speculations to more rigorous analysis. The emergence of what Ronald J. Deibert (chapter 1) calls a global "hypermedia" has dramatically changed the environment for the conduct of diplomacy and raised questions about the continuing relevance of foreign ministries. The authors in this study test and examine these questions through the lenses of international relations theory, global media, innovations in communication technology, and the emergence of more activist social movements. The Canadian Department of Foreign Affairs and International Trade (DFAIT) is presented as a case study of a foreign ministry that in recent years has had to make considerable adjustments in three key areas: in the management of its information technology infrastructure; in the impact of ICTs on its diplomatic culture; and in the use of communication technology to promote its public diplomacy.

Three fundamental questions are posed in this volume: How does the "information revolution" presage a fundamental change in the goals, objectives, and purposes of diplomacy? What effects might this revolution have on the policy formulation process that diplomacy serves? And what are the revolution's potential implications for the execution of policy and how will it affect diplomacy's processes and organizational structures?

AN OVERVIEW OF THE VOLUME

In chapter 1 Ronald J. Deibert provides a critical overview of how major schools of thought within the field of international relations interpret the impact of new technologies on world politics. The pictures that emerge from each theoretical perspective are strikingly unique and provide different lessons for those interested in foreign policy and diplomacy. Realists see new technologies as an interesting wrinkle and a potential new tool in the age-old game of "power politics." Yet the limited scope of their inquiry may blind them to the more fundamental changes that are rewriting the rules of the game itself. The state-centric billiard-ball approach to world politics is anachronistic in the face of advances in communications. Liberals applaud new communication technologies as harbingers of freedom and democracy, but may be inured to the systemic inequalities and fragmentizing forces unleashed in their wake. Marxists and neo-Marxists offer forceful critical perspectives on the structures of power embedded in the global market system, but may be slighting the non-economic consequences of new communication technologies.

In light of these theories' shortcomings, Deibert proceeds to look at world politics from the perspective of communications theory. He introduces the "medium theory," asserting that it is the most compelling and comprehensive framework with which to assess the effects of new communication technologies on world politics. This theory of communications, associated with the writings of Harold Innis and Marshall McLuhan among others, proposes that technologies of communication are not mere transparent vessels, but are significant causal factors in their own right. Changing modes of communication, in other words, have important effects on society and politics. According to Deibert, this approach offers the best way to understand how world politics is being transformed in a hypermedia environment. He is careful to caution against monocausality and the sort of technological determinism implicit and explicit in the writings of some techno-evangelists and communications theorists. For Deibert, although the power of technologies to shape human affairs is certainly significant, it is distorting to portray technologies as generating specific social forces, images, and ideas. Technologies place obstacles and constraints in the paths of some forces, while providing intensity and dynamism to others. Diebert writes that a new mode of communication is not an agent, but rather an environment, "a passive structural feature of the technological landscape in which human beings interact." Existing social forces and ideas will flourish or wither depending on their "fitness" or match with the new communications environment. Deibert concludes that one of the most flourishing forces, albeit not fully understood, is the emerging global society that defines itself in the absence of a clearly demarcated political space.

The Internet appears tailor-made for global social movements. To test this assumption, Peter J. Smith and Elizabeth Smythe (chapter 2) examine the increased capacity of non-governmental organizations and transnational social movement organizations (TSMOs) to use new information and communication technologies to resist multilateral trade and investment arrangements and to thereby challenge the often very secret process of diplomatic negotiations. They demonstrate the advantages and disadvantages of the new communication technologies for social movements in two "campaigns of resistance," one against the Multilateral Agreement on Investment (MAI) and the other against the World Trade Organization meeting in Seattle.

The central question raised by the authors is whether the growing presence of transnational social movements, facilitated by ICTs, indicates that these networks are becoming more effective. Like other researchers, Smith and Smythe conclude that if effectiveness implies the ability to have a much greater direct influence on policy direction, then the answer continues to be a qualified "not yet." The authors would agree with Leslie A. Pal "that information, communication, and mobilization can all increase without necessarily increasing the impact," especially if these social movements run up against tyrannical regimes that care nothing of public opinion.[13] But this is not to say that the authors see no impact. Indeed, they point to the social movements' successful campaigns against the legitimacy of the whole trade negotiation process, citing public opinion data that show the public's concern with the impact that trade agreements have on the environment, social programs, and jobs. As well, some of the demands for transparency are being heard by governments. The authors note that while states have responded in a negative way to direct action by social movements, as demonstrated by the use of barricades and tear gas, countries such as Canada have also instituted elaborate consultation processes, with the Department of Foreign Affairs and International Trade establishing a consultation division and Canadian bureaucrats and parliamentarians holding hearings prior to the negotiation of any trade deal. While Smith and Smythe acknowledge that the impact of social movements is not easy to measure, they assert that the traditional focus on states as the primary actors of politics and international relations is no longer appropriate. That the meaning of politics, and by extension of diplomacy, is itself being reconsidered is no small achievement of the networked politics of nongovernmental organizations (NGOs) and TSMOs.

In chapter 3 Eytan Gilboa argues that the so-called CNN effect, widely viewed as a harbinger of the decline of diplomacy, has been exaggerated. Although global television has certainly brought new actors into the foreign policy process, has focused the world's attention on particular crises, and has accelerated the pace of diplomatic communication, there is insufficient evidence to assert that it has stripped foreign policy decision makers of control. One of the problems, according to the author, is that the term *CNN effect* has never been adequately defined, being based on a limited number of case studies. The roots of the CNN effect, Gilboa writes, harken back to the Vietnam era and the commonly held view that that war was lost in the living rooms of America; the current variant originated in American government circles in the early 1990s in connection with demands to intervene militarily on humanitarian grounds in countries experiencing gross human rights violations (e.g., Bosnia, Somalia, Rwanda).

Gilboa asserts that a credible answer to how CNN has affected contemporary diplomacy requires not only a careful look at the nature of global television and the major international events of the last decade, but also a close examination of how officials have coped with them. The chapter shows that even in the television age governments have been able to limit media coverage and control the degree to which sensitive information reaches the media and public. Despite the heightened transparency brought about by the emergence of global media, governments have still been able to engage in secret or semi-secret negotiations (what Gilboa refers to as "closed-door diplomacy") and media diplomacy in their attempts to resolve some of the most serious international crises of the last half century. For Gilboa, the major underlying condition that must exist for the media to be a dominant actor in the foreign policy process is governments' failure to exercise leadership and to articulate coherent approaches to foreign policy problems.

In chapter 4 Steven Livingston describes how we are fast moving into a "post–'CNN effect'" era of global transparency. The creation of smaller, lighter transmission equipment (e.g., satellite telephones and satellite uplink equipment), the miniaturization of surveillance mechanisms (e.g., micro-air vehicles), the reduction of satellite transmission costs, and the introduction of commercial high-resolution remote-sensing satellites will together create unprecedented levels of global transparency in public (and private) affairs. Livingston avers that the host of new technologies, previously only available to governments, are leading to a new phase of global transparency. The chapter considers whether the diplomat's position of authority within his or her own government and on the world stage, resulting from privileged access to information, is slipping away because these new technologies will be in civilian hands.

Livingston reports that such are the advances in technology on the civilian side that in 1990 the Sandia National Laboratories, using relatively imprecise ten-metre resolution SPOT satellite images, were able to detect the elements of the U.S. Army during the preparatory stage of the ground war in the Persian Gulf. Nine years later, an American satellite imaging company would launch the world's first one-metre resolution commercial satellite. Micro air vehicles, costing a few hundred dollars each, no more than six inches in length, height, or width, and weighing only a few ounces, will be able to provide reconnaissance and surveillance, battle-damage assessment, sensor placement, communications relay, and sensing of chemical, nuclear or biological hazards. Livingston believes that the lower cost of increasingly sophisticated equipment will mean that, unlike the situation today, where cost is a major factor in dictating international coverage, more images will be available from more remote locations. These images will be as likely to be found on an NGO website as on network news channels. A plethora of non-state actors armed with these new tools may also help governments in their efforts to control rogue states or prevent humanitarian crises. As Livingston writes, "The avalanche of information may ironically produce an effect similar to no information at all." Echoing the conclusions of Wolfe, he observes that the glut of information arising from this new level of transparency will in fact increase rather than lessen the need for diplomats, since there will be a strong need for credible and informed analysis from a national perspective.[14]

Andrew F. Cooper offers in chapter 5 two discrete case studies of the emergent use of new communication technologies to advance diplomatic objectives. Greenpeace's campaign against French nuclear testing in the South Pacific shows how a resource-rich NGO skilfully used new and old communication technologies to generate worldwide publicity in order to force political mobilization around a single issue. In the absence of an effective counter-communications campaign by the French government, Greenpeace was able to frame the issue largely on its own terms. That is not to say, however, that Greenpeace was successful in preventing the French nuclear testing, just in raising international public opinion against France on this issue. Indeed, the case pits the use of information as a "weapon" by an NGO against a state's traditional reservoir of coercive power in the form of military intervention, which was what France used to board the Greenpeace vessels. The other case, in which the resident Spanish ambassador to Canada attempted to use the Internet as the centrepiece in a campaign of public diplomacy during the "fish war" between Spain and Canada in 1994–95, highlights the limitations of the new technology. Although the Spanish embassy's use of the Internet was on balance not very effective in influencing public opinion (especially in Canada) and Spain was widely viewed as having lost the public relations war with Canada, this case is nonetheless an example of one of the earliest uses of the Internet in a public diplomacy campaign during a crisis.

The central lesson that Cooper draws from the two case studies is that societal actors as well as states have the capacity to exploit new technology. This is especially the case with NGOs, which do not have the same concerns about security and confidentiality that states have. NGOs can use the "anarchy" of the Net to their advantage, while states must adapt uneasily and slowly to the ongoing changes. The other lesson is that the new technology is still very much a novelty and cannot compensate for the lack of an integrated communications strategy or a compelling message.

In chapter 6 Gordon Smith and Allen Sutherland contend that rather than drifting into irrelevance, the nation-state is responding to the new communications environment by reinventing itself. The "government of the information age," they predict, will have adapted to the growing number of transnational issues "through a dense web of relations among regulatory agencies, courts, line departments, and international bureaus throughout the world." The core building blocks of such a transgovernmental order remain the nation-state and with it the foreign ministries that will be tasked to coordinate these relationships. Smith and Sutherland state that middle powers such as Canada will be well suited to the coming era of "networked diplomacy."

The authors give a number of examples of how Canada's Department of Foreign Affairs and International Trade has worked to integrate information technologies into its strategies and operating procedures. With the end of the Cold War and the proliferation of new states, DFAIT found that micro-missions, made possible through ICTs, are an excellent way of extending Canada's presence and influence to new parts of the world. Whereas it once took weeks or even months to establish a new embassy, Canada can now establish "just in time and place" operational effectiveness within a few hours. DFAIT uses virtual teams to respond to diplomatic crises, and it is clear that major initiatives (e.g., the campaign to ban landmines, known as the Ottawa Process) require significant coordination with civil society, facilitated through ICTs. The authors remind us that ICTs are also important vehicles for government program delivery. Foreign ministries serve as Canada's public face and as access points for a growing number of citizens abroad, which means that consular services will have to be integrated with broader government electronic service delivery, such as website travel advisories. Finally, the authors emphasize that knowledge management, including innovative use of ICTs, must be cultivated at the organizational level to a far greater extent than is currently the case in many diplomatic organizations.

Following Smith and Sutherland's more general discussion of DFAIT, Evan H. Potter argues in chapter 7 that with the growing array of non-traditional security issues (drug trafficking, infectious diseases, terrorism) and the increasing availability of, access to, and speed of delivery of information (all of which are giving social movements new competencies and confidence), governments' ability to promote their views to foreign publics has become a central feature of diplomacy. Advances in ICTs offer an opportunity to redefine public diplomacy, to move it from the sidelines to the core of diplomacy. This chapter shows that Canada, as a middle power with limited military might but possessing an international reputation as a coalition builder, as a country with a highly educated population, and as a leader in the development of communication technology, is in an ideal position to redefine its public diplomacy.

Canada should be able to use the leverage of its know-how in the new technology to promote its intellectual leadership on a multiplicity of fronts and in so doing enhance its "soft power." However, as Potter explains, the paradox of Canadian diplomacy has been that despite these favourable conditions, Canadian interests are at risk of being drowned out "amid a cacophony of competing voices" in the international arena.

Potter writes that in the face of a decade's worth of declining Foreign Affairs' budgets, the new and old communication technologies' potential to advance Canada's interests to foreign audiences has not been fully exploited. For example, Ottawa, in contrast to its main competitors, has not identified international broadcasting as a key element in its public diplomacy approach. Potter is concerned that Canada is not taking full advantage of the opportunities to position itself in a networked world. Without a coordinated and adequately funded international information strategy, Canada risks having a declining national presence.

MAIN THEMES AND DEBATES

Six main themes run through this study. The first concerns *the enabling power of information technologies,* allowing individuals to interact and organize at unprecedented levels. Several authors reflect on how the very nature of the technology – its looseness and low cost – has allowed small organizations and individuals to achieve levels of influence that would have been unimaginable in the past. Cooper reminds us that almost three decades ago Canadian scholar James Eayrs predicted that technological advances in electronic communication and easy availability of information would allow "reasonably literate, fairly persistent, moderately affluent," and one assumes fairly average *individuals* to make their marks on history by setting up their own foreign ministries in their basements.[15] And as Pal has noted in his portrait of the on-line human rights community of the late 1990s, one of the most popular human rights websites was the fruit of just one person's labours.[16] Private citizens, then, can now use technology against the superior resources of government or business, to level the playing field. Ironically, what we see in one of Cooper's case studies is that the empowered individual in question is actually a government official – the Spanish ambassador to Canada – who takes it upon himself, with little support from his own government, to use the Internet to fight an information war with the Canadian government. The point is that the wide availability of the new technology invites innovative use by everyone; it is profoundly democratic.

The second theme concerns *technological determinism*, which is implicit if not explicit in much of the commentary on the effects of the new technology. The authors in this volume would agree that the new communication and information technologies are drivers of change, although it is recognized that they do not exist in isolation of other drivers. Perhaps what makes the current advances in communications so noteworthy in comparison to previous major changes is that the new medium is interactive, not passive like print, radio, and television. But as powerful a driver as we think ICTs may be, as Keohane and Nye assert, "[p]olitics will affect the information revolution as much as vice versa."[17] Indeed, the assembled authors are very cautious about making sweeping predictions about the ultimate impact of ICTs on social, economic, and political life. What their chapters provide are examples, vignettes, and case studies indicating possible (if not probable) changes in the conduct of diplomacy.

Referring to Greenpeace's campaign against the French, Cooper notes that it is unlikely that this organization, despite its size, would have been able to feed into the groundswell of citizen activism around the world to anywhere near the degree that it did in the absence of the new technology. While technology was certainly responsible for the increased activism, the question is whether it caused this activism. An answer is provided in Pal's observation that the new communications environment – and the existence of the World Wide Web in particular – created the conditions for new human rights organizations to come into existence, which supports Deibert's assertion that communication technology is not an agent but rather an "environment," allowing certain social forces either to flourish or to wither.

The third theme refers to *the normative judgments surrounding the issue of secrecy and exclusivity in the domain of foreign affairs*. Most of the authors in this volume bemoan the culture of secrecy and exclusivity that pervades classic diplomacy, in effect taking a leaf out of the spirited debate in intellectual circles on the existing "democratic deficit" and growing citizen alienation from government in Western societies. Smith and Sutherland write that "a sophisticated citizenry, able to access multiple sources of information, is suspicious of leaders and will no longer tolerate secrecy." As the debate over the MAI showed in 1998, traditionally hidebound institutions such as foreign ministries will no longer be given the latitude to make all major decisions behind closed doors and to plead the sanctity of state-to-state negotiations. Citizens want to feel that they have been consulted on governmental directions, including on matters of foreign policy. Foreign ministries, from the U.K.'s Foreign and Commonwealth Office to Canada's Department of Foreign Affairs and International Trade to the U.S. State Department, are attempting to embark on more collaborative relationships with the public by creating and maintaining attractive, more interactive websites and by making an effort to connect with their citizens through enhanced domestic outreach programs.[18] In a networked world, foreign ministries of one country will not only consult regularly with their own citizens but will also consult the citizens of their target countries more frequently and directly.

Smith and Smythe, Livingston, and Smith and Sutherland all see ICTs as fundamental to the new clout of NGOs and as formidable artillery to be used against the walls of exclusivity so carefully constructed by the diplomatic corps. Decentralized networks coexist and interact uneasily with the hierarchical nature of traditional bureaucratic organizations, which tend to control and compartmentalize information. Nevertheless, the increased transparency of a networked world is a powerful incentive for government officials to increase and strengthen their connections with civil society. For the authors, this is an inherently positive effect of advances in communications technologies.

That being said, a number of authors refer to the challenges inherent in creating a culture of openness in foreign ministries. Despite the acknowledged influence that social movements are gaining, Smith and Smythe, based on their examination of the Canadian Department of Foreign Affairs and International Trade, note that very few foreign ministries have developed sophisticated protocols to enhance interactive contact with citizens. For example, public diplomacy continues to be very passive and to consist largely of putting information on websites in contrast to actively engaging the interested public. Smith and Sutherland comment on the generational divide in foreign ministries, with the more senior diplomats still suspicious of the new openness being brought about by the technology.

Additionally, the evidence compiled by the authors reminds us that total transparency – even if possible – is not in the best interests of the state and its society, and that the benefits of multi-directionality do not just accrue to civil society. The authors would agree that there is a legitimate role for exclusivity and secrecy in state-to-state and state–civil society relations. Using the Arab-Israeli peace process as an example, Gilboa points out that successful diplomacy (like most forms of negotiations) still requires some degree of secrecy. And in an era of economic diplomacy, where foreign ministries and ambassadors are increasingly being tasked to support commercial interests, it is crucial for governments to guarantee that information circulating between themselves and their business communities will remain confidential. Furthermore, a foreign ministry's official representatives abroad, even in down-sized one-person offices made possible by communication technology, provide privileged information to their home governments by virtue of their private (and often personal) access to local government elites, a source of access that is often not available to the international media or international NGOs.

The above discussion cautions us not to exaggerate the benefits of the total transparency of a networked age, but we need not focus exclusively on the interests of the state to reach this conclusion. Pal has described how an Amnesty International campaign was derailed because of insufficient secrecy. Amnesty, by using e-mail action messages to build opposition against an execution in Texas, unwittingly ended up allowing supporters of the execution (once alerted to Amnesty's intentions on the Internet) to mobilize a counter-campaign. It turns out that the pro-execution campaign mobilized more citizens to send in letters to the Texas governor than did Amnesty's.[19]

Finally, while the World Wide Web, low-level private spy satellites, miniaturized highly mobile communications, and 24-hour global television networks all challenge the diplomat's exclusive access to timely, relevant information, we must remember that these same technologies can also be used by the diplomat for a multitude of purposes, including advocacy, surveillance, and disinformation. In other words, just as the networked world can increase the power of civil society, it can also increase the power of governments and their foreign ministries.

The fourth theme concerns the *credibility of information*. Credibility will be the new "edge" in international relations in the face of information overload.[20] Livingston writes that the paradox of the information age is the inverse relationship between information flow and information reliability. The overabundance of information risks drowning out any knowledge, a phenomenon that will actually raise rather than lessen the import and profile of foreign ministries. Though this may seem counter-intuitive given the earlier acknowledgment that government is losing its monopoly on information, it remains that foreign ministries are quintessential knowledge organizations. Using their analysts, linguists, and networks of representatives abroad to sift through and critically evaluate often contradictory information from a multiplicity of sources, foreign ministries will play key roles in helping their governments to formulate policy based on credible analysis.

Further, it is tempting to jump to the conclusion that NGOs will be competing with states, and winning, in information wars in an age of civilian satellites and inexpensive micro air vehicles. But, as Livingston cautions, the fact remains that the use of experts – for example, to interpret photo imagery – will still be required. It so happens that many of these "knowledge workers" are trained and employed by governments. In an information era when credibility is crucial, inaccurate interpretation by well-intentioned amateurs is a real risk and could do incalculable damage to organizations that depend on donations for their survival. Indeed, some NGOs have already learned the hard way that there is a high price to pay if they dabble in exaggeration as they make use of the real-time news environment. As journalist Nik Gowing points out in his examination of the reaction of certain NGOs during the Great Lakes crisis of 1996–97, the medium- to long-term cost in credibility, integrity, and image to NGOs is likely to be far higher than any short-term tactical advantage.[21]

The authors of this volume would agree that, despite often lagging behind the private sector in the introduction of new technologies, states continue to have the institutional capacity and authority to provide – should they choose to – credible information. For this reason Gilboa opines that states should be given much more credit for their ability to frame news reporting, even in a multi-source media environment. Indeed, it is this very environment of increasingly diverse information sources that is forcing states to strive to achieve more credibility with their publics.

The fifth theme is *the operational adaptation of foreign ministries to the new information technologies*. While it is important to abandon outmoded computer systems and to upgrade the mobility of operations, as Smith and Sutherland make clear, the major challenge for foreign ministries will be to change organizational culture. In the case of Canada's foreign ministry, Smith and Sutherland conclude that 85 per cent of the challenge involves staffing practices and operating procedures. With regard to the latter, although the impact of the Internet should not be exaggerated, it appears that foreign ministries are under-utilizing the capacity of the web to engage in interactive information exchange. Many sites, although very attractive and professional, are not much more than electronic versions of printed materials.

Foreign ministries must also be consistent. With so many sources of information, they can no longer speak differently to different audiences, although, as Pal has recommended, when it comes to on-line interactions, foreign ministries should take more care in calibrating their approaches to the different types of groups on the Internet (e.g., campaign activists, informational and network groups). There is also a need to use new language, since civil society groups – businesses, NGOs, or ethnic minorities at home – are using the language of "emotional persuasion" rather than the technical discourse of traditional diplomacy.[22]

New communication technologies provide new opportunities for diplomats to reach target audiences, domestic and foreign. The greater the public dimension to foreign policy, the greater the incentive for foreign ministries to use the new media to bypass traditional filters such as the mainstream media. But this should in no way imply that the mainstream media is no longer being used as the principal instrument in talking to foreign and domestic publics. The fact remains that while audiences may be fragmenting, foreign ministries will continue to rely heavily on mainstream media to check public opinion and to deliver key messages.[23] And with regard to efforts to reach foreign publics, Cooper highlights in his case study of the Canada-Spain fisheries dispute that for high-profile public diplomacy campaigns to be a success there must be a symbiotic relationship between the use of new media (e.g., the Internet) and traditional, state-to-state confidential personal diplomacy. One of the reasons that Spain lost this information "war" to Canada was that its traditional diplomatic efforts ("working" the Canadian political system from the inside through private meetings with senior Canadian officials) were not synchronized with its attempt to use information technologies to support its bottom-up public diplomacy campaign.

As government is being asked to be more accountable and transparent, foreign ministries are responding by using information technology to provide the public with an entrée into the decision-making process. They are setting up dedicated websites for high-profile initiatives in order to better inform and consult with both domestic and foreign audiences. In addition to the bricks and mortar of legations, these sites will increasingly become vital national showcases, allowing countries to brand themselves and promote their advantages to the world twenty-four hours a day. What is apparent is that the pressure to "keep up," technologically speaking, is relentless, yet there is a realization that there is no choice.

The last theme is *the confluence of information technology, the democratization of foreign policy, and the notion of soft power*. As mentioned, narrow security concerns no longer dominate the diplomatic agenda. In addition to the rise of economic diplomacy, new transnational issues such as infectious diseases, the environment, natural resources, terrorism, and drug trafficking have become much more important. These so-called cooperative security issues are areas that require extensive lobbying of domestic and foreign audiences, including increasingly foreign civil societies. Foreign ministries are using communications technology to support the use of soft power, which can be defined as the art of attracting "willing followers" and persuading and lobbying nations to support one's foreign policy initiatives. It can be argued, for example, that during the Cold War, with the international system divided among the East, West, and the non-aligned nations, the creation of such willing followers was not really possible, since any issue-specific alliances (especially if they cut across camps) were invariably affected by the prevailing East-West confrontation. Today, with the international agenda expanded beyond traditional security issues, not only are such alliances emerging regularly, but the lobbying of civil societies and the and building of coalitions with them (both at home and abroad) are core elements of the successful projection of soft power. This is why public diplomacy has been raised as key to the diplomacy of the future. Coalition building with civil society actors has become an increasingly significant part of the diplomatic function. In this regard, new technology has made NGOs increasingly effective sources of information, highly useful in gauging international and domestic support for national policies.

CONCLUSION

The rapid evolution of ICTs makes it difficult to predict the exact shape of the cultural revolution being brought about by the new information age. It is still unclear how mass communications and the new information technologies are affecting the balance of power between the state and other actors in the international system. The most extreme scenarios foresee unscrupulous individuals or groups holding governments and their societies hostage through info-terrorism. At the other extreme is the view that ICTs will give governments unchecked powers of surveillance and control. This volume supports the view that some state capacities will be enhanced by ICTs, but that on balance the impact of the new information age will see a reduction in state authority as other non-state actors become more influential. Certainly, advances in ICTs are ensuring that the balance will shift, but the power of the state will not wither away quickly. A full transfer of authority away from the state is still generations away. The reason is largely self-evident: the nation-state quite simply retains an organizational capacity that continues to eclipse those of most non-governmental communities.

Whatever the changes, they do not signal the end of diplomacy; the professional diplomat will not fade into "deliquescence."[24] For all the prognostications of the techno-evangelists and the post-modernists, governments' abilities to pursue policy objectives have not yet been deeply compromised by a hypermedia environment. A far more positive, yet realistic, tone concerning the role of the state pervades the writing of the contributors to this volume. The authors do not hear the death-knell of traditional diplomacy; what they see as passé is the pursuit of a diplomacy that self-consciously diminishes and underfunds its public face. Indeed, the chapters point out that diplomacy is remarkably resilient. What becomes clear is not that diplomacy is in decline, but that it has the ability to adapt – albeit slowly in the case of some foreign ministries – to the promises and challenges of the networked age.

The following are some concluding observations based on the findings in this volume:

1 Information technology and the rise of the mass media, while levelling the playing field, do not portend an inexorable decline in the utility of foreign ministries – quite the opposite in fact. The explosion of information increases the need for credible sources of information. Diplomatic missions therefore will continue to play a key role in turning information into knowledge for national decision makers.
2 The same technologies that are heralded as ushering a new age of transparency are the ones that can be used by the state to increase its own surveillance, reconnaissance, and communication needs.
3 It has been fashionable to point out that the new media led by the Internet and expanding global media organizations have radically changed the power equation between government and the media. What is less frequently pointed out is that governments lose control of the policy-making agenda to the media when they fail to exercise strong leadership and that media technology is rarely as powerful in the hands of journalists as it is in the hands of government officials and politicians.
4 The public diplomacy activities of foreign ministries have been characterized as either the propaganda arm of foreign ministries or relics of the Cold War. However, the end of the Cold War has allowed for a statecraft that accords greater importance to mission-oriented diplomacy that cuts across traditional cleavages in the international system. As a result, public diplomacy has become a more important instrument for dealing with post–Cold War challenges. Of all the public diplomacy tools, those affected most by the new technology are international broadcasting – radio, television, and the new media. Whereas in the post-war period these instruments were used to attempt to change ideological "mind space," today there is a need to use these instruments for "peace broadcasting" in zones of conflict (e.g., former Yugoslavia) and, in light of the 11 September 2001 attack on the United States, for a coordinated and more intensive use of the international broadcasting arms of the American, British, German, and Canadian governments to help clarify and explain the West's actions to the Islamic world.

5 While Internet access is severely limited today in many countries, within a decade it will be available practically everywhere. This fact raises one major caveat: "The price of admission is no longer measured in kilowattage or broadcast hours, but in the quality and presentation of the information."[25] The same can be said for foreign ministries' use of the Internet. While their presence on all media is important, presence alone will not be enough. It will have to be combined with high-quality and distinctive programming.

NOTES

1 Barry Fulton, *Reinventing Diplomacy in the Information Age: Final Draft* (Washington, D.C.: Center for Strategic and International Studies, 9 October 1998), www.csis.org/ics/dia, 13 (hereafter referred to as CSIS report). I disagree with the CSIS report's contention that the "Westphalian world in which modern diplomacy was born is no longer recognizable." Since 1998, a number of studies have reviewed the changing nature of diplomacy. Their titles and the websites on which they are available are as follows: "America's Overseas Presence in the 21st Century," at www.state.gov/www/publications/9911 opap/rpt-9911 opap instructions.html; "Equipped for the Future: Managing U.S. Foreign Affairs in the 21st century," at www.stimson.org/pubs/ausia/ausrl.pdf; "Global Trends 2015: A dialogue about the Future with Nongovernment Expets," at www.cia.gov/cia/publications/globaltrends2015/index.html; and "Information Age diplomacy," at www.ndu.edu/ndu/nwc/Public/SymposiumWebsite/symposium main.htm.
2 Harold A. Innis, *The Bias of Communication* (Toronto: University of Toronto Press, 1951), 31 (as quoted in CSIS report, 13); and CSIS report, 13.
3 Ibid., 8.
4 Ibid., 8–9.
5 I have drawn on the definitions of interconnectivity, decentralization, acceleration, and amplification from David J. Rothkopf, "Cyberpolitik: The Changing Nature of Power in the Information Age," *Journal of International Affairs* 51, no. 2 (Spring 1998): 334–6. On hypertextuality, see Derrick de Kerckhove, *Connected Intelligence: The Arrival of Web Society* (Toronto: Somerville House Publishing, 1997), xxviii.
6 As Keohane and Nye point out, the most important challenge in the "information age" is not the adjustment to the speed of transmission

(after all, as they note, the Atlantic cable in 1866 reduced the time of communications between London and New York from about a week to a few minutes) but rather the adjustment to the increased connectivity combined with "vastly reduced costs" (236), which means that the "scarce resource" in our age is the capacity to attract attention (219), which in turn raises the issue of how actors maintain credibility for their actions. Robert Keohane and Joseph S. Nye, *Power and Interdependence*, 3rd ed. (New York: Longman, 2001).

7 Peter van Ham, "The Rise of the Brand State: The Postmodern Politics of Image and Reputation," *Foreign Affairs* 80, no. 5 (September/October 2001).

8 For a definition of hypermedia, see chapter 1.

9 See Johanna Neuman, *Lights, Camera, War: Is Media Technology Driving International Politics?* (New York: St Martin's Press, 1996).

10 Rosenau, quoted in CSIS report, 31.

11 CSIS report, 32.

12 Ibid., 8.

13 Leslie A. Pal, "Bits of Justice: Human Rights on the Internet," unpublished manuscript, 1998.

14 This is the thrust of Robert Wolfe's chapter ("The Many Diplomatic Missions of Canada's Ambassadors," esp. 19–20, 23) in Robert Wolfe, ed., *Diplomatic Missions: The Ambassador in Canadian Foreign Policy* (Kingston, Ont.: School of Policy Studies, Queen's University and Canadian Centre for Foreign Policy Development, 1998).

15 James Eayrs, *Diplomacy and Its Discontents* (Toronto: University of Toronto Press, 1971), 78.

16 Pal, "Bits of Justice."

17 Robert O. Keohane and Joseph S. Nye, Jr, "Power and Interdependence in the Information Age," *Foreign Affairs* 77, no. 5: 85.

18 The U.K.'s Foreign and Commonwealth Office (FCO), while recognized for the quality of its websites and their feedback mechanisms, does not have a comprehensive domestic outreach program.

19 Pal, "Bits of Justice."

20 See Joseph S. Nye, Jr, and William A. Owens, "America's Information Edge," *Foreign Affairs* 75, no. 2 (March-April 1996): 20–36.

21 Nik Gowing, "New Challenges and Problems for Information Management in Complex Emergencies," ECHO, May 1998, 66. Gowing states that [w]hile an effective information control campaign was being waged against them, NGOs responded in desperation during the Great Lakes crisis by providing wild estimates to a media, which then turned on them."

22 Chris Langdon, "The Global Information Revolution and International Relations," Summary Notes of Wilton Park Conference, 14–18 September 1998, Wilton Park, Sussex, U.K., 2.
23 There has been a greater effort by DFAIT in recent years to direct its communications beyond Ottawa's press gallery and to target community newspapers and the ethnic press. There is no corporate monitoring of the Internet as there would be for, say, the daily print and broadcast media. Monitoring of the Internet is left to individual divisions.
24 Eayrs, *Diplomacy*, 69.
25 CSIS report, 66; for example, Radio Moscow, during the Soviet period, blanketed the short-wave frequencies with its programming, but this did not ensure that anyone was listening, given other choices such as the BBC. I am indebted to my colleague Gaston Barban for this observation.

1 Hyper-Realities of World Politics: Theorizing the Communications Revolution

RONALD J. DEIBERT

We live in a world deeply saturated with new technologies of digital-electronic telecommunications, what I call *hypermedia*.[1] Most everyone senses that these technologies are transforming economics, society, and politics. Yet beyond this intuitive feeling that change is occurring, there is wide disagreement over its precise direction or nature. Such disagreement is fuelled by two factors: widespread speculation on the implications of hypermedia coupled with the radical explosion in the means of disseminating such opinions to a global audience. One of the consequences of the "democratization" of mass broadcasting unleashed by the World Wide Web, in other words, is that anyone can present his or her views – however hastily conceived – to a potentially global audience.

Most often, the views put forth boil down to one or the other of two propositions. In one formulation, we are told that the "information revolution" is breaking down hierarchies, authoritarian regimes, and closed societies while generating openness, integration, freedom, and democratic tranquillity.[2] In the other popular view, we are warned that the "panoptic" power of states and corporations allows these bodies, with the aid of cyberspatial tools of surveillance, to penetrate the most private lives of individuals.[3] If we were to follow these projections to their logical conclusion, we would be left with two mutually exclusive types of world order: a globally integrated, hyper-libertarian system on the one hand, and a tightly compartmentalized, state-centric, "corporatist" system on the other. Digging further, we would find that at the root of these projections is the simplistic and deterministic assumption that the new technologies are technologies either of "freedom" or "control." With this discovery, however, we would be left with empty compliments to nothing, for technologies are never inherently "of" anything apart from the social context in which they are situated. To say that hypermedia are technologies of freedom or control is to beg the questions, "freedom from what?", "freedom for whom?", "control over what?", and "control by whom?"

Such assertions should come as no surprise to those who study communications, for they echo refrains that have been voiced with every abrupt technological change in history. The idea that technologies of communication radically affect the societies that employ them can be traced as far back as the first communication technologies themselves. Although we now attribute the invention of writing in ancient civilizations to the pressures of urbanization and economics, cultures at the time looked upon them with a sense of religious awe and mystery, believing them to be the gifts of omnipotent gods.[4] Indeed, so seemingly powerful are the inventions of communication technologies that they have nearly always elicited hyperbole from those living at the time. Those witnessing the invention of the telegraph, for example, spoke of the "annihilation of space," while the anarchist Petr Kropotkin, in a phrase that would echo again years later with Marshall McLuhan, believed that electronics would rescue civilization from the horrors of modern industrialism by creating blissful "industrial villages."[5] Of course, it is difficult to provide a true account of fundamental changes as one lives through them, with exaggeration in one direction or the other an ever-present temptation, but if the past is any guide, we can probably safely assume that a pure utopia, or its absolute negation, will not be the outcome of only the latest (and certainly not the last) technological change in communications.

To raise the level of discussion beyond such fantastic speculation, we need to think theoretically about how communication technologies are affecting world politics. Yet in an attempt to do so, we run up against the relative scarcity of available theories. There are very few research studies of communications and world politics, and thus few theories on the subject. The main subfield in political science devoted to the study of world politics – international relations (IR) – has largely ignored communication technologies until very recently. A quick scan of the last decade's worth of research in the main journals – *International Organization*, *International Secu-*

rity, and *World Politics* – reveals only a handful of articles with even a passing relevance to the topic. The discipline formed around the study of communications, on the other hand, has operated largely unaware of the theories and traditions of the IR field. Moreover, communications studies have tended to concentrate on "societies" in the abstract (typically with the British or American societies as the default) as opposed to relations between existing states or societies. Studies of "international" communications in the communications field have been rare.

In this chapter, I provide a critical overview of different theories of communications and world politics. For the most part, the overview concentrates on how existing schools or paradigms treat communications within the international relations field. Finding all of the major paradigms lacking in one respect or another, I turn in the second half of the chapter to an approach derived from the communications field, but not applied to world politics per se, called *medium theory*. In accord with the ideas of Harold Innis, Marshall McLuhan, and others, the basic proposition of medium theory is that technologies of communication are not mere transparent vessels, but are significant causal factors in their own right. Changing modes of communication, in other words, have important effects on society and politics. With appropriate modifications, I argue that this approach offers the most useful lens through which to view how world politics is being transformed in the global hypermedia environment. In the chapter's conclusion, I sketch some trends that may provide grounds for further research. As I will suggest below, new communication technologies are fundamentally altering the landscape of world politics in several ways: dispersing authority to multiple domains; transforming the nature of states; facilitating the rise of powerful global capitalist forces; and fuelling the emergence of a nebulous global civil society. In the face of these changes, the state-centric, billiard-ball approach to world politics is becoming increasingly useless.

THEORIES OF COMMUNICATIONS AND WORLD POLITICS

Realism

The dominant theoretical approach to world politics in the international relations field is called *realism*, a somewhat loose collection of insights, hypotheses, shared orientations, and assumptions about politics reaching back to ancient Greece. It is difficult to capture within a single frame a tradition of theorizing that purportedly spans writers as diverse as Thucydides, Augustine, Machiavelli, Hobbes, Hans Morgenthau, and Kenneth Waltz, among others. Yet within the latter half of the twentieth century, the realist approach to world politics has crystallized into a recognizable set of core assumptions. Of these, the two most important are that self-interested states are the most important actors and that anarchy is the ordering principle of the international system.[6] From these initial assumptions, several interrelated hypotheses follow, most of which centre on the inherently conflictual nature of world politics. Realism is, generally, a pessimistic account of international relations, with cooperation rare and the recourse to war always imminent.

Since so much of the realist picture of the world operates as bedrock assumption, it is not surprising that realists have been slow to contemplate how communication technologies may be changing world politics. At best, realists situate technological changes as aspects of shifts in the composition of power wielded by states or state-like units. Robert Gilpin thus argues that the most important effect of technological change in the transportation and communications arena involves "the loss of strength gradient" – that is, the degree to which effective military power of a state or political unit diminishes as distance from the centre increases.[7] More recent analyses of "the revolution in military affairs" associated with communications focus, likewise, on changes in techniques of warfare that might, in turn, affect the relative power, influence, and capabilities of states.[8] Also reflecting realist impulses would be those who see a shift to "soft power" competition among states, which means a reallocation of resources to cultural, as opposed to military, capabilities.[9] In each case, new communication technologies are framed in terms of their impact upon state power or strategic competition between states.

What is interesting, for the purposes of this chapter, is how much fails to register on the realist theoretical radar screen. Given realists' underlying, unchanging assumptions about the character of world politics, this is to be expected. For realists, communication technologies may change "the play of power politics" but not the stage upon which that play is performed.[10] Yet it may be on the stage itself that the most interesting consequences of new communication technologies are unfolding. Obscured and overlooked by realists, then, are the myriad of new social actors and groups that are flourishing in the hypermedia environment: transnational corporations, massive multi-media conglomerates, bond-rating agencies, multinational investment firms, civil society activists, and networks of feminists, gays, deep ecologists, cults, religious sects (what Smythe and Smith call Transnational Social Movement Organizations, see chapter 2), international institutions, regimes, and organizations. Whether these groups are serving to "unbundle" identities, authorities, territoriality, and/or sovereignty is – to be sure – a contentious question. Yet realism provides no leverage on this issue because it conceals the question from theoretical view. Such a blinder is all the more conspicuous given that the origins of the state system itself (which serves as the backdrop and starting point for realism) coincided with the last major shift in communication technologies: the invention of the printing press.[11]

Liberalism

While a case could be made that the bulk of social science has been carried on within the framework of a broadly *liberal* paradigm, liberals have been in the minority within the international relations field. In part, this is related to the object of study – the *Westphalian* international system – which throughout the modern period has been characterized mostly by the absence of governance. The division of political authority into territorially distinct sovereign states after the Peace of Westphalia in 1648 created conditions for the "good life" within state boundaries, but projected outward an anarchic system between them.[12] Realists have employed this historical condition as a first-order assumption; liberals, on the other hand, have viewed it as something to be overcome in time by rules, laws, and international institutions.[13] Given that the success of the latter has happened in fits and starts, and has only become slowly entrenched since the end of the Second World War, it is not surprising that liberals have been among the minority in the field.

One interpretation of the liberal IR tradition suggests that it is characterized by three main assumptions: (1) individual human beings, or collections of individual human beings, are the most important actors; (2) their interests or values (and hence the interests and values of states) are multiple and changing; and (3) international relations and politics generally – driven by processes of modernization

– are pushing history in the direction of greater "progress" and welfare.[14] Although each of these assumptions raises interesting issues and debates, it is the last of them that is the most relevant to the liberal view on how new communication technologies may be affecting world politics.

Liberals see processes of modernization, and developments in communications in particular, as serving to diminish the persistent insecurity of the international system in several overlapping ways. First, increased flows of communication are viewed as offering the prospect of enhanced mutual understanding and cooperation between states and individuals around the world. Karl Deutsch, one of the few international relations scholars to devote the bulk of his research program to communications, was the major exponent of this view.[15] For Deutsch, the uneven division of political authority among nation-states was a reflection of the "uneven distribution of overlapping clusters of communications facilities." Deutsch believed that increased flows of communications across borders would generate expanded "we-feelings" among disparate peoples, integrating political communities and creating supra-nations in regions like Europe and elsewhere – "pluralistic security communities" as he called them. For Deutsch and for liberals in general, such a view reflected an underlying belief that people are inherently good and that, once supplied with enough information and knowledge, they would overcome the ignorance that breeds conflict and develop common identities and mutual understanding.

Liberals also believe that, in addition to nurturing we-feelings, increased flows in communication have a material-structural effect. New communication technologies, it is argued, increase mutual interdependence and interpenetration between states, a process generally encouraged by liberals. The causal process runs as follows: increased flows of communications across borders generate growing interdependence; and greater interdependence, in turn, creates rational disincentives against going to war, as well as a mutual interest in working problems out peacefully through international institutions. The latter binds states together in webs of cooperation; international anarchy, in turn, is gradually overcome by ever-expanding layers of international governance and communication flows between states. From these circumstances we may surmise that the basic state of the human condition (if such a thing can be generalized in global terms) is on the upswing, grounded in ever more deeply entrenched systems of international law and complex interdependence.[16]

The third liberal argument, similar to the first, is that new communication technologies place obstacles in the path of centralized, hierarchical forms of political rule. Authoritarian states, and all forms of hierarchy in general, are said to be unsustainable in the face of digital telecommunications and networked computing, whose communications are difficult, if not impossible, to control and contain.[17] A common illustration used to bolster this argument is the failed Soviet coup attempt in 1991.[18] Following the coup, the authorities who had usurped power found that they could not reimpose centralized control over communications within and outside the Soviet Union. Similar forces are said to be bearing down today on authoritarian states like Singapore and China, in Asia, and Iran and Saudi Arabia, in the Middle East. Liberals believe that the properties of hypermedia naturally encourage liberal-democratic, non-hierarchical forms of political rule.

The basic arguments comprising the liberal position cited above can also be found in government policies, in scattered popular media accounts, and in more substantive academic studies of global politics. Former U.S. vice-president Al Gore, for example, heralded the Internet and the development of a "global information infrastructure" as a harbinger of progress towards democracy and freedom around the world. The popular *Wired* magazine has issued a lengthy treatise on the so-called Long Boom of economic prosperity, openness, and international cooperation unleashed by new digital-telecommunication technologies.[19] And Kenichi Ohmae has coined perhaps the most succinct eulogism of the liberal position on world politics and communications: the coming "borderless world."[20]

Certainly a great many trends could be identified today that seem to bear out the plausibility of the liberal position. In the last few decades, states around the world have been drawn increasingly into international regimes representing a wide array of issue areas in order to facilitate the smooth functioning of those areas of public policy that cross national borders or impinge another state's affairs.[21] The European Union, the North American Free Trade Agreement, the World Trade Organization, and the Asia-Pacific Economic Co-operation Forum group are only a small sample of some of the more prominent. Coordination of domestic policies through these regimes has internationalized states in ways suggestive of the widening "pluralistic security community" among major industrialized states theorized by Deutsch and others. Indeed, today it is hard to imagine a realistic scenario involving any of the great powers threatening another with military force. And however much states like Singapore, China, and Iran attempt to smother or control communication flows, information leaks through in seemingly incessant ways, from illicit satellite dishes to anonymous re-mailers and encrypted e-mail over computer networks. Today, with earth-orbiting satellites, personal camcorders, and transnational interest groups and activists wired into networked computers, transparency has been raised to such a level that central state authorities cannot hide much of significance from the rest of the world (see chapter 4 by Steven Livingston).

Equally impressive, however, are the many trends contrary to liberal expectations. While liberal-democratic states have arguably formed a "zone of peace," no doubt encouraged by economic globalization, supra-national we-feelings have been lagging far behind. Indeed, at the same time as globalization proceeds apace, what seems to be occurring is a revivification of national and other parochial sentiments.[22] Some have argued there is a kind of dialectical relationship between the two trends. Globalization – with its distant markets, hyper-financial flows of capital, and bland global images – cannot generate a meaningful sense of community, so people naturally turn inward to more familiar, parochial identities, be these religious or ethno-national.[23] No doubt exacerbating these reactions are the increasing disparities of wealth between rich and poor, both within and among states around the world. Thus, while integration is pulling states together in webs of governance, fragmentation is pulling them apart from within – hardly the one-way street to the liberal "End of History" so confidently predicted by Francis Fukuyama at the end of the Cold War.[24]

The liberal position on communications is perhaps better seen as a form of ideology than as theory per se. It tells a story of utopia, points in its direction, and then speaks of its coming in the "language of inevitability."[25] Implicit or not, there is a hope of self-fulfilling prophecy behind all of this. If only enough people behaved as if the liberal position were accurate, it would come true. The problem, however, is that globalization and liberalization have side-effects that manifest themselves in such things as chronic unemployment, lost social safety nets, crumbling education and health infrastructures, widespread anomie and violence, labour unrest, and the paving over of cultural difference by the forces of "McWorld." In the face of these, and alongside billion-dollar annual bank profits and other manifestations of wealth concentration, it is a hard story for any but the most gullible to swallow. Today, if liberalism is to offer any guide, it must be seen as a project worth fighting for, rather than as an inevitability unfolding naturally in the course of history.

Marxism

If the liberal perspective lacks an appreciation of the social relations of power and communications, the Marxist position more than makes up for it. In Marxist interpretations of global communications, ownership of media and the ensuing control over content are given prominent attention. Marxists situate today's changes in communication technologies as part of much larger processes of economic transformation. The productive forces in societies that, according to Marxists, have always driven broader social patterns are today in the midst of yet another epochal transformation, this time in the direction of a global, post-Fordist regime of flexible accumulation.[26] The consequences for world politics are no less profound – though certainly less well received – than those sketched out by liberals, and communication technologies play an important, if not first-order, role in them.

While there is no one single Marxist theory, all forms of Marxism share a view of the importance of economic class in relation to modes of production in determining social and political relations. Marxist theories of communications and world politics range from those that deal in a somewhat orthodox manner with ownership of media and control over mass communications content to those that employ a more nuanced interpretation of the structural constraints unleashed by transnational capital and global communications. In the former, the actual material properties of communication technologies are abstracted away as relatively insignificant. For Marxist theories of control, whether the medium is print, radio, television, or the Internet matters less than who owns the medium itself. A classic example of such an approach is Noam Chomsky's "Propaganda Model," which "traces the routes by which money and power are able to filter out the news fit to print, marginalize dissent, and allow the government and dominant private interests to get their messages across to the public."[27] Chomsky's model should not be taken for a conspiratorial view of society, with editors and capitalist barons acting in concert to censor the news. It draws attention, rather, to those systemic factors that structure the news in specific ways advantageous to the workings of capitalism. Because private media must cater to advertisers, "stories" and information running contrary to the interests of the capitalist system tend to be winnowed away or sifted out. Ideology or culture is, in this way, moulded around the economic base of society.

Theories on the other side of the Marxist spectrum take a much more holistic approach to communications and world politics, typically employing a perspective influenced by the neo-Marxist Antonio Gramsci.[28] Here, the emphasis is not simply on the relations between communications control and content, but on the "structural" power of capital, which is now able to move more freely and rapidly across territorial-political boundaries because of telecommunications. Economic class is still the most important unit of analysis, but the concept of hegemony is introduced to provide a more subtle, less reductionist view of the way dominant cultural frameworks are produced and recreated (as opposed to imposed) by elites than do the more orthodox variants of Marxism described above.

The divisions sketched above between Marxist schools are somewhat stylistic, with many analyses falling somewhere in between or employing skilful combinations of both. For example, Edward Comor's analysis of U.S. foreign communications policy unearths both the structural constraints of transnational capital and the active promotion of a worldwide liberal economic regime by U.S. elites.[29] Likewise, Stephen Gill and David Law point to the structural power of internationally mobile capital as well as to the construction of a dominant neo-liberal ideology through the conduits of such elite media as the *Wall Street Journal* and the *Economist*, and by organizations like the Group of Seven (G7) and the Trilateral Commission.[30] In contrast to liberal perspectives, these Marxian-inspired "critical" approaches are much more illuminating of the power relationships that underpin today's construction of a global information infrastructure. Given the extent to which transnational capital and global media conglomerates have grown in importance in recent years, such analyses are particularly valuable contributions. Neo-Marxism tells us why states around the world have adopted, almost en masse, macroeconomic policies favourable to global market forces, policies that typically result in cutbacks, downsizing, labour unrest, and layoffs. It explains why global corporate advertising campaigns paint a placid picture of multicultural harmony and global communications while ignoring mass migrations, nationalist xenophobia, and the spread of infectious diseases. It tells us why ardently faithful National Hockey League franchises in Winnipeg and Quebec are moved south of the border to such hockey oases as Arizona, North Carolina, and Nashville while Fox Network broadcasts of hockey games feature the "glowing" puck. It highlights, in other words, the political economy of global communications.

What, if any, are the limitations of the Marxist theories of global communications? Critics argue that Marxist approaches are too reductionist, meaning that everything is seen through the lens of the mode of production and economic class. Such a limitation might obscure many of the primarily non-economic effects related to new communication technologies. Relatedly, it might underestimate the autonomous impact of communication technologies altogether. For example, one increasingly well-known effect of the Internet is that it has facilitated the activities of transnational social movements and civil society networks, groups like Amnesty International, Greenpeace, and Earth First, many of which work to limit the excesses of the global market system. The same technologies, in other words, that link foreign exchange traders in the 24-hour marketplace provide the tools by which activists resist the spread of global consumer culture.

Indeed, this obscuring points to a much more fundamental limitation of Marxian-inspired approaches, particularly those of the more orthodox variety. Such analyses are based on a tight link between increasing concentration of media ownership within a few large transnational corporate empires and communications content. Yet one of the novel aspects of the World Wide Web is the way it allows people to communicate with each other and to disseminate information, largely outside of any corporate or state filters. The World Wide Web allows individuals to become, in essence, private broadcasters to a potentially global audience. Such a democratization of publication, though certainly still mostly an unrealized potential, would seem to challenge fundamentally the premises of, for example, Chomsky's propaganda model of communications. How do corporations place editorial blinders around communications content when the source of such content is widely dispersed and democratized?

MEDIUM THEORY OF COMMUNICATIONS

If the approaches to communications within the IR field are lacking, what of those in the communications field? Although an exhaustive survey of that discipline is beyond the scope of this analysis, one tradition of scholarship that does take as its central focus the impact of changing communication technologies on society and politics might provide an interesting starting point. The tradition of scholarship to which I refer is known as *medium theory*, an approach associated with theorists such as Harold Innis and Marshall McLuhan.[31] At the heart of medium theory is the argument that changes in modes of communication – such as the shift from primary orality to writing or the shift from print to electronic communications – have important effects on the trajectory of social evolution and the values and beliefs of societies. Medium theory traces these effects to the unique properties of different modes of communication, to the way information is stored, transmitted, and distributed through different media at different times in human history. It argues that media are not simply neutral vessels for conveying information between two environments; rather they are environments in and of themselves.

One of the major criticisms of medium theory is that the approach can tend towards technological determinism and monocausal reductionism. It is the type of thinking that attempts to reduce the sources of complex social forces or ideas to a single "master" variable.[32] Certainly McLuhan bears the brunt of this criticism (perhaps unfairly), although other medium theorists are not immune. For example, Elizabeth Eisenstein's lengthy investigation of the cultural and social consequences of the invention of printing in Europe received considerable denunciation for her use of the word "agent" to describe an inanimate technology, the printing press. Though such criticism is often a knee-jerk reaction, it is nonetheless important to avoid the many interrelated pitfalls in such a simplistic model of change. While the power of technologies to shape human affairs is certainly significant, it is distorting to portray new technologies (as technological determinists are wont to do) as entering society *de novo* – as if deposited from outer space – with certain behaviours and ideas invariably tied to them irrespective of the social or historical context in which they are developed. But is this type of technological determinism and mono-causal reductionism essential to medium theory?

Elsewhere I have made a number of modifications to medium theory so that it might be articulated in a non-deterministic, non-reductionist way.[33] The majority of these modifications are attempts to get back to the roots of this approach, so to speak – to unearth what I see as the historical materialist grounds out of which medium theory developed. Embedding medium theory in this deeper tradition of scholarship enables me to articulate a more holistic view of the role of communications technology in social evolution and thereby avoid the type of technological determinism to which other medium theorists may be prone. At the core of my modifications was an attempt to draw out one of the more prominent metaphors in medium theory analysis: modes of communication as environments.

Communications environments, defined as the material properties of communication technologies and the political and economic context in which such technologies are embedded, facilitate and constrain social forces, collective images, and ideas much as natural environments facilitate and constrain the reproduction of species. As part of the structural-material landscape in which human beings interact, communications environments do not generate social forces, collective images, and ideas *de novo*; they do not impose thought or behaviour. Rather, they place obstacles and constraints before some, while providing intensity and dynamism to others. An examination of the properties of a communications environment can thus indicate which collective images will predominate over time and, in doing so, help to trace the changing contours of the world order.[34]

While it could be misleading to stretch it too far, this environmental metaphor is particularly useful because it moves away from the technological determinist view that technologies "generate" specific social forces and ideas. It affirms that the actual genesis of social forces and ideas ultimately reflects a multiplicity of factors that cannot be reduced to a single, overarching, master variable. Instead, it argues that the existing stock of social forces and ideas will flourish or wither depending on their fitness or match with the new communications environment. From this perspective, a new mode of communication is not an agent but rather a passive, structural feature of the technological landscape in which human beings interact. It imposes certain constraints or limitations on the nature and type of possible human communications, while facilitating other types, but it does not impose thought or behaviour in any crude one-to-one fashion. It is an environment. And as in natural environments, when the communications environment changes, some species will be favoured while others will be disadvantaged, not because of an active intervention on the part of the environment itself, but rather because the functional properties of the environment either reinforce or constrain the characteristics and interests of the species within it.

Medium Theory and World Politics

Medium theory has been applied in the past to a wide range of issue areas, from the Homeric tragedies of ancient Greece to the rise of nationalism in modern Europe. How might we use it to illuminate political forces at the global level? What type of social forces will flourish as networked computing deepens and expands around the world, and which will wither? Although space precludes a detailed investigation, the following trends certainly warrant further investigation:

Transnationalization of Production. Throughout the modern period, the production of goods and services has been organized primarily on the basis of state-territorial boundaries. The vast majority of economic transactions have (and still continue to be) "domestic" as opposed to "inter-national." In part, this reflects the subordination of the low politics of economics to the high politics of state security. Through most of the modern period, economics was seen as serving the needs of states and societies, and not the other way around. Those economic transactions that crossed sovereign boundaries were primarily of the arm's-length variety, with goods or services produced in one country being shipped and traded with those of another country, and vice versa. In the hypermedia environment, however, the organization of production has begun to diffuse across territorial boundaries. Production processes have been disaggregated and dispersed into multiple, national locations to take advantage of low labour costs, favourable regulatory climates, or specialized preferential policies. Whereas at one time this type of transnational production was the exception, in the hypermedia environment it is fast becoming the norm, as reflected in statistics on foreign direct investment and world trade in services.[35]

The Globalization of Finance. As with production, finance throughout the modern period (with exceptions) was primarily a national affair. Capital provided the grease for the so-called real economy of production, and was mostly confined to transactions within territorial boundaries. In the hypermedia environment, in contrast, financial activities have transmogrified and globalized to such an extent as to comprise an entirely new autonomous power on the world political landscape. Billions of dollars bristle in a constant circulation of planetary networked flows, rippling across political spheres in market repercussions. The structural power of this 24-hour, planetary financial sphere over state macroeconomic policy has been well documented.[36] Central state authorities are increasingly bound by the dictates of the market, as the numerous policy changes in the direction of privatization and liberalization across the world indicate.[37] Along with the changes in production outlined above, unbridled global finance has increasingly whittled states into "transmission belts" or conduits for the global economy.[38]

Transnational Civil Society Networks. While global market forces are hegemonic in the hypermedia environment, the same technologies have facilitated the rise of a myriad of transnational interest groups, activists, militia movements, terrorists, cults, religious movements and sects, and other assorted groups. While these groups lack the shared values that translate the micro-decisions of individual capitalists into the structural influence of global market forces, they have what might be called "inter-stitial" power – influence, that is, on the margins and in specific issue-areas.[39] Groups like Greenpeace and Amnesty International now wield legitimate influence in the environment and human rights areas, and are increasingly seen as important actors alongside states in the world political arena. Greenpeace has its own satellite link-up; Kurdistan national liberation movements have their own television shows; the webpages of UFO cults, neo-pagan groups, religious sects, and various rock music idolatries plaster the World Wide Web like the walls of a postmodern agora. What is perhaps most interesting is the way these communities define themselves in the absence of a clearly demarcated political space. As with production and finance, collective identities, it seems, are also unbundling.

Postmodern Mentalities. The philosophical and artistic movement known as postmodernism arose during the mid-twentieth century as a curiously abstract and elite Western phenomenon. Its ideas of plural worlds, and multi-perspectivism and its scepticism of truth as corresponding to reality challenged many of the core tenets of mainstream social science. In the hypermedia environment, such ideas have found a niche and have flourished, not so much among elites as among the younger generations of cybernauts and websurfers. Today, postmodernism resonates, if only implicitly, in computer games, Imax theatres, videos, cineplexes, and television advertisements, where plural worlds and multiple realities are taken to the extreme in digital simulations and images. Teenagers today are proto-Derrideans and Baudrillardians-in-the-making, entirely comfortable with the idea of constructed worlds, created realities, and de-centred selves, since most of their communications experience is through the de-centred, hyper-real environment of digital-electronic computer networks. Whereas English professors and philosophers write about created worlds and multiple realities, youths today experience them directly as downloaded "shareware" games, such as Doom and Quake. As this hypermedia environment deepens and expands, the ideas of postmodernism will resonate and flourish, as predominant a spatial bias in the future as was the precise linearity of the early modern period.

International to Intra-planetary Security. Throughout the modern period, the primary threat to people's physical security was violence from inter-state war. States constructed military technologies and personnel to defend their territories from encroachment or invasion. The logic of this inter-state insecurity gradually evolved – with changes in ballistic missile, transportation, and communication technologies – into the global superpower competition of the Cold War, a strategic game that divided states into two competing blocs whose rivalry covered the entire planet. Although the Cold War has subsided, its surveillance and intelligence infrastructure remains largely intact; in fact, it has grown in density and scope with the shift to environmental monitoring. The difference today is that instead of two superpowers monitoring each other's behaviour, the focus of surveillance has shifted inward on a single, undifferentiated global economic and security system, with the centres of surveillance dispersing to a much wider domain. Planet Earth is under constant surveillance from a variety of actors, ringed by an increasingly dense web of inward-focusing optical, electronic-eavesdropping, thermal imaging, and radar satellites used for commercial, military, and environmental purposes.

CONCLUSION

In this chapter, I have sketched some of the different theoretical frameworks that could be employed to interpret the way world politics are undergoing transformation because of new communication technologies. The pictures that emerge from each theoretical perspective are strikingly different and provide different lessons for those interested in foreign policy, diplomacy, and the character of world politics. Realists see new technologies as an interesting wrinkle and a potential new tool in the age-old game of power politics. Yet the limited scope of their inquiry may blind them to the more fundamental changes that are rewriting the rules of the game itself. Liberals applaud new communication technologies as harbingers of freedom and democracy, but may be inured to the systemic inequalities and fragmenting forces unleashed in their wake. While Marxists and neo-Marxists offer forceful critical perspectives on the structures of power embedded in the global market system, they may be slighting non-economic consequences of new communication technologies. Because of these theories' various shortcomings, I believe, a medium theory perspective provides the most compelling and comprehensive framework with which to assess the effects of new communication technologies on world politics.

The changes that I describe above point to the emergence of a fundamentally different era of world politics. Whereas once political rule was parcelled and fragmented into territorially distinct and mutually exclusive sovereign states, today authority is dispersing and de-centring to multiple domains – to transnational corporations, global bond-rating agencies, transnational civil society activists, non-governmental organizations, religious cults and sects, multimedia conglomerates, software empires, and international regimes. Whereas once state was a container-like meta-organization that ordered social, economic, and political relations within its territory and acted as representative for its people in affairs beyond its borders, today the state is transforming into one of many "transmission belts" for global market forces and flows of information. States are meso-layers of authority, conduits between the local and the global. Whereas once a clear demarcation could be made between politics within a state and politics beyond – that is, between domestic and international spheres – today it has almost become a cliché to describe such boundaries as being blurred, as fragmenting, or as dissolving into a pastiche-like ordering of postmodern political spaces. Local, national, non-territorial, and global domains coexist in a montage of virtual flows and cyberspaces. Today world politics is multi-perspectivism writ large, characterized not by balances but by mutual penetration and hence paralysis of political power.[40] It is a quasi-feudal, polytheistic world order embedded in a transparent environment of increasingly intense enclosed encounters. In such an environment, attempting to implement a coherent diplomacy is like trying to tap-dance in a three-dimensional cobweb.

NOTES

1 See Ronald J. Deibert, *Parchment, Printing, and Hypermedia: Communication in World Order Transformation* (New York: Columbia University Press, 1997).
2 See, in particular, Peter Schwartz and Peter Leyden, "The Long Boom: A History of the Future, 1980–2020," *Wired* 5, no. 7 (July 1997).
3 "Panoptic" is derived from Jeremy Bentham's design for an all-seeing prison, which he called a "Panopticon." The idea of the panopticon has been appropriated by postmodern theorists as a metaphor for modern surveillance by corporations and states. See Oscar Gandy, *The Panoptic Sort: A Political Economy of Personal Information* (Boulder: Westview Press, 1993), for a useful overview.
4 See Harold Innis, *Empire and Communications* (Oxford: Oxford University Press, 1950).
5 James Carey, *Communication and Culture: Essays on Media and Society* (New York: Routledge Press, 1989).
6 See Robert Keohane, ed., *NeoRealism and Its Critics* (New York: Columbia University Press, 1986); and Kenneth Waltz, *Theory of International Politics* (New York: Random House, 1979).
7 Robert Gilpin, *War and Change in World Politics* (Cambridge: Cambridge University Press, 1981), 56.

8 See Stuart E. Johnson and Martin C. Libicki, eds, *Dominant Battlespace Knowledge: The Winning Edge* (Washington, D.C.: National Defence University Press, 1995).
9 David Rothkopf, "In Praise of Cultural Imperialism?" *Foreign Policy*, Summer 1997: 38–53; Joseph Nye and William Owens, "America's Information Edge," *Foreign Affairs* 75 (March/April 1996): 20–36; and Ann Medina, "Canada's Information Edge," *Canadian Foreign Policy* 4, no. 2 (Fall 1996): 71–85.
10 John Gerard Ruggie, "Territoriality and Beyond: Problematizing Modernity in International Relations," *International Organization* 47 (Winter 1993): 139.
11 See Deibert, *Parchment, Printing, and Hypermedia*, for an overview of the relationship between printing and the rise of the modern state system.
12 See Hedley Bull, *The Anarchical Society: A Study of Order in World Politics* (London: Macmillan Press, 1977).
13 For an overview, see Mark Zacher, "The Decaying Pillars of the Westphalian Temple," in *Governance without Government: Order and Change in World Politics*, Ernst Otto-Czempiel and James N. Rosenau, eds (Cambridge: Cambridge University Press, 1992).
14 Mark Zacher and Richard Matthew, "Liberal International Theory: Common Threads, Divergent Strands," in *Controversies in International Relations Theory: Realism and the Neo-Liberal Challenge*, Charles Kegley, ed. (New York: St Martin's Press, 1995), 107–50.
15 See particularly Karl Deutsch et al., *Political Community and the North Altantic Area: International Organization in the Light of Historical Experience* (Princeton: Princeton University Press, 1957); and Karl Deutsch, *Nationalism and Social Communication* (Cambridge, Mass.: MIT Press, 1966).
16 For such a view, see, among others, Zacher, "The Decaying Pillars of the Westphalian Temple"; Robert Keohane and Joseph Nye, eds., *Transnational Relations and World Politics* (Cambridge, Mass.: Harvard University Press, 1971); Robert Keohane and Joseph Nye, *Power and Interdependence: World Politics in Transition*, 2nd ed. (Glenview, Ill.: Scott, Foresman, 1989); and Edward Morse, *Modernization and the Transformation of International Relations* (New York: Basic Books, 1976).
17 See, for example, Allen E. Goodman, *A Brief History of the Future: The United States in a Changing World Order* (Boulder, Colo: Westview Press, 1993).

18 Scott Shane, *Dismantling Utopia: How Information Ended the Soviet Union* (Chicago: Ivan R. Dee, 1994).
19 See note 2 above.
20 Kenichi Ohmae, *The Borderless World: Power and Strategy in the New Interlinked Economy* (New York: HarperCollins, 1990).
21 Mark Zacher, *Governing Global Networks* (Cambridge: Cambridge University Press, 1996).
22 Benjamin Barber, *Jihad vs. McWorld* (New York: Ballentine Books, 1995).
23 Anthony Smith, "Is There a Global Culture?" *Theory, Culture, and Society* 7, nos 2–3 (1990).
24 Francis Fukuyama, *The End of History and the Last Man* (New York: Avon Books, 1992).
25 For discussion, see Louis Pauly, "Capital mobility, State Autonomy and Political Legitimacy," in *Journal of International Affairs* 48, no. 2 (Winter 1995): 369–88.
26 See David Harvey, *The Condition of Postmodernity: An Enquiry into the Origins of Cultural Change* (Cambridge, Mass.: Blackwell, 1989).
27 Edward S. Herman and Noam Chomsky, *Manufacturing Consent: The Political Economy of the Mass Media* (New York: Pantheon Books, 1988).
28 See Antonio Gramsci, *Selections from the Prison Notebooks*, Quintin Hoare and Geoffrey Nowell Smith, eds (New York: International Publishers, 1971).
29 Edward A. Comor, ed., *The Global Political Economy of Communication: Hegemony, Telecommunication and the Information Economy* (London: Macmillan Press, 1994).
30 Stephen Gill and David Law, "Global Hegemony and the Structural Power of Capital," *International Studies Quarterly* 33 (1989): 475–99.
31 See especially Marshall McLuhan, *The Gutenberg Galaxy* (Toronto: University of Toronto Press, 1962); and idem, *Understanding Media: The Extensions of Man* (New York: McGraw-Hill, 1964).
32 A technological determinist would make an assertion like "the Reformation is the child of the printing press" or "the printing press created individuality," claims that clearly break down upon closer historical investigation.
33 Deibert, *Parchment, Printing, and Hypermedia*.
34 For example, the development of the printing environment in early modern Europe constrained the strategic interest of the Roman Catholic Church while facilitating heretical movements, capitalist

entrepreneurs, national-linguistic identities, and centralized-state bureaucratic modes of governance, all of which contributed to a shift in world order at the time. For an explanation, see Deibert, *Parchment, Printing, and Hypermedia*, Part 1.
35 See United Nations Conference on Trade and Development (UNCTAD), *World Investment Report, 1997*. As that report noted, "[t]he global FDI stock, a measure of the investment underlying international production, increased fourfold between 1982 and 1994; over the same period, it doubled as a percentage of world gross domestic product to 9 per cent. In 1996, the global FDI stock was valued at $3.2 trillion. Its rate of growth over the past decade (1986–1995) was more than twice that of gross fixed capital formation, indicating an increasing internationalization of national production systems."
36 See, in particular, J. Goodman and L. Pauly, "The Obsolescence of Capital Controls? Economic Management in an Age of Global Markets," *World Politics* 46 (1993): 50–82.
37 For documentation, see UNCTAD, *World Investment Report, 1997*.
38 See Robert Cox, "Global Restructuring: Making Sense of the Changing International Political Economy," in *Political Economy and the Changing Global Order*, Richard Stubbs and Geoffrey Underhill, eds (Toronto: McClelland and Stewart, 1994).
39 See, among others, Paul Wapner, "Politics beyond the State: Environmental Activism and World Civic Politics," *World Politics* 47 (April 1993): 311–40.
40 It should be clear that I am not arguing that states are going to "disappear" any time soon. Quite the contrary: I expect states to continue to exist for the indefinite future. What has changed, however, is the significance of states as actors in world politics that monopolize political authority and within which the organization of economics, community, and identity is bundled. That architecture of political authority, which defined world politics throughout the modern period since at least the late eighteenth century (if not before), is now fast transforming into something else. A change in world order, in other words, does not hinge on whether states are here or not.

2 New Technologies and Networks of Resistance

ELIZABETH SMYTHE
AND PETER J. SMITH

While transnational political activity by non-governmental organizations (NGOs) has long had an impact on world politics, it has only been in recent years that its importance has become undeniable. While figures vary, they all portray a veritable explosion in the numbers and activities of transnational NGOs and transnational social movement organizations (TSMOs). It is estimated that the number of international NGOs in the 1990s increased from 6,000 to 26,000.[1] Rare is the international issue that does not attract a transnational network of NGOs, TSMOs, and informal associations that organize and mobilize to express their point of view. Examples abound: the groups in sympathy with the Zapatista rebellion against the Mexican government; the forces aligned against the implementation of the North American Free Trade Agreement (NAFTA); the International Campaign to Ban Landmines; and the transnational campaigns against the Multilateral Agreement on Investment (MAI) and the World Trade Organization (WTO) meetings in Seattle, Washington, and elsewhere.

While serving different goals, these efforts had a number of commonalities. First, their ability to communicate, network, and interact on a transnational level was considerably enhanced by new communication technologies, particularly the Internet. For example, when the Mexican government responded to the peasant rebellion with repression, an amorphous network of NGOs used the Internet to mobilize a worldwide protest, with the result that the Mexican government stayed the hand of repression. Second, the ensuing politics surrounding all these issues was contentious, particularly so vis-à-vis the campaigns against the NAFTA, the MAI, and WTO. These three represent transnational campaigns of opposition to the growing neo-liberal agenda of economic integration, continentally in the instance of the NAFTA, globally in the case of the MAI and WTO. The MAI and WTO campaigns are illustrative of the political opportunity given NGOs and social movements by neo-liberal trade and investment negotiations to challenge both domestic and global institutional economic agendas.[2]

Clearly, just as nation-states can network at a multilateral level, so can NGOs and TSMOs. The result is an institutional dialectic of domination and resistance at the transnational level. With the rise of a global information economy, we are witnessing not only the efforts of states and corporations to shape this economy according to neo-liberal ideology, but also the concurrent attempts of NGOs and TSMOs to resist the impact these trade and investment arrangements are having, or are anticipated to have, at the national and local levels.

This chapter examines the increased capacity of NGOs and TSMOs to resist multilateral trade and investment arrangements and thereby to challenge the privileged and often very secret process of diplomatic negotiations. In the first section, we will discuss how new information and communication technologies (ICTs) are allowing NGOs and social movements to organize and mobilize beyond the nation-state to create globalization from below. Like their corporate counterparts, NGOs and TSMOs are becoming networked organizations at a rate exceeding government bureaucracies, which have been slower to make use of these new technologies. In effect, the networking revolution, propelled by new forms of communications, is accelerating the formation of networked organizations and eroding the privileged place the vertically organized state once had in international relations. In the second section of this chapter, we will examine two campaigns of resistance, the MAI and the WTO, focusing on the role played by new technologies and their advantages and disadvantages for NGOs and TSMOs. Finally, we will examine the impact these campaigns have had at both the national and the international level. After all is said and done, have they made a difference?

THE ASSOCIATIONAL REVOLUTION, NEW TECHNOLOGY, AND THE DEVELOPMENT OF NETWORKS

The process of economic globalization has led, as Cleaver notes, to a "growing uniformity of policies and international agreements among governments to implement world wide sets of rules."[3] At the same time, however, this growing homogeneity of institutions and policies has promoted a situation where increasing numbers of people, despite a host of cultural, linguistic, and geographical differences, are uniting in opposition to these institutions and policies as they increasingly impinge on their lives. In brief, power and domination (globalization and politics from above) are encountering resistance (globalization and politics from below). As Manuel Castells so aptly puts it:

With the exception of a small elite ... people all over the world resent loss of control over their lives, over their environment, over their jobs, over their economies, over their governments, over their countries, and, ultimately, over the fate of the Earth. Thus, following an old law of social evolution, resistance confronts domination, empowerment reacts against powerlessness, and alternative projects challenge the logic embedded in the new global order, increasingly sensed as disorder by people around the planet.[4]

Among those newly empowered are civil society–based NGOs and social movements. These non-state actors have demonstrated a remarkable ability to organize and network on a transnational basis. For example, the NGOs that came to Seattle in 1999 to protest against the WTO meetings were "better prepared and more knowledgeable than many, if not most, international organizations and their secretariats or the government ministers and officials about trade theories, the UR [Uruguay Round] and their impact on countries."[5] It has become clear that NGOs and TSMOs are more able than ever before to challenge the process of neo-liberal economic globalization.

In considerable measure the growing empowerment of non-state actors is due to their adept use of new ICTs, in particular the Internet. Information and communication technologies, we argue, are essential components of the globalization process, and but they are also indicators of how complex, contradictory, paradoxical, and messy globalization actually is. The Internet, for example, is both an essential means of global capital growth and a tool of democratic resistance.

What is it about ICTs that facilitates the formation of networks of resistance? According to Reg Whitaker, "Big Brother," the panoptic state, has increasingly lost pre-eminence as a means of social control.[6] The result is that the rational, centralized administrative state, along with other bureaucratic institutions in society, is losing its monopoly over key sources of its power, information and the capacity of surveillance. From the perspective of Michel Foucault, it could be argued that ICTs, particularly the Internet, are dismantling the vertical Panopticon that had isolated and disciplined individuals. With the advent of the networked society, panoptic power has been reorganized along horizontal lines. This new, de-centred Panopticon "facilitates unmediated horizontal communications among the panoptic subjects and the capacity of the subjects to 'watch the watchers,' to carry out potentially democratic surveillance from below."[7] At the same time, the Internet represents a significant departure from earlier media in that it permits horizontal bi-directional and multilateral communications, a boon to associational activity. One result, Whitaker argues, is that "the globalization of capitalism will almost certainly be paralleled by a globalization of resistance networks ... just as the flexible capitalist enterprise forms and reforms virtual organizations for particular ventures."[8] In sum, as economic globalization spreads, so do potential means of resistance. They are two sides of the same coin.

We may therefore be part of a historic shift, from modernity, with its emphasis on centralized, hierarchical mechanisms of control, to a new era in which horizontally linked, networked organizations predominate. This, essentially, is the argument of Manuel Castells, who writes that the rise of a global informational economy is accelerating a "shift from vertical bureaucracies to the horizontal corporation."[9] In effect, the horizontal corporation is a networked organization based on decentralization, participation, and coordination. Networks, argues Castells, "are the fundamental stuff of which new organizations are and will be made."[10] Consistent with the argument of Castells, James Rosenau maintains that new technologies have created a relational revolution with profound implications for voluntary associations, NGOs, and civil society.[11] One consequence is that these organizations have increased in number as they have gained the ability to act upon a global stage and challenge the privileged state-to-state discourse that was once the sole domain of foreign ministries.

New communication technologies, particularly the Internet, provide a variety of advantages to NGOs, TSMOs, and associations engaging in grassroots activism, three of which will discussed here. First, the Internet has levelled the playing field between horizontal and vertical organizations. With this technology, the incentive to centralize communications processes has disappeared. Previously, bureaucratic structures relied upon an elaborate hierarchical information system involving written files and print to ensure clarity of communication, a very costly process. Today, thanks to the Internet, complex messages can be transmitted, accurately and clearly, within complex horizontal networks at a much lower cost than ever before. As a result, claims Hans Geser, "the Internet is indispensable for combining decentralized fact-gathering and mobilization with speedy diffusion and knowledge, consensus building and effective transnational action."[12] In some respects, vertically organized bureaucratic structures, especially hierarchical organizations such as foreign ministries, are at a disadvantage in a networked informational society. They rely, for example, on a system of top-down communication and formal protocol, which means delayed responses.

A second related advantage of the Internet is that it frees NGOs and social movements from associational relationships based on territory, allowing them instead to form relationships based on function. And, as Leslie A. Pal's detailed examination of the topography of web-based human rights networks shows, different types of groups have different communications functions on the network: "The campaign/activist groups are focussed on results; the informational groups are geared to reflection and analysis; and network groups stress relationships and links."[13] Geographical space is no longer a factor in the formation of organizations. Networked organizations can move quickly upward and outward, inserting themselves into a rich network of existing groups at a variety of levels.

With respect to the third advantage to be discussed here, governments and traditional mass media have lost their virtual monopoly over information and publicity. With digitization allowing NGOs and TSMOs to project themselves quickly and directly onto a global stage, governments find it more difficult to keep negotiations secret and to manage information flows to the public (though Gilboa shows in chapter 3 that the state still has the power to keep certain negotiations closed to public scrutiny); the mass media is gradually losing its position as unchallenged intermediary, making it all the more difficult to impose a particular world view on mass audiences.[14]

The rise of new communication technologies, the compression of space and time, and the increasing irrelevance of traditional borders have thus facilitated campaigns of resistance and globalization from below. With the proliferation of NGOs and the increased transnational efficacy of social movements, global governance becomes less state-centric and more messy, complex, dispersed, contradictory, and paradoxical than ever before.

CAMPAIGNS OF RESISTANCE INFORMATION AND COMMUNICATION TECHNOLOGY

In this section we will examine networks of resistance and the extent to which ICTs have played a role in them. We will do this by looking at two transnational campaigns of resistance, both of which have had a major impact on trade and investment negotiations and both of which used ICTs to organize, educate, and mobilize citizens. Before discussing the role of ICTs in the MAI, Seattle, and subsequent campaigns, we must acknowledge that ICTs did not create these networks or the groups and movements. Many grew out of and alongside the governmental and corporate process of embedding economic liberalism in the global political economy through the bilateral and multilateral negotiation of rules. Networks of resistance have deep roots; in the cases we are studying many go back to the 1980s, originating in national and international campaigns against, for example, the Canada-U.S. Free Trade Agreement and the NAFTA. Many North American environmental groups were heavily involved on several fronts: in the NAFTA campaign, in United Nations (UN) environmental programs and conferences (in Rio, for example), and in battles with the World Bank in the 1980s and 1990s. The more radical critics of the World Bank, including environmental, development, women's, and other groups, were also part of the Fifty Years Is Enough Campaign against the bank. With the growing evidence of the devastation caused by Third World debt, an international coalition of faith and development groups, among others, in the North and the South mounted the Jubilee 2000 campaign, targeting the largest economies and their chief tool of debt enforcement, the International Monetary Fund.

Clearly, it would be wrong to claim that ICTs are responsible for the development of networks. The above examples show that many of these networks had already developed around and against a set of international organizations and rules associated with globalization. Furthermore, ICTs are not the only technologies that have profoundly affected citizens, groups, and social movements around the world. We argue instead that these technologies have facilitated, in a major way, the further development of horizontal international networks of resistance by permitting a wide variety of groups and individuals to share resources and information and collaborate internationally in a much faster, easier, and lower-cost way than was previously possible. The ICTs have both increased the ease of organization on a global basis and, perhaps even more important, broken the traditional monopoly of information that characterized states and international economic negotiations in the postwar period. Finally, these technologies have enhanced the NGOs' cultural impact on public and international agendas through their capacity to provide alternative media and channels of communication for the like-minded and thereby allow the public and global debates on globalization to be reframed.[15]

Information and communication are not enough, however. As the social movement literature indicates, there must also be the appropriate political environment (see chapter 1 by Ronald Deibert), a space that has opened to allow this contestation to occur.[16] We argue that this space had opened by the mid-1990s as a result of a number of factors, including, first, the ever deeper impact of the rules governing international trade and investment on domestic laws and regulations; second, the uneven impact of globalization within and between economies; third, the erosion of the postwar liberal bargain and the shrinking state-sponsored domestic compensation for losers; and fourth, the division within state elites and among states within these intergovernmental organizations (IGOs), partly as a result of expanding state memberships and agendas. In addition, the weakening of the link between international rules and democratic political systems, in the context of the post–Cold War triumphal rhetoric of democratization, created real legitimacy problems within member countries and the IGOs themselves. Thus, it is the application of these new facilitating technologies by groups with established networks, at a time of emerging political opportunities, that accounts for the rapid rise and development of these networks of resistance at the end of the twentieth century.

The Multilateral Agreement on Investment Campaign

While the MAI campaign is well known, we include it here for several reasons. First, many groups involved in campaigns of resistance see it as a turning-point in bringing home the value of transnational activity, radicalizing some groups, calling into question the inevitability of globalization, and challenging globalization's status as an undisputed good. Second, many groups and observers and those involved in the negotiations have pointed to the role that ICTs have played in the campaign of opposition to the MAI. Finally, in many ways the campaign against the WTO in Seattle was linked to the MAI campaign.

The following discussion summarizes earlier research by the authors, including an analysis of over 300 websites and detailed interviews with individuals from a number of the groups most active in the anti-MAI campaign.[17] We begin, then, with a brief review of the events of the MAI case.

The MAI negotiations were drawn out over three and half years, ending on 3 December 1998.[18] The negotiations had been formally launched in May 1995 at the Organization for Economic Co-operation and Development (OECD) ministerial meeting, largely as a result of a U.S.-led and business-supported initiative. The idea was to create a binding, free-standing agreement, thought to be easier to achieve within a small, like-minded group of wealthier economies. Non-OECD states would then accede to the agreement on a negotiated, case-by-case basis. It was hoped that the agreement would establish a high standard of investment liberalization, a benchmark to which larger developing countries in Latin America and Asia, the favoured destination of much foreign investment, would need to rise in order to join the agreement. The agreement would discipline the investment regulations of these states and facilitate and protect foreign investment.

The negotiations began in the fall of 1995, and while not a secret, they failed to attract the attention of the mainstream media.

Following the prevailing practice, the talks were conducted behind closed doors. The OECD generally gives consultative status to business and labour groups from member countries, but these interest groups were excluded from the MAI negotiating table. Initially, state negotiators seemed to be making rapid progress on the main principles, such as national treatment (i.e., no discrimination against foreign investors and foreign-based firms) and strong investor protection against uncompensated state expropriation. The draft also included a clause establishing the right of investors to lodge complaints against states and seek compensation in the event that the complaints were successful, a provision similar to chapter 11 of the NAFTA. The key political issue for the OECD members revolved around which economic sectors or state policies (culture, for example) would be exempted from these general obligations, although it was not fully addressed until the winter of 1997. Discontent with the process and real political divisions became apparent in March and April 1997 as member states lodged their reservations against the obligations contained in the draft text.

Around the same time, a copy of the February 1997 draft text was leaked, ending up in the hands, and on the websites, of two public policy advocacy groups in North America. It was quickly and widely shared via the Internet with groups around the world. With the leak and the dramatic pronouncements of critics came an increase in media coverage in a number of member countries. As the pressure on the negotiators increased because of growing public disquiet about the negotiations, so too did the number of state reservations lodged against the obligations of the agreement. Legislative hearings and inquiries were held in a number of member countries, including Australia, Canada, France, the United Kingdom, and the European Parliament.

A fractious meeting between an international coalition of NGOs and the OECD negotiating group, held 27 October 1997, marked a turning-point for the opposition. When a suspension in the negotiations was not forthcoming, anti-MAI groups mobilized an all-out campaign in various countries to stop the MAI process. Recognizing that the likelihood of reaching an effective agreement, one that would bring real gains in liberalizing investment regulation, was slipping away, the OECD negotiators attempted to save the situation at a high-level political meeting in February 1998. When it failed, it became clear to a number of key players, especially the United

States, that whatever limited agreement might ultimately emerge from the process was unlikely to be worth the political costs.

As enthusiasm for the MAI waned, some of the states under the most pressure, including France, successfully pressed for a hiatus in the negotiations in April 1998. Opposition continued to mount, and when the negotiations were set to resume in mid-October, the French government, under pressure from Greens and Communists within its coalition and after the release of an inquiry report very critical of the agreement, withdrew from the negotiations, thereby ending any hope of agreement.[19]

Negotiators and groups involved in the anti-MAI campaign believe that the Internet played an important role. Table 2.1 suggests the rich variety of groups and individuals that used the web to communicate their concerns about the MAI. There is a general impression that in the anti-MAI campaign the Internet was a tool of NGOs, usually thought of as non-profit groups, separate from the political process. However, although a number of advocacy NGOs (e.g., Public Citizen and the Council of Canadians) did play a major role in leaking the draft text and providing detailed critiques of the MAI, a surprising number of websites were in fact sponsored by elected members of legislatures and political parties (in most cases, opposition), business groups (e.g., law offices), individuals, media organizations (including both broadcast and print), and government agencies. The data suggest that NGOs were not the only networking organizations and that their use of websites generated a response. Websites often came in waves, with many of the media and government (departments, agencies, parliaments, and even municipalities) websites following in response to those of the advocacy, environmental, and development NGOs.

We tried to get a sense of the countries that were home to organizations that were active on the web (see Table 2.2).[20] Unfortunately, our linguistic limitations led us to under-report the total number of sites, especially in Asia. Nevertheless, we found range of factors at play. As many studies have indicated, access to the Internet is still uneven and largely a function of the level of wealth of an economy, the telecommunications infrastructure, and the cost of connection. A couple of aspects of the results in Table 2.2 are interesting. The significant number of U.S. sites is no surprise, but the relatively large number of Canadian sites reflects how extensive the MAI controversy was. A similar comment could be made about Australia,

Table 2.1
Websites by Type of Sponsoring Organization

Type of Group Sponsoring Site	Number of Sites	Per Cent of Total Sites
Public policy advocacy	53	15.1
Political parties and MP sites	45	12.8
Media organizations	37	10.5
Government agencies, all levels	35	10
Individual/Personal	30	8.5
Business organizations (incl. law offices)	26	7.4
Broad, anti-MAI coalitions	20	5.7
Environmental organizations	19	5.4
Trade unions	16	4.6
International organizations	17	4.8
Research institutes/centres	15	4.3
Student groups	9	2.6
Other (unable to classify)	9	2.6
Arts/Cultural organizations	8	2.3
Church/Religious	5	1.4
Total	352	100

New Zealand, and Austria. Surprising, too, were the number of websites in Spanish over all and the number in Latin America countries, which, with the exception of Mexico, were not OECD members. Brazil, Chile, and Argentina were, however, major candidates for accession to the agreement and were courted by the OECD, sitting as observers during the negotiations. This may have drawn some attention to the issue in this region, as did NAFTA, perhaps, and the Free Trade of the Americas negotiations.

The Internet, many have argued, facilitates collaboration, information sharing, and networking via the use of hypertext links and the capacity to download and access information easily. While this reproducing and sharing has been the bane of copyright lawyers, it has been a cheap and effective way for groups with very limited resources to have virtually instant access to the information gener-

Table 2.2
Websites by Country

Country	Number of Websites	Per Cent of Total
United States	129	31.9
Canada	71	17.6
Australia	36	8.9
Germany	32	7.9
United Kingdom	17	4.2
Spain	16	4
New Zealand	14	3.5
Austria	12	3
Mexico	10	2.5
Sweden	8	2
Uruguay	6	1.5
Nicaragua	4	1
Argentina	4	1
Switzerland	4	1
South Africa	3	.7
Norway	3	.7
Netherlands	3	.7
Japan	3	.7
Denmark	3	.7
Chile	3	.7
Brazil	2	.5
Singapore	2	.5
France	2	.5
Other countries	15	4.5
Total	400	100

ated by groups with more resources. According to commentators like de Brie of *Le Monde Diplomatique*, this aspect of the Internet was key in redressing the traditional monopoly on complex, technical information held by large corporations, governments, and the media. As Table 2.3 indicates, virtually all of the websites we coded had external links (650) to other sites that provided information. Our researcher was able to track the most frequently occurring links within the websites and thereby identify which organizations were major sources of information. While links allowed groups the opportunity to access detailed analyses of the MAI and the official OECD information on the agreement, there was no privileging of the OECD information over that of other very critical sources, which in many cases, such as the MAI-Not site, ran on a shoestring budget with a few dedicated volunteers.

NGOs were strikingly similar in the way they used the Internet. Almost all of the organizations used a website, e-mail, and a listserv as part of their anti-MAI activities. Websites were generally targeted at a broader public than just members and were not, by and large, used to fund-raise for campaigns or carry out more routine communications with members. Rather, their main functions were to gather and share information and to mobilize those concerned about the agreement. One respondent described the process as a giant relay of obtaining and quickly passing on information. Some of the larger advocacy and environmental groups shared detailed technical, and often legal, analyses of the draft MAI texts. Many used their sites to mobilize concerned citizens, providing accessible means to lobby decision makers, such as draft faxes, open letters that citizens could sign and send automatically, and press releases that local groups could use to garner more media coverage.

Electronic mail – especially automated mailing lists, in some cases involving as many as several thousand names – was used by all groups to maintain links with other activists and concerned citizens both within and outside their own countries. For the larger groups actively involved in the anti-MAI campaign, such as World Wide Fund for Nature (WWFN) and Friends of the Earth (FOE), electronic mail was used to link local, national, and international organizations so that they could share strategy and intelligence and coordinate their activities with allied groups. Some groups maintained two or more separate mailing lists, one for contacting concerned and interested groups and individuals and another for reaching key contacts and activists in other groups. The latter was a smaller, closed list of those with whom they shared strategy, often based on previous campaigns (e.g., anti-NAFTA or World Bank networks).

Table 2.3
Top Ten Organizations Appearing as Links in Websites

Name of Organization	Frequency	Rank
OECD	95	1
MAI-Not (Flora)-OPIRG-Carleton U.	87	2
National Centre for Sustainability (Victoria, B.C.)	25	3
Appleton (law office, Toronto)	23	4
YUCC (personal site, York U. law student)	22	5
Public Citizen (Washington, D.C.)	21	6
Preamble Centre (Washington, D.C.)	21	6
Friends of the Earth-U.S. (Washington, D.C.)	19	7
Multinational Monitor (U.S.-linked to Public Cit)	17	8
Council of Canadians	16	9
Canadian Centre for Policy Alternatives (Ottawa)	12	10
Stop MAI (Australia)	12	10

The key advantages of the Internet to anti-MAI campaigners were its speed, its capacity to move large amounts of information easily, and the overall lower costs for NGOs in comparison to traditional methods such as mail-outs. E-mail also allowed anti-MAI strategists to share intelligence and strategy quickly and to compare notes in a timely way as events unfolded. The speed, the ease, and the low cost made publishing and sharing complex technical information easier. In essence, the Internet helped to break the information monopoly enjoyed by business, government leaders, and OECD officials. With instant access to the latest analysis of the long complicated draft texts, as well as to the state of play of the negotiations, citizens were able to challenge both their own government officials and OECD officials.

There were, however, concerns about the new technology. First, there was the general problem of uneven access to the Internet both within and across societies. Second, the Internet carries huge volumes of information of uneven quality. For small organizations, the management of information and the task of updating websites became burdensome.

Overall, the groups we contacted felt that the Internet campaign had an effect on the domestic and international public debate on the MAI. In particular, many pointed to the greater coordination of activities and the sharing of information among groups. Coupled with the limited mainstream media coverage of the negotiations in many countries, this led to a situation where NGOs, by late 1997 and early 1998, had already set the terms of the public debate. Most importantly, the MAI campaign had provided a lesson for groups, and, as we shall see, for governments, on the potential of new technology in the globalization debate.

THE INTERNET, THE BATTLE OF SEATTLE, AND BEYOND

The ministerial meeting of the World Trade Organization in Seattle provides another valuable case to help us assess the role of ICTs in facilitating networks of resistance to globalization. It differs, however, in a number of ways from the MAI case, which suggests the further growth and development of these networks. Three differences stand out. First, while the anti-MAI groups coordinated internationally and organized a few demonstrations at the OECD in Paris, the primary focus of the MAI campaign was to educate citizens within member countries and mobilize them to express and demonstrate strong opposition to the agreement and thereby influence their own government. In the case of Seattle, ICTs became part of an effort not only to educate and mobilize groups and individuals to pressure their governments to rein in the WTO, but also to facilitate direct citizen action through a wide variety of forms of protest at the venue of the IGO meeting itself, a trend that has characterized subsequent actions on the part of anti-globalization forces. Second, the Seattle case illustrates the expanding global reach of such campaigns, as national NGOs in both the North and the South quickly became part of this network, reflecting the broad membership and coverage of WTO rules. Third, a new set of actors emerged in the WTO resistance process. We call them facilitators, public space providers, and/or alternative media entities; they reflect in part the increased capacity of the Internet to handle voice and image and thereby permit sophisticated broadcasting. Organizations such as the Association for Progressive Communications and WebNet gave a range of organizations both technical support and unmediated channels via the provision of webspace so that they could get their message out directly. Thus, this set of actors is helping the opponents of globalization voice their experience and alternative vision.

The WTO had by 1999 become a target of choice for the resistance campaign for a number of reasons. First, the Uruguay Round of negotiations had resulted in the imposition of new regulations in areas not traditionally considered part of international trade, such as intellectual property, services, and the treatment of investors. Second, because of the contentious nature of some issues and the lengthy negotiations, the Uruguay Round left much unfinished business for the Seattle ministerial to pick up. Other contentious issues such as labour standards, unresolved from the 1996 Singapore meeting, were also likely to be on the table, given the looming U.S. election. In addition, since NGOs, as a result of the eighteen-month MAI campaign, were well aware that the European Union, Japan, and Canada were willing to negotiate the investment agreement at the WTO, they were determined to stop any new round that included MAI-type investment rules. Further, several WTO dispute resolution decisions (Tuna-Dolphin, Shrimp-Turtle) raised fears on the part of environmentalists that WTO obligations, despite the exemption of Article 20 with respect to environmental regulations, would further undermine domestic environmental regulations, even as the Multilateral Environmental Agreements remained largely unenforceable.

Key decisions about future WTO negotiations are left to a consensus of member states that meet every two years. In Seattle in 1999 the big decisions that the trade ministers had to make were how and when the mandated negotiations in agriculture and services would go forward and whether and what additional issues (such as investment rules) should be added to the negotiating agenda. The likelihood for severe conflict among WTO members in Seattle was already very high, given the presence of agriculture on the agenda. There was also evidence of real discontent among representatives of developing countries, which had taken on new and onerous obligations, as a result of the Uruguay Round, in areas such as intellectual property in return for little real results in improved market access for their goods in developed economies. Ministers thus came to Seattle with few areas of agreement mapped out in advance.

In contrast, NGO preparations had been under way more than a year in advance of the meeting and went into high gear once Seattle had been chosen as the venue. In Seattle, a coalition of groups (including the Washington, D.C.–based advocacy organization Public Citizen [founded by Ralph Nader], its trade arm Global Trade Watch, and major labour unions such as the AFL-CIO, the Teamsters, and the Steelworkers, united in a coalition called Citizens Trade Campaign) created a local Washington group, People for Fair Trade. This group established a Seattle office and began organizing on the ground with an army of volunteers drawn from churches, universities (where an anti-sweatshop movement had been having great success), and a host of local organizations that plugged their own efforts into a broader series of events at the alternative citizens' summit. Similarly, in Washington, D.C., Public Citizen and Friends of the Earth coordinated another fifty groups. Environmental groups, already well organized, angered by WTO decisions but buoyed by successful boycotts of several major firms and retailers, coordinated other groups and concerned citizens in cooperation with organizers. Internationally, Public Citizen's Lori Wallach, representatives of seven other organizations, and other key individuals (many of them veterans of the MAI battle) coordinated the campaign through regular contact via e-mail and conference calls every four weeks.[21] A series of closed listservs kept strategists in touch, and other listservs, such as STOP WTO round, were instrumental in widely circulating information and intelligence about developments at the WTO and ideas and information about mobilization and campaigns in various countries. A number of other organizations, such as the International Center for Trade and Sustainable Development in Geneva and the Institute for Agriculture and Trade Policy in Minnesota, made widely available on the Internet regular newsletters and information about issues and developments related to the WTO.

Others, such as the International Forum on Globalization (itself a coalition of representatives from other NGOs), Public Citizen, West Coast Environmental Law (British Columbia), and the Preamble Center (Washington, D.C.), published accessible citizen guides to the WTO and participated or organized events designed to educate both other activists and citizens in general.[22] In addition, groups were able to use two face-to-face gatherings of NGOs, including one in Geneva in March 1999, to hammer out strategy and finalize a civil society statement on the WTO, called "No New Round Turnaround," which formed the set of principles around which over two thousand NGOs ultimately united.

The events that unfolded in Seattle are well known, especially the major protests that delayed the opening of the meeting and the subsequent protests throughout the week. What was not captured in the press coverage were the teach-ins, workshops, lectures, and other educational events along with the vast array of colourful and symbolic actions, ranging from street theatre to hanging freeway banners.[23] Moreover, the focus on the events in the streets also misses the fact that 767 NGOs were officially registered and had access to the convention centre, where they could engage in very traditional lobbying of trade ministers and delegates. Many of those representing official NGOs also took part in street actions and events, thus bridging both the official meetings and the resistance in the streets.

What role did new technology play in organizing and facilitating the process of contesting globalization on the ground in Seattle? As described by many of the activists involved in the Seattle campaign, it had three aspects – organizing, educating, and mobilizing. For many NGOs, the Internet proved invaluable in the work of coordinating and organizing the activities of thousands of groups and individuals, much of it done by e-mail. Electronic mail, especially listservs, allowed groups and individuals to get messages out to other groups very quickly and cheaply. As in the MAI case, this meant that intelligence on what was happening at the WTO and in key capitals could be shared quickly. The Internet also permitted, through closed lists, the sharing of strategy and ideas. In addition, many websites provided places where citizens could connect and interact directly with each other to chat, exchange information, share resources, and in some cases participate in interactive workshops on WTO issues.

In terms of creating greater public awareness about the WTO, a key aim of all the organizations, many groups found the Internet's capacity to permit the sharing of very detailed analyses of aspects of the WTO and the ministerial invaluable. The lesson of the leaked draft agreement on the MAI had shown the potential of the Internet in this area. Material posted on websites could be downloaded and/or reproduced on other websites. Many organizations strived to simplify and communicate issues in accessible language, highlighting how trade issues directly affected people and the environment. For some of the smaller research organizations that specialized in trade issues and disputes, websites were a cheap and effective way to distribute their research to a worldwide audience.

Even more than the MAI case, the WTO campaign highlighted the Internet's use as a tool of mobilization. Many organizations, especially in North America, used their sites to encourage and call on citizens to come to Seattle. Many provided detailed information on practical matters such as housing and helped pair people up for rides. Some groups organized cross-continent caravans over the web; activists could spread the word and post daily journals and bulletins to the websites, along with video footage, accounts, testimonials, and pictures inspiring others to become involved.

The impact of these efforts was reflected in the increased traffic on many sites and in the huge volume of e-mail, the latter in excess of several hundred messages a day for some groups. Groups continued to rely on e-mail and the ever-present cell phone as they organized activities and events up to and during the week of the ministerial meetings. It should be noted, however, that the Internet was only one of several tools, facilitating but not replacing traditional ways of organizing. Groups also worked for weeks on the ground in Seattle with an army of volunteers prior to the ministerial meeting.

Unlike in the MAI campaign, resistance to globalization in Seattle and elsewhere has been accompanied by large demonstrations at the venues of international meetings, often involving a wide variety of actions and a heavy police presence and response. In these cases, the Internet has provided an alternative view and interpretation of events to mainstream media and a means by which many activists could express their views directly.

Through the independent media based on the web, NGOs got their message out. Even more important, they provided alternative perspectives and information on what was going on in Seattle, some of it filmed by the demonstrators themselves. Technology has directly contributed to the ease with which this can be done. One individual described how, with the help of an intern and access to websites, a few people were able to publish a daily newspaper, the *WTO Observer*, for the whole week in Seattle, covering events there and around the world connected to the ministerial. A major audience for this paper, he claimed, consisted of mainstream media journalists, many of whom were unaware of (or could not get to) many of the things going on in the street. The use of digital video cameras allowed protestors to video events in the street, including police attacks, from their own perspective and download them onto websites. Thus, the Internet facilitated both a mobilization beyond the dreams of most activists and a way for them to continue to frame the debate over globalization and the events in Seattle. This has been particularly crucial in subsequent protests as well in countering the focus of the media on sensational incidents and confrontations with the police – a focus that often makes it difficult for groups to get the content of their message heard in the mainstream media.

Much of the activity of organizing, educating, and mobilizing for Seattle took place on websites around the world. A range of groups and individuals, including both those who opposed a new round and those who supported one, used websites to influence the debate. Because of the huge explosion of websites that dealt with the WTO (in comparison to the MAI), we could only examine the larger sites and a sample of the thousands of smaller ones that we were able to identify.

As Table 2.4 indicates, we again see a wide array of organizations, but a greater presence in this case of labour, farmer, and anarchist groups. There is also evidence of a much greater presence of official sites, a reflection of how organizations like the OECD, the WTO, and numerous government agencies (such as foreign and trade ministries) have learned from the MAI experience the value of getting their own unmediated message out on the Internet. It also reflects the desire of many governments and IGOs to enhance their legitimacy by claiming or showing a greater transparency in the negotiation process.

Our web research also suggests a much larger presence of media organizations than in the MAI case. Many of these are mainstream press, television, and radio media, but we also found a notable presence of net-based alternative media and hybrid organizations that coupled activist networks with alternative media. The appearance of One World, Corporate Watch, the Institute for Global Communications, and Indymedia are examples of web-based broadcasting systems that contained thousands of written items, but also audio and video files and news stories from around the world submitted by activists as well as groups that have been hurt by globalization. Our data indicate that even among traditional organizations websites have increasingly used audio and video and searchable archives of information.

Table 2.4
Websites by Organization Types

Type of Organization	Number of Sites	Per Cent of Total
Public advocacy	94	18.3
Media organizations	88	17.2
Other (includes anarchist and feminist organizations)	75	14.6
Government agencies (all levels)	52	10.1
Environmental and conservation organizations (incl. animal welfare)	44	8.6
Business organizations	41	7.8
Trade unions	33	6.4
Development organizations	32	6.2
Political parties	20	3.9
Farmer organizations	18	3.5
International organizations (e.g., WTO, OECD)	16	3.1
Total	513	100

An examination of the external links on the websites indicates the extent of collaboration. For example, groups that might be considered potential competitors formed links with each other.[24] The links also indicate that a number of these web-based groups serve as alternative sources of information. Many websites linked official sources and both mainstream and alternative media without privileging one source over the other. For example, an Internet group such as Corporate Europe Observatory, though operating on a shoestring budget, can nevertheless widely disseminate its research on corporate influence on trade and investment issues at the EU. In other cases, the Internet has allowed groups and activists from industrialized countries to access a Southern perspective online through such bodies as OneWorld, the Third World Network, and Focus on the Global South. One group, for example, reported over 135,000 hits in a four-month period, the vast majority originating in the North.

Table 2.5
Top Twenty Organizations Appearing as Links on Websites

Organization	Frequency	Rank
World Trade Organization	2,129	1
Seattle Post-Intelligencer	732	2
OECD	322	3
OneWorld Online	348	4
Washington Council on International Trade (host org to wtoseattle.org)	127	5
Financial Times	125	6
Seattle Times	123	7
Institute de recherche pour le développement (IRD)	122	8
Third World Network	116	9
Institute for Global Communications	111	10
Le Monde-Diplomatique	107	11
Trade and Development Centre (joint initiative of WTO and World Bank)	99	12
United States Mission to the European Union	98	13
Seattlewto.org (sponsored site of NGO coalition against WTO)	92	14
International Center for Trade and Sustainable Development	85	15
Corporate European Observatory	83	16
Corporate Watch	74	17
Southbound (Penang)	73	18
Institute for Agriculture and Trade Policy	71	19
DFAIT-MAECI, Government of Canada	70	20

Based on our interviews with groups involved in the Seattle campaign and an inventory of data on about seventy-seven groups that have been actively involved in resistance, it is clear that the Internet is an important tool for a wide range of groups in their efforts to organize networks of resistance.[25] Virtually all of the groups had access to the Internet and used e-mail, and the vast majority had websites. For most groups, the key goal in Seattle was not to shut down the meetings *per se* but rather to raise awareness of the role of the WTO and its impact. Groups used a wide array of tactics to mobilize citizens in opposition. The tactic most favoured was dissemination of information through various forms of popular education, and here the Internet was particularly effective. While for some groups it was a secondary, rather than a primary, means to achieve their goals, the Internet still played an important role. Many groups feel they were successful in raising awareness through its use, and some of the data on public opinion appears to corroborate their claims.

With the near worldwide membership of the campaigns against the WTO and the IMF/World Bank, the groups we interviewed remain concerned about the digital divides, especially of the North-South variety. A number were concerned, as well, about the dominance of English on the web. However, an increasing number of groups, especially in the South, are posting more and more in other languages. Our research did indicate a wide geographic array of websites, including thirty-six different country codes, in every region of the world. In addition, as a number of those we interviewed pointed out, in many areas of the world one central NGO is connected on-line as part of a broader international network and serves as a conduit for passing information to groups that are not connected. Thus, the on-line information does connect with and reach groups off-line. Moreover, as part of a competitiveness strategy in the globalization process, many states and IGOs, such as the World Bank, are encouraging more connectivity for NGOs and, in the case of some governments, providing funding and grants so that groups can go on-line.[26]

To what extent, however, can these evolving networks of resistance, facilitated as they are by technology, be considered a serious and sustainable counterbalance to the power of transnational corporations and states? In the sociology literature, social movements are defined as networks involving shared values and identities that engage in contentious – that is, non-mainstream – politics. But can a loose coalition of NGOs around the world connected largely online and often mobilized around a particular issue be considered a network in the social movement sense?

Our research indicates that the diversity of groups involved is striking in terms of resources, sectors, tactics, and cultural differences. Do they share values? Many involved in these networks would argue "yes." Maude Barlow and Tony Clarke, for example, claim that the groups broadly agree on the need to address four issues: the negative impact of globalization on the ecosystem, the inequalities globalization has generated, the excessive power amassed by transnational corporations, and massive poverty and financial instability caused by deregulated capital flows.[27] Others emphasize common values of community, sovereignty, and diversity.[28] Still others point to the recent movement to go beyond simple opposition to facets of globalization and instead create forums to articulate alternatives; an example is the World Social Forum in Porto Alegre in 2001, which attracted a huge number of activists and was partly organized with the use of ICTs. The more than 150 organizations involved in the Porto Alegre meeting raised concerns about "equity, social justice, democracy and security of everyone" and the need to rebalance a system that privileges private capital and the market in favour of one that asserts "the supremacy of human, ecological and social rights over the demands of finance and investment."[29] The threatened erosion of democracy by the forces of neo-liberal globalization is the other strong and recurrent theme shared by the groups. Many activists are disillusioned and disappointed with their own government's role in the process of facilitating globalization in response to corporate demands, one of the reasons why the incentive to network across borders is so strong. Many of the groups share a sense of global citizenship as well, indicated by their view of accountability. While many (especially more traditional organizations like trade unions) identify members, or funders, as those to whom they are accountable, many also identify the global community and in some cases the earth itself.

A second question raised by social movement analysts concerns continuity.[30] On-line connections, while they can bridge distances, are thin and issue-based and do not correspond to the broader basis of contact and trust, or memory, which develops in real communities, thus limiting the endurance of opposition in comparison to that of transnational corporations (TNCs) and states. As one activist reminded us, "the Internet is a tool, not a movement." As we have indicated, groups do not rely solely on electronic connection. As legitimacy problems have mounted, the rise of IGOs and inter-state conferences have led to the funding of regular parallel meetings at which many NGO leaders can renew links face to face. Thus, the growth of IGOs and inter-state networks has facilitated the creation and viability of NGO networks. Moreover, many non-governmental organizations are part of overlapping and intersecting networks that cut across issues. For example, the Council of Canadians, part of the International Forum on Globalization, is also part of both the Canadian Common Front on the WTO and Common Frontiers. The latter is a forum connecting a number of Canadian groups with groups in Latin America that oppose the FTAA; most recently, it became involved in a new international coalition, the Blue Planet Project, which opposes the privatization and commodification of water. A number of groups involved in the MAI meetings in Paris were also in Seattle, and they frequently meet in Geneva and New York as well. Smaller NGOs with local roots are often inserted into these broader networks through a larger organization, and ICTs provide a very cost-effective way to share information and fit local strategies and concerns within this broader movement. Many groups and activists are on several different listservs and receive cross-postings so that there is cross-fertilization in information and ideas and many nodes of intersection among networks, offering them a broader, global perspective.

Finally, we need to be a bit more sceptical about the imbalance of resources among states, TNCs, and NGOs. While a number of organizations have a sizeable paid staff and large budgets (especially trade unions, the larger environmental organizations, and legal foundations), most NGOs operate with predominantly volunteer staffs and limited, and in many cases uncertain, funding. Their resources cannot compete with the bureaucracies of major states or the vast corporate legal and financial resources that groups representing business interests can call upon. As the agenda of global economic rule-making has expanded, however, states have had to address increasingly complex issues; in some cases, dozens of ministries and a vast array of personnel have had to face onerous challenges of coordination. At the same time, the processes of privatizing and downsizing, subcontracting and intensifying the use of ICTs have weakened institutional continuity and memory in these bureaucracies. In the case of TNCs, while resources abound, surveys indicate that the public's trust in them and sense of their legitimacy are in shorter supply. A determined and well-connected international network that raises moral and ethical questions (such as the campaign of Médecins sans Frontières against multinational pharmaceuticals with respect to the HIV/AIDS crisis in South Africa) can sometimes even bring large multinationals to heel.

THE IMPACT OF NETWORKS OF RESISTANCE

While we have demonstrated that the rise of transnational networks has been greatly facilitated by ICTs, we still face the question of how much impact the networks have actually had. Many past studies have focused on issues such as human rights in this regard, but only a few have addressed trade and investment issues.[31] Moreover, assessing the impact of networks of resistance, given the short time frame, may be somewhat premature. At best, we may be able to outline some measures of impact, examine some short-term trends, and outline some broader questions for the future.

In terms of their own immediate goals for the Seattle, IMF/World Bank, and other campaigns (for example, against the FTAA), most groups put educating citizens about these organizations and agreements high on their list of goals. Many point out that the first step is to raise awareness, the basis for citizen mobilization. Have their efforts succeeded in raising awareness and reshaping public attitudes? In the case of the April 2000 IMF/World Bank campaign and protests in Washington, a Pew Centre poll reported in May 2000 that a mere 24 per cent of those polled in the United States had followed the issue somewhat or very closely – less than had followed the Elian Gonzalez case. Clearly, the general public's obsession with the fate of the Cuban boy indicates the important role that mainstream media still play in shaping the public agenda. Other surveys in the United States, Canada, and elsewhere do show high levels of support for international trade; however, they also show a more mixed picture for specific trade agreements and a certain amount of public concern about the impact of agreements on the environment, social programs, and jobs. A survey by Ekos Research Associates in 2001, for example, indicates that in Canada there was "enormously high recall of media coverage of the [anti-globalization] protests ... Moreover, many respondents [could] offer cogent, detailed descriptions of the perceived points the protestors aim to get across."[32] A slim majority of Canadians (53 per cent) reported in this survey that the protests reflected issues of concern to a great many Canadians and did not represent a small set of "fringe" groups. Many polls also show that the public regards large multinational corporations as the prime beneficiaries of such agreements. Clearly, we need more comparative data over a much longer time frame, along with with a more subtle probing of public attitudes, to make a reliable assessment of the networks' impact in this sense.

A second way to assess impact is in terms of how groups were able to shape events. Here most NGOs are rather cautious and realistic about their influence. Most of those involved in the Seattle meetings were quite surprised at the extent of the disruption they were able to cause. While they have publicly claimed a role in causing the meeting's failure, most will also admit the importance of the opposition of many developing countries to the process, as well as of disagreements between the United States and the European Union. Still, the WTO built-in negotiations are moving forward in both agriculture and services, despite the Stop GATS Attack network of groups that has been working to oppose an expanded services agreement. In more subtle ways, however, it could be argued that the campaigns have had an effect on the WTO and a number of member countries. Most of this impact relates to the critique of the legitimacy of the whole negotiation process alluded to above. Because of the widespread acceptance, at least at the level of rhetoric, of democratic values, a number of WTO members have pushed for greater transparency in terms of the release of documents, mainly on the enhanced WTO website, and more opportunities, both at the WTO and in national capitals, for NGOs' voices to be heard. This has taken the form of NGO briefings, an enhanced WTO external relations office, occasional symposia for NGOs, and an NGO-dedicated portion of the WTO website. Admittedly, much of this consultation has been by invitation and highly structured, leaving groups frustrated and fearful of co-option attempts. There has also been a move to release a larger number of documents and some discussion of a role for input from third parties in the dispute resolution system. Nevertheless, negotiations – and most importantly the decisions on key trade-offs and bargains – still take place behind closed doors.

In the national capitals of some members, the process of consultation with NGOs has become quite elaborate, involving both bureaucrats and parliamentarians holding extensive and unprecedented hearings prior to the negotiating of any deal. Some countries have released their positions and proposals and identified their negotiating teams, again, in an effort to demonstrate transparency. In the case of the FTAA, Canada's trade minister pushed for a release of the draft text, although the text came out long after the protests. Even so, a controversial portion of the text on investment was leaked and available on the Internet much earlier. There is less evidence of any dramatic change in state negotiating positions, although some caution on controversial issues such as investment is evident on the part of negotiators.

That said, there is evidence that departments of foreign affairs and trade are beginning to adapt organizationally to the increasing complexity of consultation. In 1999, for example, the Canadian Department of Foreign Affairs and International Trade established the Trade Policy Consultation and Liaison division in order "to facilitate and stimulate the involvement of Canadians in the development and implementation of Canada's trade policy agenda," according to a draft mission statement dated February 2001. This involvement includes consultation with NGOs. In the same year, the Australian Department of Foreign Affairs and Trade appointed an individual to coordinate consultations with NGOs. To date, however, on-line consultation has remained limited, in part because of a preference of the public and NGOs for more traditional means of consultation – letters and face-to-face meetings, for example. In both the Canadian and Australian cases, officials have reported that funding and staffing are already inadequate to undertake enhanced consultations, given the daunting information overload and the challenge of synthesis facing them. While reliance on departmental websites is increasing, these are still primarily used to disseminate information, as instruments of public diplomacy, not as an interactive means of consulting with a broader public. As interaction with the networked world of NGOs increases, officials have noted two key issues, authenticity and representation – that is, who is really speaking and just whom do they represent?[33]

States hosting international meetings have responded in a more negative way to direct action and protests. Best described as a closed-border, barricades, and tear gas model, this reaction has been increasingly in evidence since the April 2000 IMF meetings. On the other hand, this pattern of escalating repression and turmoil has made many host states and cities think twice about welcoming such meetings. Thus, the WTO selected Doha in Qatar for its ministerial in 2001 as a result of a dearth of offers to host the meeting elsewhere.

It is probably at the level of public policy discourse among elites in states, IGOs, and corporations that we can see the networks' influence on the globalization debate. Already in the run-up to Seattle, WTO and state representatives were trying to re-brand a new round of negotiations as a development round. Issues of importance to the poorest countries, such as their debt situation, have moved a little higher on the IMF's agenda. Even the World Economic Forum acknowledged the issue of growing inequalities in a globalizing world in its conference theme for 2001.

Transnational business has also reacted to the networks' pressure; it has tried, for example, to demonstrate a commitment to values such as environmental sustainability and human rights, best exemplified in the Global Compact, an agreement with the UN on a set of commitments and principles that remain unenforceable. In addition, corporate-funded think-tanks, such as the Institute for International Economics in Washington, have been producing studies that seek to show more clearly the benefits of globalization and the problems inherent in the misguided efforts of activists.[34] The new Cordell Hull Institute in Washington, D.C., is specifically charged with expounding the benefits of globalization. More crude responses of some globalization supporters have been to monitor closely, discredit, or try to limit the funding of some NGOs.

Finally, as Pal observes, "it must be acknowledged that information, communication, and mobilization can all increase without necessarily increasing impact."[35] He goes on to point out that the only resource that the on-line organizations have is information and that, as the discussion above highlights, their impact will depend on "how vulnerable targets are to the dissemination of information, combined with the pressures of mass appeals." Brutal dictatorships often care nothing about world opinion and are immune to pressure, whether of the traditional kind in the form of mass demonstrations abroad in front of their embassies or through the use of ICTs. That being said, there is some evidence that in addition to the successes achieved by the campaigns against the MAI and the WTO at Seattle, high-visibility human rights campaigns (e.g., Free Burma) have had some measure of success, using websites and other public relations and organizational tools, in shaming Western corporations in the eyes of consumers and thereby forcing them to pull their operations out of countries with poor human rights records.[36]

A NEW POLITICS IN THE MAKING?

While the impact of the networks of resistance is not always easy to measure, one thing is clear: the traditional focus on states as the primary actors in politics and international relations is no longer appropriate. In a larger sense, then, our understanding of what politics is and where it takes place is being contested. That the meaning of politics itself is being reconsidered is no small achievement of the networked politics of NGOs and TSMOs. What, we must ask, are the features of the new politics and what are its implications for political practice and international relations? Of equal importance, what is the relationship between the new politics and ICTs?

In considering this question, we should first remind ourselves that horizontal networks are not new forms of organization or necessarily derivative of ICTs. In fact, the major organizational trends occurring today are products of earlier trends in the economy and in the social movements themselves. What ICTs have done is facilitate and accelerate the trend towards a new networked organizational form. The result is a rebirth of associational activity, a renewal of social capital.

It would be an understatement today to say that international relations are in a state of contestation and uncertainty. ICTs have permitted NGOs and TSMOs to project alternative values and norms more readily, to contest the hegemonic discourse of economic globalization. However, whether oppositional movements can (or even desire to) coalesce to form a coherent counter-hegemonic alternative to economic globalization is another question. If, indeed, ICTs reflect a new horizontal bias in communications, one that will continue for the foreseeable future to facilitate horizontal associational networking, independent voices, and contestation, then any hegemony or counter-hegemony may not be possible. Neo-liberal global hegemonists and anti-global counter-hegemonists are alike in that they both envision a world beyond politics, one shaped either by markets and regulations or by issues beyond capitalism.

Politics in the future may be more open-ended and uncertain than today. Civil society may increasingly be a realm of contested social space. In a world of decentred politics and dispersed power, what centre or citadel will there be to capture? We might find a clue in a European visitor's response to an American immigration agent's question in 1950s McCarthy-era America. The agent had asked the visitor whether or not he intended to overthrow the government of the United States. The response: "I wouldn't know where to start." Many NGOs and social movements today are not entities that desire to or are able to capture political power. Given the premium these networked organizations place upon plurality and diversity, a counter-hegemonic alternative with its implications of singularity of outlook may not be desirable. Perhaps, in fact, a variety of alternatives to globalization may emerge.

The new politics of resistance is, then, messy and uncertain. It is also far more than a battle of opposites, of centralization and decentralization, of universalism and particularism, of space and place, of the global and the local – to highlight some of the opposites accentuated by information technologies. Rather, the new politics is paradoxical, often taking a hybrid form. One finds, for example, a highly nationalist organization, the Council of Canadians, employing ICTs – networking on a global stage – to defend the democratic, sovereign right of the Canadian state to protect its water and public services from the WTO.

The new politics emerging in international relations is, thus, highly complex. ICTs facilitate, as indicated in the MAI and WTO campaigns, not only on-line politics, but also more traditional forms of politics, whether these be protests, face-to-face meetings with other activists or politicians, lobbying efforts directed at government decision makers or officials of multilateral organizations, or other citizen activity such as letter writing or making telephone calls. Yet, the nature of the new politics' ultimate impact on globalization is highly uncertain. Even though there has already been a clear impact, much is still unknown. For example, can these expanding networks of resistance be sustained? Can they be co-opted? Are they too thin and issue and campaign oriented? Do they, in fact, constitute a movement? Moreover, while ICTs permit NGOs and TSMOs to disseminate critiques and alternative visions, the identity of their audience remains a very important question. Will the new politics be only a politics at the margins? Can NGOs move to the national and multilateral stages and participate around the table(s) where decisions are made? Do they want to? Ultimately, what are the implications for foreign and trade policy making?

While there are no definitive answers to these questions at this early stage, a number of tentative conclusions emerge. Clearly, as this chapter has shown through its case studies of the MAI and Seattle campaigns, governments no longer exercise monopoly control over fields of public policy. For state bureaucrats, especially negotiators, these networked activists and their technology have been seen as a nuisance, but one that is clearly not going to go away, and thus the response in some capitals has been an *ad hoc* one of selectively consulting some groups and attempting to deal with the loss of the information monopoly by putting resources into ICTs as well, to ensure that the state perspective is also presented to citizens in an unmediated way. For political leaders, these groups represent a challenge to the political legitimacy of the international economic rule-making process, raising difficult questions about who is being represented in that process and what that means for democracy. Thus, for all those involved in the postwar process of multilateral clubs, with state elites making economic rules on the bases of the selected input of a few of the largest economic stakeholders, the new politics signals the end of an era.

Policy makers must now recognize the Internet as an important new tool in diplomacy and in projecting national interests abroad. The potential of the Internet should not be exaggerated, but it is clear that governments must join the networked world. They must do a better job of using the new technologies to inform and consult citizens through the development of interactive protocols in their agencies and departments, and they must make more of an effort to understand the particular characteristics of the on-line communities with which they will have to deal on a more frequent basis.

NOTES

Authors' Note: The authors would like to acknowledge the financial assistance of Athabasca University, Concordia University College of Alberta, the Centre for Trade Policy and Law at Carleton University, the Kahanoff Foundation, and the Non-profit Sector Research Initiative at Queen's University School of Policy Studies. Research was provided by Leonard Stoleriu-Falchidi and Janet Ilin Mou. An earlier version of the article was presented at the International Studies Convention, Hong Kong, 28 July 2001.

1 Robert Keohane and Joseph Nye, "Globalization: What's New? What's Not (And So What?)," *Foreign Policy*, Spring 2000: 116.
2 See Jeffrey Ayres, "Transnational Political Processes and Contention against the Global Political Economy," *Mobilization* 6, no. 1

(Spring 2001): 55–68; and Jackie Smith, "Globalizing Resistance: The Battle of Seattle and the Future of Social Movements," *Mobilization* 6, no. 1 (Spring 2001): 1–20.

3 Cleaver, quoted in Hans Geser, "On the Function and Consequences of the Internet for Social Movements and Voluntary Associations," Sociology in Switzerland on-line publications: *Social Movements, Pressure Groups and Political Parties*, April 2000: 20.

4 Manuel Castells, *The Information Age: Economy, Society and Culture*, vol. 2: *The Power of Identity* (Oxford: Blackwell Publishers, 1997), 69.

5 Raghavan, quoted in Ray Goldstein, "The Contest for Civil Society: The Emergence of Global Civil Society and Global Agenda Setting," paper presented at the annual meeting of the International Studies Association, Chicago, 23 February 2001: 6.

6 Reg Whitaker, *The End of Privacy: How Total Surveillance Is Becoming a Reality* (New York: The New Press, 1999), 175.

7 Ibid., 176.

8 Ibid., 177.

9 Manuel Castells, *The Information Age: Economy, Society and Culture*, vol. 1: *The Rise of Network Society* (Oxford: Blackwell Publishers, 1996), 164.

10 Ibid., 17.

11 See James Rosenau, "Three Overlapping Revolutions: One Neutral, All Powerful," paper presented at the annual meeting of the International Studies Association, Chicago, 22 February 2001.

12 Geser, "On the Function and Consequences," 31.

13 Leslie A. Pal, "Bits of Justice: Human Rights on the Internet," unpublished manuscript, 1998.

14 See chapter 3 of this volume.

15 See Paul Wapner, "Horizontal Politics: Transcendental Environmental Activism and Global Cultural Change," paper presented at the annual meeting of the International Studies Association, Chicago, February 2001.

16 See Donatella Della Porta and Mario Diani, *Social Movements: An Introduction* (Oxford: Blackwell Publishers, 1999); and chapter 1 of this volume.

17 See Peter J. Smith and Elizabeth Smythe, "Globalization, Citizenship and Technology: The MAI Meets the Internet," *Canadian Foreign Policy* 7, no. 2 (Winter): 83–106.

18 For a discussion of the MAI negotiations and the opposition to them, see Elizabeth Smythe, "The Multilateral Agreement on Investment: A Charter of Rights for Global Investors or Just Another Agreement?" in Fen Osler Hampson and Maureen Appel Molot, eds, *Canada among Nations 1998* (Oxford University Press, 1999), 239–67; and William A. Dymond, "The MAI: A Sad and Melancholy Tale," in Fen Osler Hampson, Michael Hart, and Martin Rudner, eds, *Canada among Nations 1999* (Oxford University Press, 2000), 25–55.

19 See Pascal Riché, "Jospin: adieu l'Ami, salut les copains," *Liberation* (15 October 1998).

20 Not all URLs contain a country code, and it is quite possible that a site sponsored by a group in one country could be on a website in another.

21 These included Maude Barlow and Tony Clarke in Canada, Martin Khor of the Third World Network, Vandana Shiva in India, Takomo Sakuma of Peoples Forum 2000 in Japan, Agnes Bertrand of Ecoropa in France, and Olivier Hoedeman of the Corporate Europe Observatory based in Amsterdam.

22 See, for example, Stephen Shrybman, *A Citizen's Guide to the WTO* (Toronto: James Lorimer and Canadian Centre for Policy Alternatives, 1999); and Lori Wallach and Michelle Sforza, *Whose Trade Organization* (Washington, D.C.: Public Citizen, 1999).

23 These are described in greater detail in Peter J. Smith and Elizabeth Smythe, "Sleepless in Seattle: Challenging the WTO in a Globalizing World," paper presented at the annual meeting of the International Studies Association, Chicago, 23 February 2001.

24 See Melissa Wall, "The Battle of Seattle: How Nongovernmental Organizations used Web Sites in Their Challenge to the WTO," paper presented at the International Communications Conference, Washington, D.C., 24–28 May 2001.

25 The groups were identified by cross-referencing lists of groups involved in major events in Seattle (e.g., workshops, teach-ins), lists of officially registered NGOs attending the ministerial, website links, and references to key actors arising from interview data.

26 For example, in Canada, the Department of Industry funds VolNet, a program of grants that is designed to "connect voluntary organizations to the power of the Internet" and provides hardware, software, connection costs, and some training, enabling voluntary organizations to get on-line.

27 Maude Barlow and Tony Clarke, *Global Showdown: How the New Activists Are Fighting Global Corporate Rule* (Toronto: Stoddart, 2001), 26.
28 See Amory Starr, *Naming the Enemy: Anti-Corporate Movements Confront Globalization* (New York/London: Zed Books, 2000).
29 *Porto Alegre Call for Mobilization*, World Social Forum, 10 January 2001 (www.forumsocialmundial.org).
30 See Sidney Tarrow, "Fishnets, Internets and Catnets: Globalization and Transnational Collective Action," in Michael Hanigan et al., eds, *Challenging Authority: The Historical Study of Contentious Politics* (Minneapolis: University of Minnesota Press, 1998), 228–44.
31 See Robert O'Brien, Anne-Marie Goetz, Jan Aart Scholte, and Marc Williams, *Contesting Global Governance: Multilateral Economic Institutions and Global Social Movements* (Cambridge: Cambridge University Press, 2000); and Pal, "Bits of Justice."
32 Ekos Research Associates, "Canadian Attitudes towards International Trade," presentation to the Department of Foreign Affairs and International Trade (Canada) in June 2001. Available on the department's main website: www.dfait-maeci.gc.ca.
33 Interviews with officials of the Canadian Department of Foreign Affairs and International Trade, February and May 2001, and with officials of the Australian Department of Foreign Affairs and Trade, August 2001.
34 See Edward Graham, *Fighting the Wrong Enemy: Antiglobal Activists and Multinational Enterprises* (Washington, D.C.: Institute for International Economics, 2000).
35 Pal, "Bits of Justice."
36 Ibid.

3 Real-Time Diplomacy: Myth and Reality

EYTAN GILBOA

INTRODUCTION

This chapter explores the effects global communication is having on the conduct of contemporary diplomacy. It focuses primarily on global television networks, such as Cable News Network (CNN), and not on the new media. However, the difference between television and the new media will soon be moot. With the convergence of technologies, television will be the Internet and the Internet will be television. Thus, the findings and conclusions of this study should be relevant and valid for both present and future cyber-diplomacy.

The term *diplomacy* has been used interchangeably to describe foreign policy in general, one of several instruments of foreign policy, inter-governmental negotiations, and the official activities of diplomats in representating their country, such as providing information and protecting national interests. Although diplomacy may have many functions, negotiations are centrally involved in all of them. The definition of diplomacy used in this study is a revised and expanded version of a formulation suggested by D. Fransworth.[1] It refers to a communication system through which state and non-state actors, including politicians, officials, and professional diplomats, express and defend their interests, state their grievances, and issue threats and ultimatums. Diplomacy is a channel of contact for clarifying positions, probing for information, and convincing states and other actors to support one's position.

Traditional diplomacy was highly personal, formal, slow, and usually protected by secrecy.[2] The *new diplomacy* that emerged after the First World War is primarily associated with the exposing of the diplomatic process to the media and the public. In 1918 President Woodrow Wilson said that secret diplomacy had been one of the major causes of the First World War; he advocated "open covenants of peace, openly arrived at, after which there shall be no private international understandings of any kind but diplomacy shall proceed always frankly and in the public view."[3] For Abba Eban, who served for many years as ambassador and foreign minister of Israel, the new diplomacy refers both to the exposing of negotiations to the public and to the direct conduct of negotiations by politicians and high-ranking officials.[4] He named summit diplomacy as an example of this new form of international negotiations. Today, heads of state and foreign ministers do not have to travel extensively; they frequently exchange views and conduct diplomacy on secured telephone lines. This practice is known in diplomatic circles as "Rolodex diplomacy."

The exposure of diplomacy to the media and the public has had an enormous impact on the making of foreign policy and the conduct of diplomacy. Commenting recently on diplomacy, Eban wrote that "nothing has done more to revolutionize the diplomatic craft than the current vogue of persistent media attention ... [and] there is no way of putting the clock back to an era in which negotiations were sheltered from domestic constituencies."[5] This dramatic change was primarily the result of interrelated revolutionary changes in politics, international relations, and mass communication.

The revolution in politics has generated growing mass participation in political processes and the transformation of many societies from autocracy to democracy. A revolution in international relations is occurring as a result of a new source of power – *soft power*. Joseph Nye, Jr, and William Owens explain that soft power, defined as "the ability to achieve desired outcomes in international affairs through attraction rather than coercion," is gradually replacing military and economic power.[6] "Attraction" requires the effective use of global communication to persuade people around the world to support one's causes. The revolution in communication technologies – the capability to broadcast, often live, almost every significant development in world events to almost every place on the globe – has led to the globalization of electronic journalism and to substantial growth in networks, stations, and communication consumers worldwide.[7] Consequently, it is not only the military and economic power of nations that determines their status and capabilities in the international community; rather it is increasingly the images they project of themselves and their leaders, as well as the scope of the information and information technologies available to them.

Politicians and journalists have suggested that the convergence of the revolutions in international relations, politics, and communications has created a new media-dominated governing system. U.S. senator Richard Lugar called this system "medialism," and David Gergen, a media adviser to presidents Ronald Reagan and Bill Clinton, called it "teledemocracy."[8] A few observers have argued that in foreign policy this transformation in media power has inspired a phenomenon known as the CNN *effect* or *curve*.[9] These terms refer to the media's various effects on diplomacy, primarily to decision makers' loss of control to the news media, particularly in humanitarian crisis situations. The foreign editor of *USA Today*, Johanna Neuman, described the CNN effect in the following way: "It suggests that when CNN floods the airwaves with news of foreign crisis, policymakers have no choice but to redirect their attention to the crisis at hand. It also suggests that crisis coverage evokes an emotional outcry from the public to 'do something' about the latest incident, forcing political leaders to change course or risk unpopularity."[10]

For President Wilson and Foreign Minister Eban, there were only two modes of interaction between media and diplomacy, secret and open. Since their time, fundamental changes in diplomacy, politics, and global communication have created new modes of interaction between media and diplomacy. In turn, these have prompted a scramble for new terms and definitions, such as media diplomacy, teleplomacy, photoplomacy, soundbite diplomacy, instant diplomacy, and real-time diplomacy. A few of these terms are no more than linguistic gimmicks, but they do represent an effort to capture in one word the effects of the new global media, television in particular, on diplomacy.

The media's expanding role in diplomacy and the growing effects of this role on negotiators have not received sufficient scholarly attention in the relevant disciplines of political science, international relations, and communications. Existing knowledge is fragmented and deals only with limited facets of media-diplomacy interactions.

Surprisingly, perhaps, journalists and officials (elected politicians and appointed professional civil servants) have addressed this topic much more fully than have scholars, who have lagged behind in understanding the significance of political communication in domestic and international affairs. Marvin Kalb, a former diplomatic correspondent and currently a professor at Harvard University, correctly observed a few years ago that "academics are now coming to appreciate what successful politicians have known for decades – that the press is a key player in the process of governance."[11]

While this awareness is now becoming more widespread, the highly complex interdisciplinary nature of research on media and diplomacy and the lack of analytical tools have inhibited progress in the field. Politicians, scholars, and observers have lumped together very different media-diplomacy interactions under fashionable but tautological terms such as media diplomacy, television diplomacy, or the CNN effect, resulting in conceptual confusion.

In other works, I have developed models and theoretical frameworks in an attempt to correct the conceptual confusion.[12] In this study, I offer a more complex perspective on the effects of global communication on the conduct of modern diplomacy. Although there is wide consensus that the media has transformed diplomacy, the question remains whether the media has functioned primarily as an independent controlling actor, as suggested by one version of the CNN effect theory, or whether it has become a sophisticated tool in the hands of leaders and officials. A credible answer to this question requires a careful look not only at the challenges of global communication and the particular crises that have demanded humanitarian intervention, but also at the ways and means by which officials have coped with them.

The CNN effect theory has been most applicable with respect to humanitarian crises, and it has carried the implication that officials have lost control over the entire process of policy making in defence and foreign affairs. This study takes a much broader view, showing that while global communication constrains leaders and officials, it also provides them with opportunities to advance their foreign policy and diplomatic agenda. The study demonstrates that even in this age of global communication, officials have found innovative ways to insulate sensitive negotiations from the media and the public. Moreover, officials have shown considerable ability to harness the growing power of global communication to achieve their goals at home and abroad. Officials have often had more control over the media's roles than the journalists themselves, except when they failed to exercise leadership and formulate coherent strategy.

GLOBAL TELEVISION AND POLICY MAKING: THE CNN EFFECT

The roles played by global television, particularly by CNN, in major crises and wars over the last decade provide the background for the development of the CNN effect theory. These crises include the Chinese government crackdown on the students' protest in Beijing's Tiananmen Square in June 1989; the 1990–91 Persian Gulf crisis and war following Iraq's invasion and occupation of Kuwait; the Russian coup attempt of August 1991; and the civil wars in Somalia, Rwanda, Northern Iraq, Bosnia, and Kosovo. CNN was given special credit for directly affecting and channelling the Russian coup attempt while it was happening and for the humanitarian interventions in Somalia and Bosnia.[13]

The end of the Cold War effectively removed any rationale for American military intervention abroad except in clear cases of direct threat to American economic and strategic interests, such as the Iraqi invasion and occupation of Kuwait in August 1990, and even then, the United States went to war only after it had built a large fighting international coalition, had negotiated for several months with Saddam Hussein, and had received authorization from the UN to use force. American policy makers were reluctant to intervene in civil wars in Somalia, Rwanda, Bosnia, and Kosovo, but they have said that pictures of massacres or starvation shown repeatedly on CNN and other networks had pressured them to send soldiers to these trouble zones.

Rozanne Ridgway, an assistant secretary of state, described this effect as CNN's ability to prompt a public demand for action by displaying images of starvation or of other human tragedies, only to reverse this sentiment when Americans are killed while trying to help.[14] Clinton's adviser, George Stephanopoulos, said that CNN became a universal and immediate actor and that "we're often forced to respond to them as much as to actual activity."[15] The veteran diplomat George Kennan claimed that there was no rational reason for the U.S. humanitarian intervention in Somalia beyond the congressional and public emotional reactions aroused by television coverage.[16] These perceptions were not held only by Americans. Officials from international organizations and other countries have described CNN's power and influence in a similar way. Former UN secretary general Boutros Boutros-Ghali was of the opinion that "CNN is the sixteenth member of the Security Council."[17] In 1993 British secretary of state for foreign affairs Douglas Hurd blamed foreign correspondents covering the Bosnia War for the military intervention, calling them the founding members of the "something must be done" school.[18]

The above statements, all by senior officials, imply loss of policy control to global television; implicit is the idea that major policy makers don't make decisions on the basis of interests but rather are driven by emotional public opinion aroused by television pictures. This represents the most extreme version of the CNN effect theory. Several empirical studies using a variety of research methods applied to one or several case studies have raised serious questions about the validity of this version. Nik Gowing, for example, agreed that CNN coverage has indeed drawn attention to crises and may have evoked emotional public reactions, but after interviewing policy makers in several countries, he concluded that these officials resisted the pressure to act solely in response to television news reports.[19] He noted that in 1991 the U.S. and other Western governments refrained from intervening in the Bosnia crisis despite substantial news coverage of atrocities. Gowing sees the CNN effect as a necessary, but insufficient on its own, condition for intervention. Using careful content analysis and interviews with decision makers in Washington and Africa, S. Livingston and T. Eachus concluded that the U.S. decision to intervene militarily in Somalia for humanitarian reasons "was the result of diplomatic and bureaucratic operations, with news coverage coming *in response* to those decisions" (emphasis added).[20]

Several foreign policy makers have offered a more complex view of the CNN effect, considering the global network's coverage as one factor that is weighted against other considerations. Clinton's national security adviser, Anthony Lake, said, for example, that public pressure driven by televised images was increasingly a factor in decision making on humanitarian engagement, but added that other considerations were equally significant, such as "feasibility; the permanence of the improvement our assistance will bring; the willingness of regional and international bodies to do their part; and the likelihood that our actions will generate broader security benefits for the people of the region in question."[21]

Peter Jakobsen examined the role of some of the factors mentioned by Lake in the initiation of peace enforcement operations in five crises: Kuwait, Northern Iraq, Somalia, Rwanda, and Haiti.[22] The factors he investigated were the CNN effect, a clear humanitarian or legal case, national interest, chance of success, and domestic support. Jakobsen confirmed Lake's statement and Gowing's conclusions, finding that CNN coverage was an important factor in four of the five crises because it placed them on the agenda, but that the ultimate decision to intervene was made on the basis of perceived chances for success. At a more general level, W. Lance Bennett suggested that reporters "index" the slant of their coverage to reflect the range of opinion that exists within the government.[23] Jonathan Mermin used this theory to examine coverage of foreign policy crises since Vietnam, including the post–Cold War crises, and found "indexing" a major factor.[24]

The findings of these and other studies essentially contradict the theory that officials lose policy control to the media.[25] If a government decides to intervene, it may need dramatic global coverage of atrocities to win public support for its policy, but dramatic coverage alone is usually insufficient to convince leaders of the necessity to intervene. This conclusion is supported by those who make the ultimate decisions. For example, President Bill Clinton, Secretary of State James Baker, and Chairman of the Joint Chiefs of Staff Colin Powell have all said that while they experienced pressure from television coverage to intervene in crisis situations, they were able to resist it.[26]

REAL-TIME CONSTRAINTS AND ADVANTAGES

More moderate formulations of the CNN effect have focused on the increased speed of diplomatic messages following the rise of new media technologies and global television, going from weeks to minutes. This change in the pace of diplomatic communication has challenged policy makers and the foreign affairs bureaucracy, but at the same time has allowed them to respond more quickly and effectively to emerging diplomatic events and crises.

In traditional diplomacy, ambassadors and state representatives had a monopoly over several important areas of diplomacy: representing their countries, communicating their government's positions, negotiating and concluding agreements, gathering information about the countries to which they were posted, and recommending actions to policy makers back home. The communication and information revolutions, however, have substantially eroded the ambassadors' central position in all four areas. The 1992 U.S. presidential candidate Ross Perot made the following observation: "Embassies are relics of the days of sailing ships. At one time, when you had no world communication, your ambassador spoke for you in that country. But now, with instantaneous communication around the world, the ambassador is primarily in a social role."[27] Indeed, heads of state and ministers of government talk and negotiate directly, in secrecy or in public, with their counterparts. Their negotiations are conducted primarily through official and unofficial meetings and visits, but also via mass and interpersonal communication.

Leaders have always used the press, particularly the "elite newspapers," to obtain information and insights on other countries and world affairs, but global television has become a much more dramatic and powerful source than print media. The faster pace of diplomatic exchanges conducted on global television alters standard decision-making processes, particularly in acute crisis situations. Valuable information, observations, and suggestions from traditional overseas diplomatic and intelligence sources may no longer arrive in time to have the desired influence on decisions, and even when information does arrive in time, it can hardly compete with dramatic televised images and the ongoing reportage of crises and foreign policy issues.

In several recent crises, global television coverage has replaced ambassadors and experts as the authoritative sources of critical information and analysis of what is happening in the world. An American official acknowledged that "diplomatic communications just can't keep up with CNN."[28] President George Bush's press secretary, Marlin Fitzwater, said that in international crises "we virtually cut out the State Department and the desk officers ... Their reports are still important, but they often don't get here in time for the basic decisions to be made."[29] President Bush himself admitted during the 1990–91 Gulf crisis: "I learn more from CNN than I do from the CIA."[30] Apparently, Soviet leaders also used global television as a quick way to get information on other countries. In December 1988 Alexander Bessmertnykh, then the Soviet first deputy foreign minister, congratulated Colin Powell in a meeting at the United Nations for being promoted that day to a four-star general. Powell wondered how the Soviets had learned so quickly about his promotion. Bessmertnykh said he had learned of it on CNN: "I have it in my office and I watch it all day long." Powell said he did too, joking that the two countries could save a lot on communication and intelligence just by relying on CNN.[31]

Sometimes conventional diplomatic messages, regardless of their depth and sophistication, do not have the same effect on policy makers as do televised images from the field. Hurd acknowledged that "when it comes to distant but important conflict, even all the Foreign Office cables do not have the same impact as a couple of minutes of news video."[32] Fitzwater recalled that during the violence in Tiananmen Square they were getting reports and cables from the American Embassy in Beijing, "but they didn't have the sting, the demand for a government response that the television pictures had."[33] The U.S. response in this case was based almost entirely on what the administration's officials saw on television.

A similar phenomenon occurred during the 1991 Russian coup attempt. In the absence of Mikhail Gorbachev, who was seized by rebels, Boris Yeltsin's phone messages to Washington did not impress Bush until the actual arrival of photos from Moscow showing Yeltsin's visible and viable resistance to the coup. Only then did the U.S. administration become convinced that the resistance was serious, and proceeded to take actions to support Gorbachev.[34] The live CNN coverage led Bush to believe that Gorbachev's government had a chance to survive and that when he, Bush, spoke out at news conferences in support of the democratic forces in Moscow, his words "would travel much swifter by global TV than by any diplomatic channel. These facts, in addition to the pictures of resistance inside and outside the Russian Parliament building, energized the resisters."[35]

In addition, for non-secret messages, policy makers now bypass established diplomatic channels and instead use the new technologies of global communication to transmit these messages directly to leaders of state and non-state actors as well as to their respective publics. For example, when the Bush administration first heard about the coup attempt in Russia, its first consideration was not how to cable instructions to American diplomats, but how to get a statement on CNN that could shape the response of America's allies. Likewise, during the 1990–91 Gulf crisis, when Saddam Hussein proposed a peace plan perceived in Washington as a false proposal, Bush proceeded to inform all twenty-six members of the international coalition confronting Iraq of the White House's position. Fitzwater later recalled how the quickest and most effective way for transmitting this evaluation was via CNN, because "all countries in the world had it and were watching it on a real-time basis."[36] During the same crisis, Secretary of State James Baker delivered the last ultimatum to Saddam Hussein through CNN, and not through the U.S. ambassador to Iraq.[37] This growing practice has further eroded the status and main functions of professional diplomats.

The faster speed of diplomatic exchanges on global television presents major dilemmas to all the main participating actors in the foreign policy process: political leaders, experts, diplomats, and journalists. Michael Beschloss argued that this speed may force hurried responses based on intuition rather than on careful extensive policy deliberation, and that this may lead to dangerous policy mistakes.[38] He wondered whether under the pressure of global television President Kennedy would have had the time to give careful consideration to the options as he sought to resolve the highly inflammable Cuban missile crisis. This argument points to a difficult dilemma that today's political leaders face: if they respond immediately without taking the time to consider policy options carefully, they might make a mistake; but if they tell the public they need more time to think or have no comment for the time being, they create the impression, both at home and abroad of confusion or of losing control over events. Leaders often try to get around admitting they need additional time to deliberate their decision by providing an initial response.

The foreign affairs bureaucracy is facing another dilemma: how to compete effectively with real-time information provided on the screen without compromising professional standards of analysis and recommendations. If foreign policy experts, intelligence officers, and diplomats make a quick analysis based on incomplete information and severe time pressure, they might make bad policy recommendations. Conversely, if they take the necessary time to verify and integrate information and ideas from a variety of sources and produce in-depth reliable reports and recommendations, they may find that their efforts have been futile if policy makers have had to make immediate decisions in response to challenges and pressure emanating from coverage on global television.

Global communication may also function as a "perceived constraint." "Too often in recent years," observed David Gergen, "U.S. officials have substituted the power of television for the power of their own reasoning, believing that successful policies must first and foremost please the Great God of Public Opinion."[39] He added that "what too often counts is how well the policy will 'play,' how the pictures will look, whether the right signals are being sent, and whether the public will be impressed by the swiftness of the government's response – not whether the policy promotes America's long-term interests." Based on his practical experience, former secretary of state Henry Kissinger confirmed this observation, commenting that diplomats seeking his advice used to ask him what they should *do* but now they ask him what should they *say*.[40] Philip Powlick found that American foreign policy officials generally accord greater weight to public opinion than is sometimes thought, and that they use news media along with elected officials as their major sources of information about public opinion.[41]

The CNN effect theory has never been adequately defined. It probably originated in American government circles, primarily in connection with demands to intervene militarily abroad for humanitarian purposes, but it has also been used in reference to other effects of global television on diplomacy and foreign policy making. These effects include the following: decision makers' loss of policy control to the media; a tendency to replace ambassadors for the purposes of getting information and exchanging diplomatic messages; the speeding up of diplomatic communication and increased pressure for immediate responses; and a "perceived constraint" on policy makers' consideration of policy options. The loss of policy control version of the CNN effect theory has received the most attention in policy-making circles and the most criticism in scholarly forums. Both the officials' perceptions and the scholarly criticism, however, have focused on recent crises, particularly the humanitarian intervention crises. Global television plays larger and more diversified roles in diplomacy both when it is absent from and when it is involved in international negotiations.

TAKING THE MEDIA OUT OF NEGOTIATIONS

Politicians and officials prefer to conduct negotiations far away from television cameras because of the nature of international negotiations and their desire for immunity from political cost in case of failure. Hurd said that open diplomacy "doesn't work on matters of high importance ... If you want to arrive at it openly, you are unlikely to arrive at all."[42] Michael Ledeen claimed that "if secrets – of various sorts – cannot be kept, good policy and good relations are impossible."[43] These positions are based on a practical principle: negotiations to resolve difficult international conflicts entail long and hard bargaining that moves in stages, from the initial presentation of tough opening demands, through the making of often painful and risky concessions, to a final compromise based on reciprocal concessions on both sides.

Diplomats believe that premature disclosure of initial negotiating positions and tactics, as well as of the potential to make concessions, exposes them to pressure from both the other side's negotiators and their own domestic public. Such stressful conditions could end negotiations prematurely or hamper diplomacy with unnecessarily long discussions, resulting in less effective agreements. The media invokes the public's "right to know" and demands to cover every aspect and detail of international negotiations, while diplomats claim the right to negotiate peace freely without being subjected to constant domestic pressure. The result is a built-in conflict of interest between the diplomat and the journalist; "what one seeks to conceal," Eban wrote, "the other seeks to reveal."[44] I. Claude, Jr, cited critics who argue that "open diplomacy is a contradiction in terms; we may have publicity or we may have diplomacy, but we cannot have both."[45]

Secret diplomacy is characterized by the total isolation and exclusion of both the media and the public from negotiations and related policy making: journalists, the public, and most non-participating politicians and officials are unaware that meetings are taking place, proposals are being exchanged, and agreements are being negotiated and agreed upon.[46] As the world has become more democratic and more accessible to the media, it has become more difficult to conduct diplomacy in secrecy. The public demands information about negotiations and, in general, the media satisfies this demand.

The higher the rank and the status of the negotiators, the more challenging it has been to maintain secret talks. Gone are the days when presidents and prime ministers, by invoking national security, could successfully convince editors to suppress publication of stories. Today, because of the stiff competition among them, media outlets and the Internet are pressured to publish even the most sensitive information as soon as they receive it. Yet, in a few critical and highly sensitive cases, even well-known, high-level policy makers have been able to pursue secret negotiations.

Secret diplomacy produced historical breakthroughs in both American-Chinese and Arab-Israeli relations. In July 1971 Henry Kissinger undertook a secret mission to Communist China to investigate the potential for American-Chinese rapprochement.[47] The results of this visit paved the way for President Nixon's historic 1972 visit to China, one of the most dramatic shifts in American foreign policy in the twentieth century. Secret meetings held in Morocco between Israeli foreign minister Moshe Dayan and Egyptian deputy prime minister Hassan Tuhamy, facilitated President Sadat's historic visit to Jerusalem in November 1977, a spectacular media event leading to a formal peace agreement between Israel and Egypt.[48] In 1993 a few high-ranking Israeli officials negotiated secretly with high-level Palestine Liberation Organization (PLO) officials in Oslo.[49] The negotiations lasted several months and yielded a dramatic breakthrough in Israeli-Palestinian relations. Secret negotiations were also critical in the successful resolution of the violent conflict in Northern Ireland.[50]

In order to keep negotiations secret successfully, officials must create and maintain certain conditions.[51] The following factors were present both in the U.S.-China and the Arab-Israeli secret talks: the talks were designed to produce a breakthrough or transformation in the hostile relations between the actors; the mere contact between the sides was highly sensitive or even legally prohibited, involving actors who had publicly committed themselves never to negotiate; the negotiators knew that if the existence of the talks were leaked before the achievement of acceptable results, the talks would end immediately and the negotiators would face serious domestic criticism: only a small number of negotiators were involved in the talks, and very few other officials knew about them. The talks were held in remote locations far from the media's attention and were organized by discrete and cooperative third parties. Morocco helped to arrange the first Israeli-Egyptian secret talks, Pakistan helped to organize Kissinger's secret visit to China, and Norway assisted Israelis and Palestinians in conducting the Oslo talks.[52]

Secrecy cannot always be assured in high-level negotiations among ministers or heads of state should these negotiations last for an extended time. While politicians and officials are able to deceive the media and disappear for a few hours or a weekend, they cannot leave their offices for long periods without arousing media attention and speculation. High-level politicians who need several days for intensive negotiations and want to minimize the adverse effects of open diplomacy can use *closed-door diplomacy*. This term means limiting the information exposed to the media to the technical aspects of the negotiations for the most part, while excluding the more substantive aspects. The media and the public are aware of the dates when negotiations are scheduled to begin, of the venue for the talks, and of the identity and ranks of the participants. But once the actual negotiations begin, a news blackout is drawn over the talks with only limited information being provided about the actual progress of the talks. In this way, the participants are effectively isolated from their respective domestic publics, as well as from opposition forces, pressure groups, other states, international organizations, and transnational actors, as long as the negotiations continue.

Three major peacemaking conferences – the first at Camp David in 1978; the second at Wright-Patterson Air Force Base in Ohio (WP-AFB) in 1995; and the third at Wye Plantation in 1998 – are good examples of successful closed-door diplomacy at the highest level of leadership.

In September 1978 President Jimmy Carter invited Egyptian president Anwar Sadat and Israeli prime minister Menachem Begin to a summit meeting at the secluded U.S. presidential retreat of Camp David, the goal being to save the Egyptian-Israeli peace process. Carter excluded the media from the conference and later explained: "[I]t was imperative that there be a minimum of posturing by Egyptians or Israelis, and an absence of public statements, which would become frozen positions that could not subsequently be changed."[53]

In 1995 President Clinton invited presidents Slobodan Milosevic of Serbia, Alija Izetbegovic of Bosnia, and Franjo Tudjman of Croatia to a summit meeting at WP-AFB outside Dayton, Ohio. The goal of this conference was to end the civil war in Bosnia that had taken the lives of over 250,000 people.[54] American officials selected the military base largely to isolate the three Balkan presidents from the media. A State Department official explained, "[W]e did not want the work to be interrupted by opportunities for posturing before the cameras."[55] In October 1998, in an effort to save the Israeli-Palestinian peace process, Clinton invited Israeli prime minister Benjamin Netanyahu and the chairman of the Palestinian Authority Yasser Arafat to a critical summit meeting at Wye Plantation.

Analysis of these three examples of closed-door diplomacy suggests that if officials wish to keep negotiations behind closed doors, they must maintain certain conditions. The physical seclusion in the chosen locations increases the chance of maintaining closed doors. Camp David, WP-AFB in Ohio, and Wye Plantation were selected as the sites for the respective conferences precisely because they were secluded or highly protected, with only a few narrow roads leading to them. The reporters covering these summits were forced to camp outside the closed main entrances. In Ohio, one observer noted that the rival negotiators were unable "to hop a taxi to a TV studio and in a few minutes be on a camera denouncing one another, as they might have in Washington or New York City."[56]

Skilled and forceful mediators must determine the negotiation rules, which would include the imposition of a news blackout. Carter and Clinton successfully performed this role at Camp David and Wye Plantation by the sheer authority of the presidency. In Ohio, with the full backing of Clinton and Secretary of State Warren Christopher, the American mediator Richard Holbrooke effectively commanded the talks and set the rules for media coverage. Appointing one spokesperson for all the participating delegations helps to ensure a news blackout. Presidential Press Secretary Jody Powell effectively performed this role at Camp David.[57] State Department spokespersons Nicholas Burns and James Rubin respectively were the only officials authorized to issue statements in Ohio and Wye Plantation.

This brief presentation and analysis shows that when officials wish to take the media out of negotiations, they have the means to do it. In all the above cases, secret or closed-door diplomacy was quite effective and substantially helped the leaders to reach significant agreements. However, new communication technologies such as the

Internet and cellular phones may allow reporters access to restricted sites. This happened, albeit in a limited way, in the 1998 Wye conference. Hosts and mediators can respond to breaches of security by jamming cellular communications around sites and blocking Internet lines, but the best guarantee for a complete news blackout remains the strong commitment of all participants to secrecy. One should note, however, that while secret or closed diplomacy may be necessary for successful negotiations, in itself it is an insufficient condition. Despite the use of this method, in July 2000 Clinton failed to broker at Camp David a comprehensive peace agreement between Israeli prime minister Ehud Barak and Palestinian leader Yasser Arafat.

USING THE MEDIA TO ADVANCE NEGOTIATIONS

The previous section demonstrates how officials were able to take the media out of negotiations through secret or closed-door diplomacy. This section shows the opposite phenomenon, how officials use the media extensively, particularly global television, to advance negotiations and conflict resolution. These uses have come to be known as media diplomacy.[58] Bosah Ebo, for example, defines this too broadly as "the use of the media to articulate and promote foreign policy."[59] I suggest a more specific and thus more useful definition: media diplomacy refers to uses of the media by leaders to express interest in negotiation, to build confidence, and to mobilize public support for agreements. Media diplomacy is pursued through various routine and special media activities, including press conferences, interviews and leaks, visits by heads of state and mediators from rival countries, and spectacular media events organized to usher in a new era.

The tactic of signalling has been discussed in early studies of media diplomacy.[60] In the absence of adequate direct channels of communication, or when one side is unsure of how the other side will react to its negotiation conditions or conflict resolution proposals, officials use the media, with or without attribution, to send messages to leaders of rival states and non-state actors. After the 1973 Arab-Israeli war, Kissinger perfected the use of the media for signalling and pressure purposes during his famous and highly successful "shuttle diplomacy." His relentless efforts to achieve disengagement and interim agreements between Israel and its neighbours, Egypt and Syria, included the extensive use of senior American correspondents aboard his plane.[61] He gave them background reports, as well as information both on and off the record, that were primarily intended to extricate concessions from the negotiating parties and break deadlocks. British foreign secretaries employed a similar technique that John Dickie called "travelling diplomacy."[62]

Sometimes leaders and officials signal an interest in negotiating through their attitudes towards journalists on the other side. In January 1994, for example, Syrian leader Hafez-al Assad met with Clinton in Geneva to convey Syria's interest in peace. Assad barred Israeli reporters from participating in the press conference he held with Clinton at the end of the meeting, indicating that Syria's intentions were not sincere.[63] In September 1994, however, this attitude was reversed when Syrian foreign minister Farouq al-Shara answered for the first time a question from an Israeli reporter at a press conference in London and later consented to be interviewed, also for the first time, on Israeli television. Although the substance of these interviews was disappointing to Israel, Syria's new attitude towards Israeli journalists was seen as Syria's attempt to build the confidence that would be required for peace with Israel. In July 2001 the same foreign minister appeared again in London, but he reverted back to old negative practices when he refused to answer questions from an Israeli reporter, thus again indicating Syria's unwillingness to negotiate with Israel.

In recent years, leaders favour global communication over traditional diplomatic channels to deliver messages intended to alter an image or open a new page. For example, in January 1998 the newly elected moderate Iranian president Mohammed Khatami chose CNN to send a conciliatory message to the United States.[64] CNN and the print media around the world alerted global audiences to the interview well in advance of the broadcast, and the interview was extensively discussed afterwards.

The *new diplomacy* that developed in the twentieth century has been characterized by two principal components: (1) exposure of negotiations to the media and (2) direct talks between high-level leaders. Perhaps, more than any other phenomenon, summit meetings for the purpose of conflict resolution and possibly even longer-term reconciliation vividly demonstrate the combination of these two components. Depending on context and conditions, many high-level summits – for example, the U.S.-U.S.S.R. summits that celebrated the conclusion of peace agreements between the former adversaries – are primarily media events.[65] Dramatic media events, after all, represent media diplomacy at its best. They are broadcast live, organized outside the media, pre-planned, and presented with reverence and ceremony.[66] Live coverage of these media events interrupts scheduled broadcasting and attracts wide audiences around the world.

D. Dayan and E. Katz identify several direct effects of media events on diplomacy: (1) they trivialize the role of ambassadors, (2) they break diplomatic deadlocks and create a climate conducive to negotiations, and (3) they create a favourable climate for sealing an accord.[67] The distinction between the last two effects is significant because media events can be used at the onset of negotiations to build confidence and facilitate negotiations, or at the end of negotiations to mobilize public support for an agreement that has already been achieved. Media events can also be used to cultivate public support in the intermediary phase, *after* the conclusion of the initial phase but *before* the beginning of the next phase. This typically occurs when a breakthrough has been achieved but the sides still have a long way to go before translating a declaration of principles into a permanent legal peace agreement. The public support mobilized by media events at this stage can facilitate the next phase in the negotiations.

Gorbachev's summits with presidents Reagan and Bush demonstrate how the two superpowers became adept at exploiting the media in the transition from the Cold War to the post–Cold War era. Above all, these summits reflected the dramatic changes in superpower relations. As media events, they motivated individuals, groups, and nations "to reassess their relations with each other in light of the actions taking place live in front of their eyes."[68] The first Gorbachev-Reagan summit, in 1985, demonstrated the value of staging a media event at the beginning of the conciliation process. The next summits demonstrated the use of media events during the intermediary phase of negotiations, where each event represents a step forward in the movement from confrontation to cooperation. The climactic Gorbachev-Bush summit held in Washington in May 1990 officially ended the Cold War. Gorbachev, for his part, used the summits with Reagan and Bush to cultivate public support both at home and abroad for his major political and economic reforms. Reagan, on the other hand, used the summits to legitimize the dramatic shift in his attitudes towards the Soviet Union, branded as "the evil empire" at the beginning of his presidency.

Media events were also frequently used in Arab-Israeli peacemaking. Anwar Sadat's historic visit to Jerusalem in November 1977 and the 1991 Madrid peace conference were media events in the initial stage of negotiations, intended to facilitate the negotiation process.[69] The signing ceremonies of the three major documents – the Camp David Accords of September 1978, the PLO-Israel Declaration of Principles of September 1993, and the Israel-Jordan Washington Declaration of July 1994 – are examples of media events in the intermediary negotiation phase. The signing ceremonies of the two peace treaties – the Israeli-Egyptian Peace Treaty of March 1979 and the Israeli-Jordanian Treaty of October 1994 – are examples of media events designed to have a "sealing effect."

Leaders consider media events effective tools for building confidence and mobilizing domestic public support for difficult peacemaking processes involving painful concessions. According to the typology of media events suggested by Dayan and Katz, the Arab-Israeli media events and the U.S.-U.S.S.R. summit meetings belong to the category of conquests where a great leader is able to overcome decades of hatred, conflict, and war and usher in an era of negotiations, cooperation, and peace. Media events, however, are not always successful, as was the case in the U.S.-sponsored Arab-Israeli Madrid conference. Such ploys become far less effective, their effect diluted, when used too frequently.[70] It should be emphasized that media events are fully controlled by politicians and officials, who determine when, where, and how they are played on television. The politicians and officials serve as the producers and the directors of the television coverage, while journalists play only a marginal role.

CONCLUSION

The CNN effect theory was not developed by journalists eager to prove the media's pivotal role in the making of foreign policy and the shaping of global politics, or by scholars eager to share a new scientific discovery; rather, it was formulated by officials haunted by the Vietnam media myth, the confusion of the post–Cold War era, and the communication revolution. Despite overwhelming evidence to the contrary, many officials in many countries believe that negative television coverage was the sole cause of America's defeat in Vietnam.[71] Consequently, many officials have viewed the media as a threat to government policies in many areas, undermining, for examples, the use of force abroad and international negotiations. Following the Cold War, the United States was the only remaining superpower, but Americans preferred to concentrate on their domestic problems and American leaders were slow to adopt an appropriate strategic platform for the new era. Given this recent history, one can understand why global television has been perceived as having the power to determine American diplomacy.

Global communication plays multiple roles, constraining foreign policy officials and diplomats but at the same time helping them to achieve their goals. Increasingly it is becoming a source of rapid real-time information for policy makers; it has accelerated the pace of diplomatic communication; and it has focused world attention on crises in places such as Bosnia, Somalia, and Kosovo, and on global issues such as terrorism, global warming, and human rights. The great speed of global communication impels policy makers and foreign policy experts to respond ever more quickly to world events, while also allowing them to send important messages that, in turn, influence the outcomes of these events. Yet, the CNN effect theory, defined in terms of decision makers' loss of control, has not yet been sufficiently proven, and the media's role in diplomacy has not yet made the role of ambassador obsolete. The CNN effect theory suffers from a major research gap. It has been defined very broadly, but to test it, the researcher must apply it in a very narrow way. When this is done, as has been demonstrated in several studies, it becomes easier to disprove many of its claims and implications.

This study shows that even in the age of global communication, officials have found innovative ways to keep critical negotiations secret or semi-secret, and following the successful conclusion of negotiations, they have employed the media to cultivate public support at home and abroad for their policies and agreements with former enemies. Contrary to the assertions made by diplomats such as Eban or Hurd, officials have shown considerable ability to limit media coverage and control the degree to which negotiations are exposed to the media and the public. They have used secret or semi-secret negotiations and media diplomacy to resolve a few of the most serious crises and conflicts of the second half of the twentieth century.

Journalists and leaders agree that global television becomes a much more powerful independent actor in periods of crisis or a vacuum of leadership. When the House Foreign Affairs Committee summoned Ted Koppel of ABCNEWS *Nightline* to "a friendly lecture" on television coverage of crises in places such as Somalia and Bosnia, Koppel replied by criticizing both Bush and Clinton for failing to develop policies that could guide the cameras: "When an administration fails to set forth a clear agenda of its own, it will become the prisoner of somebody else's."[72] James Schlesinger, a veteran politician and a former secretary of defense, agrees with Koppel: "In the absence of established guideposts our policies will be determined by impulse and image. In this age image means television, and policies seem increasingly subject, especially in democracies, to the images flickering across the television screen."[73]

Even if the CNN effect theory does help to explain some of the United States' actions in certain humanitarian crises, it is certainly not a valid theory of media-government relations in defence and foreign affairs. The opposite approach, which suggests that the media blindly serves governments' national interests in world affairs or staunchly protects the liberal-capitalist system and has no interest or standing of its own, is also highly questionable.[74] Patrick O'Heffernan adopted a more realistic and balanced assessment of the relations between media and diplomacy, one that incorporates elements from the two extremes. His "mutual exploitation model" suggests that the two sides – government and the media – incorporate "each other into their own existence, sometimes for mutual benefit, sometimes for mutual injury, often both at the same time."[75] He explained that "policy-making cannot be done without the media, nor can the media cover international affairs without government cooperation." This mutual dependency, however, is not necessarily symmetrical.

Government officials have been in control of the media's roles more than the journalists themselves have. Friedland concluded that "as is evident from events such as the Gulf War and the Tiananmen Square massacre, the world television system has begun to supplement traditional diplomatic activity ... By the end of 1992, CNN was seen to be the foreign policy *tool* of choice" (emphasis added).[76] Newsom said that "in the last analysis it is the executive that has the power to dominate the news."[77] Based on long-term historical analysis, Neuman concluded that new media technologies have not changed this power equation: "media technology is rarely as powerful in the hands of journalists as it is in the hands of political figures who can summon the talent to exploit the new invention."[78] The media, therefore, have transformed diplomacy more by providing leaders and officials with new tools than by functioning as an independent controlling actor.

This study has implications for both the practice of diplomacy and research into the roles of global communication in the foreign policy process. Many leaders and officials have not yet adapted to the new realities of global communication. Foreign policy experts, intelligence officers, and diplomats have lost many of their traditional functions to journalists as well as to spokespersons and communication experts, increasingly influential in inner governmental circles. I suggest that to cope successfully with the challenges of global communication and to use new and innovative media technologies efficiently, governments must implement two sets of reforms: first, in the training of leaders, high-level policy makers, and diplomats; and second, in the planning and implementation of policies. Leaders must be prepared to handle the rapid pace of global communication and to avoid serious policy mistakes because of global television's demands for fast and effective responses, particularly in crisis situations. In addition to appreciating traditional and conventional diplomatic procedures, those undertaking sophisticated policy making in defence and foreign affairs today must have both a sensitive understanding of the global media challenges and an efficient communication strategy for dealing with them.

NOTES

1 D. Fransworth, *International Relations: An Introduction* 2nd ed. (Chicago: Nelson-Hall, 1992), 179.
2 H.G. Nicholson, *Diplomacy*, 3rd ed. (London: Oxford University Press, 1963); R.P. Barston, *Modern Diplomacy*, 2nd ed. (London: Longman, 1997).
3 W. Williams, *The Shaping of American Diplomacy* (Chicago: Rand McNally, 1971), 79.
4 A. Eban, *The New Diplomacy* (New York: Random House, 1983).
5 A. Eban, *Diplomacy for the Next Century* (New Haven and London: Yale University Press, 1998), 75.
6 J.S. Nye, Jr, "Soft Power," *Foreign Policy* 81 (1990): 153–71; J.S. Nye, Jr, and W.A. Owens, "America's Information Edge," *Foreign*

Affairs 75 (1996): 20–36; R. Keohane and J.S. Nye, Jr, "Power and Interdependence in the Information Age," *Foreign Affairs* 77 (1998): 81–94.

7 H. Mowlana, *Global Information and World Communication*, 2nd ed. (London: Sage, 1997); T. Silvia, *Global News: Perspectives on the Information Age* (Ames, Iowa: Iowa State University Press, 2001); P. Seib, *Going Live: Getting the News Right in a Real Time, Online World* (Lanham, Md: Rowman and Littlefield, 2001).

8 D. Gergen, "Diplomacy in a Television Age: The Dangers of Teledemocracy," in *The Media and Foreign Policy*, S. Serfaty, ed. (New York: St Martin's Press, 1991), 47–63.

9 N. Gowing, *Real-Time Television Coverage of Armed Conflicts and Diplomatic Crises: Does It Pressure or Distort Foreign Policy Decisions?* Working Paper 94-1 (Cambridge, Mass.: Joan Shorenstein Center on the Press, Politics and Public Policy, John F. Kennedy School of Government, Harvard University, 1994); J.F. Hoge, Jr, "Media Pervasiveness," *Foreign Affairs* 73 (1994): 136–44.

10 J. Neuman, *Lights, Camera, War: Is Media Technology Driving International Politics* (New York: St Martin's Press, 1996), 15–16.

11 M. Kalb, "Foreword," in *The Media and Foreign Policy*, S. Serfaty, ed. (New York: St Martin's Press, 1991), xiii.

12 E. Gilboa, "Media Diplomacy: Conceptual Divergence and Applications," *Harvard International Journal of Press/Politics* 3 (1998): 56–75; E. Gilboa, "Mass Communication and Diplomacy: A Theoretical Framework," *Communication Theory* 10 (2000): 275–309; E. Gilboa, "Media Coverage of International Negotiation: A Taxonomy of Levels and Effects," *International Negotiation* 5 (2000): 543–68; E. Gilboa, "Diplomacy in the Media Age: Three Models of Uses and Effects," *Diplomacy and Statecraft* 12 (2001): 1–28.

13 On CNN and the Moscow coup attempt, see G. Gerbner, "Instant History: The Case of the Moscow Coup," *Political Communication* 10 (1993): 193–203; and L. Friedland, *Covering the World: International Television News Services* (New York: Twentieth Century Fund Press, 1992), 42–5. On the intervention in Somalia, see W. Goodman, "Critic's Notebook; Re Somalia: How Much Did TV Shape Policy?" *New York Times*, 8 December 1992: C20; J.F. Hoge, Jr, "The End of Predictability," *Media Studies Journal* 7 (1993): 1–9; and J. Sharkey, "When Pictures Drive Foreign Policy," *American Journalism Review*, December 1993: 14–19.

14 W. Strobel, *Late-Breaking Foreign Policy: The News Media's Influence on Peace Operations* (Washington, D.C.: United States Institute of Peace Press, 1997), 4–5.
15 Neuman, *Lights, Camera, War*, 15.
16 G. Kennan, "If TV Drives Foreign Policy, We're in Trouble," *New York Times*, 24 October 1993: A14.
17 Cited in L. Minear, C. Scott, and T. Weiss, *The News Media, Civil War, and Humanitarian Action* (Boulder, Colo: Lynne Rienner, 1996), 4.
18 Cited in K. Hindell, "The Influence of the Media on Foreign Policy," *International Relations* 12 (1995): 73.
19 Gowing, *Real-Time Television Coverage*.
20 S. Livingston and T. Eachus, "Humanitarian Crises and U.S. Foreign Policy: Somalia and the CNN Effect Reconsidered," *Political Communication* 12:413.
21 Hoge, "Media Pervasiveness," 138–9.
22 P. Jakobsen, "National Interest, Humanitarianism or CNN: What Triggers UN Peace Enforcement after the Cold War?" *Journal of Peace Research* 33 (1996): 205–15.
23 W.L. Bennett, "Toward a Theory of Press-State Relations," *Journal of Communication* 40 (1990): 103–25.
24 J. Mermin, *Debating War and Peace* (Princeton, N.J.: Princeton University Press, 1999).
25 S. Livingston, "Beyond the 'CNN Effect': The Media-Foreign Policy Dynamic," in *Politics and the Press: The News Media and Their Influences*, P. Norris, ed. (Boulder, Colo: Lynne Riener, 1997), 291–318; P. Robinson, "The CNN Effect: Can the News Media Drive Foreign Policy," *Review of International Studies* 25 (1999): 301–9.
26 See C. Powell, *My American Journey* (New York: Ballentine, 1995), 507, 573; J.A. Baker III, *The Politics of Diplomacy: Revolution, War and Peace* (New York: Putnam, 1995), 103; D. Morris, *Behind the Oval Office* (New York: Random House, 1997), 245.
27 Neuman, *Lights, Camera, War*, 270–1.
28 D. Hoffman, "Global Communications Network Was Pivotal in Defeat of Junta," *Washington Post*, 23 August 1991: A27.
29 Cited in T. McNulty, "Television's Impact on Executive Decision-making and Diplomacy," *Fletcher Forum of World Affairs* 17 (1993): 71.
30 Friedland, *Covering the World*, 7–8.
31 B. Woodward, *The Commanders* (New York: Simon and Schuster, 1991), 53.

32 N. Hopkinson, *The Media and International Affairs after the Cold War* (London: HMSO, Wilton Park Paper 74, 1993), 11.
33 Hoge, "Media Pervasiveness," 140.
34 Friedland, *Covering the World*, 44.
35 R. Donovan and R. Scherer, *Unsilent Revolution: Television News and American Public Life, 1948–1991* (Cambridge: Cambridge University Press, 1992), 317.
36 W. Wriston, "Bits, Bytes, and Diplomacy," *Foreign Affairs* 76 (1997): 174.
37 Neuman, *Lights, Camera, War*, 2.
38 M. Beschloss, *Presidents, Television, and Foreign Crisis* (Washington, D.C.: Annenberg Washington Program, 1993).
39 Gergen, "Diplomacy in a Television Age," 48–9.
40 Neuman, *Lights, Camera, War*, 270.
41 P.J. Powlick, "The Attitudinal Bases for Responsiveness to Public Opinion among American Foreign Policy Officials," *Journal of Conflict Resolution* 35 (1991): 611–41; P.J. Powlick, "The Sources of Public Opinion for American Foreign Policy Officials," *International Studies Quarterly* 39 (1995): 427–51.
42 Hindell, *The Influence of the Media on Foreign Policy*, 82.
43 M. Ledeen, "Secrets," in *The Media and Foreign Policy*, S. Serfaty, ed. (New York: St Martin's Press, 1991), 121.
44 Eban, *The New Diplomacy*, 347.
45 I. Claude, Jr, *The Impact of Public Opinion upon Foreign Policy and Diplomacy: Open Diplomacy Revisited* (The Hague: Mouton, 1965), 9.
46 E. Gilboa, "Secret Diplomacy in the Television Age," *Gazette: The International Journal for Communication Studies* 60 (1998): 211–25.
47 H. Kissinger, *White House Years* (Boston: Little, Brown, 1979), 733–87; idem, *Diplomacy* (New York: Simon and Schuster, 1994), 726–32.
48 E. Gilboa, *American Public Opinion toward Israel and the Arab-Israeli Conflict* (Lexington, Mass.: Lexington Books, 1987), 83–101.
49 S. Peres, *The New Middle East* (New York: Henry Holt, 1993); W.I. Zartman, "Explaining Oslo," *International Negotiation* 2 (1997): 195–215.
50 C. O'Clery, *Daring Diplomacy: Clinton's Secret Search for Peace in Ireland* (Boulder, Colo: Rinehart, 1997).
51 E. Gilboa, "Media Coverage of International Negotiation," 546–52.

52 M. Dayan, *Breakthrough: A Personal Account of the Egypt-Israel Peace Negotiations* (New York: Knopf, 1981), 38; U. Savir, *The Process* (New York: Vintage, 1998).
53 J. Carter, *Keeping Faith* (New York: Bantam, 1982), 317–18.
54 R. Holbrooke, *To End a War* (New York: Random House, 1998), 231–312.
55 D. Johnson, "Bemused Dayton Awaits Peace Talks," *New York Times*, 29 October 1995: 24.
56 G. Church, "Let No More Children Die," *Time Magazine*, 6 November 1995: 20.
57 M. Kalb, T. Koppel, and J. Scali, "The Networks and Foreign News Coverage," *Washington Quarterly* 5 (1982): 41; W.C. Spragens and C.A. Terwood, "Camp David and the Networks: Reflections on the Coverage of the 1978 Summit," in *Television Coverage of International Affairs*, W. Adams, ed. (Norwood, N.J.: Ablex, 1982), 125.
58 Y. Cohen, *Media Diplomacy* (London: Cass, 1986); Gilboa, "Media Diplomacy," 62–7.
59 E. Ebo, "Media Diplomacy and Foreign Policy," in *News Media and Foreign Relations*, A. Malek, ed. (Norwood, N.J.: Ablex, 1996), 43.
60 P. Davison, "Mass Communication and Diplomacy," in *World Politics*, J. Rosenau, K. Thompson, and G. Boyd, eds (New York: The Free Press, 1976), 388–403; J. Anderson, "Delivering the Message: The Press as an Instrument of Diplomacy," *Foreign Service Journal* 71 (1994): 32–6.
61 M. Kalb and B. Kalb, *Kissinger* (Boston: Little, Brown, 1974); R. Valeriani, *Travels with Henry* (Boston: Houghton Mifflin, 1979); W. Isaacson, *Kissinger: A Biography* (New York: Simon and Schuster, 1992), 573–86.
62 J. Dickie, *The Boys on the Bongo Bus: The Media and Travelling Diplomacy* (Luton: University of Luton Press, 1997).
63 I. Rabinovich, *The Brink of Peace, Israel and Syria, 1992–1996* (Princeton: Princeton University Press, 1998), 129.
64 See texts and articles published in the *International Herald Tribune*, 9 January 1998: 10.
65 D.C. Hallin and P. Mancini, "Summits and the Constitution of an International Public Sphere: The Reagan-Gorbachev Meetings as Televised Media Events," *Communication* 12 (1994): 249–65.
66 D. Dayan and E. Katz, *Media Events: The Live Broadcasting of History* (Cambridge, Mass.: Harvard University Press, 1992), 4–9.
67 Ibid., 204–5.

68 R. Negrine, *The Communication of Politics* (London: Sage, 1996), 172.
69 M. Bagnied and S. Schneider, "Sadat Goes to Jerusalem: Televised Images, Themes, and Agenda," in *Television Coverage of the Middle East*, W. Adams, ed. (Norwood, N.J.: Ablex, 1982), 53–66; E. Bentsur, *Making Peace: A First Hand Account of the Arab-Israeli Peace Process* (Westport, Conn.: Greenwood Press, 2000).
70 T. Liebes and E. Katz, "Staging Peace: Televised Ceremonies of Reconciliation," *Communication Review* 2 (1997): 235–57.
71 D. Hallin, *The Uncensored War: The Media in Vietnam* (Berkeley, Calif.: University of California Press, 1989).
72 M. Kortanek, "When Pictures Make Policy," *Congressional Quarterly*, 30 April 1994: 1078.
73 J. Schlesinger, "Quest for a Post–Cold War Foreign Policy," *Foreign Affairs* 72 (1992–93): 17.
74 W.S. Herman and N. Chomsky, *Manufacturing Consent: The Political Economy of the Mass Media* (New York: Pantheon, 1988); T. Carpenter, *The Captive Press: Foreign Policy Crises and the First Amendment* (Washington, D.C.: Cato Institute, 1995).
75 P. O'Heffernan, "Mass Media and U.S. Foreign Policy: A Mutual Exploitation Model of Media Influence in U.S. Foreign Policy," in *Media and Public Policy*, R. Spitzer, ed. (Westport, Conn.: Praeger, 1993), 188–9.
76 Friedland, *Covering the World*, 41.
77 Newsom, *Diplomacy and the American Democracy*, 64. See also D. Newsom, *The Public Dimension of Foreign Policy* (Bloomington, Ind.: Indiana University Press, 1996).
78 Neuman, *Lights, Camera, War*, 8.

4 The New Media and Transparency: What Are the Consequences for Diplomacy?

STEVEN LIVINGSTON

In the early years of the twentieth-first century, several developments in information technology promise to further the latest phase of an electronic revolution in diplomacy that began with the development of global, real-time television two decades earlier.[1] Firstly, smaller, lightweight satellite phones, cameras, and satellite up-link equipment will diminish the costly logistical challenges now associated with gathering and transmitting live video images from remote locations. Secondly, commercial, high-resolution remote-sensing satellites will democratize spying from space, providing many nations, non-governmental organizations (NGOs), corporations, and even individuals with surveillance capabilities that were once the sole preserve of a handful of government security and intelligence agencies. Thirdly, a new generation of wireless communication devices will create a mobile, point-to-point communication capacity on a global scale.

This chapter provides an overview of these technologies and a consideration of their ramifications for diplomacy.[2] At the heart of the argument is a consideration of the further erosion of the diplomat's ability to manage the information environment concerning international events. The World Wide Web, private spy satellites, and smaller, highly mobile communication devices used by journalists and other NGOs challenge the web of embassies, intelligence agencies, and surveillance technologies at the disposal of the diplomat.

While intelligence gathering and diplomacy may enjoy advantaged positions from time to time, the relative difference between the capabilities of open-source information – such as real-time news gathering – on the one hand, and those of intelligence and diplomatic channels on the other is diminishing. What is known about the world by news organizations using advanced technologies, particularly during crises, and what is known by diplomats using government channels and resources are about to reach parity. As a result, the ability of officials to maintain control over policy agendas and the public interpretation of events has diminished. News media are no longer dependent on officials for information and analysis of ongoing events. Diplomats' position of authority within their own government and on the world stage, born of their special access to information and knowledge, is slipping away. Or is it?

Alternatively, we will consider the possibility that new technologies and the chaotic information environment they create actually strengthen the position of diplomats. Rather than being undermined, foreign policy professionals are now better positioned to serve as credible, steady analysts who can be trusted to "make sense of it all" in an increasingly rushed and chaotic world. That is the alternative vision of the new information environment. We begin our consideration of these alternatives with a review of the CNN effect and then move on to a cursory review of a handful of new technologies that expand the reach and speed of modern media.

THE CNN EFFECT

Since the early 1990s, scholars have been interested in the effects of global real-time media on international affairs policy making, usually referred to as the CNN effect. The CNN effect refers to the potential loss of policy control by officials to news media. In 1975 William Macomber wrote that the source of the tension between diplomats and the press is found in their conflicting obligations. A properly functioning press "deals with disclosure and exposure at all times, while the diplomat deals in these terms only in end results." Macomber continued: "In his dealings along the way to these results, the diplomat has learned that not only are the best results obtained through confidentiality and privacy, but that often results can be obtained in no other way."[3]

For the most part, a manageable equilibrium has existed between diplomats and journalists. Reporters have gathered enough information to tell a story and meet deadlines, while diplomats have enjoyed reasonable success at managing the overall content of the press. In fact, three decades of scholarly analysis have found that news content most often consists of official accounts of reality.[4] In other words, press briefing, background briefing, and news releases have most often accounted for most of news content. In the words of political scientist W. Lance Bennett, the parameters of political debate in traditional journalism are "indexed" to the contours of debate between official sources.[5] In the news, debate is typically limited to opposing members of political parties. As Bennett and political communication scholar Jarol Manheim found in their analysis of American news coverage of the Persian Gulf War, "As a practical matter, news organizations routinely leave policy framing and issue emphasis to political elites (generally, government officials)."[6] While some see this as the product of conspiracy and intrigue, a more reasonable explanation emphasizes the mutual benefits and rewards to journalists and officials alike through the nurturing of this symbiotic relationship. Journalists' traditional reliance on official sources provides them with a readily available story, while it provides policy makers with an opportunity to shape and manage public perception of distant events. The point of this chapter is to suggest that this symbiotic relationship has been disrupted by the introduction of global, real-time television and other advances in information technology.[7] We will focus next on why this might be true.

Global, real-time television has heightened the audience's sense of proximity to unfolding events around the world. "Policies," noted David D. Pearce, "can no longer be presented to the public in the abstract. They are constantly measured against images on television – images that are instantly available, around the clock and around the globe."[8] At times, it has seemed that decision makers and citizens share approximately the same level of understanding – or at least raw data – about unfolding events. During the opening hours of the air war against Iraq, for example, General Colin Powell and Secretary of Defense Dick Cheney declared that they were getting much of their information on the impact of the bombing from CNN.[9] "We're getting our information from the same place everyone else is, CNN," said Cheney. Perhaps Cheney was exaggerating the importance of open-source information such as that provided by CNN. One must assume that a defence secretary has access to a more complete inventory of intelligence sources. But in relative terms, global, real-time media have produced a levelling effect. What was once known to a few is now observable by almost anyone willing to pay attention. That said, there are of course important exceptions. Serb authorities were able to restrict media access to much of Kosovo during the 1999 NATO bombing campaign. Through intimidation, coercion, and other means, authorities are still quite capable of preventing direct access to news. Yet, as in Kosovo, news media were able to piece together sufficient evidence from refugees, smuggled videotape, satellite or cellular telephone interviews, and the occasional independent report to report the news. In the years since the war in Kosovo, the technological base of international reporting has grown, making it even less likely that Kosovo or any similar region can now be sealed off from observation. Commercial, high-resolution remote-sensing satellites, for example, though not available in 1999, are now operational and available to news organizations.

Advances in the technology used by news media have produced a shift in the balance of power between news media and officials. In a fashion suggestive of the way that the printing press and the subsequent spread of literacy undermined the position of the Catholic Church five hundred years ago, the creation of global, real-time television and related technologies has undermined the ability of officials to intermediate global events for the public. Just as the authority of priests to serve as the sole interpreter of theological matters was challenged by the printing press and the spread of literacy in the sixteenth century, the position of officials to establish the parameters of secular political discourse is challenged today. In short, global, real-time television challenges the policy makers' ability to shape perceptions and frames of reference.

The Gulf of Tonkin incident in August 1964 offers an example of the kind of power that may have been weakened, if not lost altogether. Daniel C. Hallin has called the incident "a classic of Cold War news management."[10] He continued, "Through its public statements, its management of information, and its action, ... the administration was able to define or frame the situation in such a way that its action appeared beyond the scope of political controversy."

President Lyndon Johnson was able to frame the events in the Gulf of Tonkin as "requiring" him to respond as he did with airstrikes against targets in North Vietnam.

In Johnson's time, a part of the president's political power was derived from his ability to manipulate symbols. "The exercise of this kind of symbolic power naturally depend[ed] to a large degree on the president's control of the news."[11] The ability to control the content, timing, and flow of information was key. Though diplomats might have disagreed with the judgment exercised by reporters and editors working in the traditional media, there was still a degree of control over news content, thanks to an editorial chain of command and a resulting degree of accountability. Foreign ministers and presidents could simply withhold information or make appeals to the patriotism of publishers to delay publication, as President Kennedy did with the *New York Times* during the Cuban Missile Crisis. No such system of control and accountability is likely to exist, at least to the same degree, in the new global information environment. Similarly, external control mechanisms imposed on traditional media by governments – such as censorship, press pool systems, and news quarantine areas – will often fail to prevent the collection and dissemination of information in the emerging information environment.

Robert J. Kurz has made this point, too: "Media access to technology that was once the exclusive domain of governments has changed the nature of who knows what and when, thus altering the terms of policy debate."[12] This is the potentially radical consequence of the "CNN effect" and of the related effects of the other technologies we will review below. If this is indeed the consequence of global, real-time media, then they have reset the terms of debate in the foreign affairs arena. New information technology weakens official control over the collection and distribution of information. The press briefing, the typical venue for official control of news content, is less important in an environment dominated by the priority of live pictures. Today's more mobile, less expensive, and more versatile news transmission equipment increases the likelihood that live pictures will be available and used. Officials are not supplanted entirely in this transaction, but the nature of their position relative to unfolding events has changed and one would expect them to be more reactive, even defensive, in their response to the flow of events and the symbols used to characterize them.

In short, in the new information environment, officials are less able to set the terms and pace of events. This said, caution is warranted before expectations about the new technology are raised too high. As significant as the establishment of global, real-time television has been, there is some risk that its importance has been overstated. In Somalia, for example, several scholars and policy makers involved in the 1992–93 crisis have questioned the presumed role of television pictures as an explanation of U.S. involvement.[13]

In addition, the networks' vaunted ability to broadcast live from anywhere in the world has been tempered by the harsh economic realities of doing so, particularly outside urban areas with satellite facilities.[14] The primary reason for this limitation has been the bulky equipment. A "flyaway" unit – everything needed to broadcast live from the field – until recently filled over a dozen cases or was "enough to fill a small van."[15] As the CNN London bureau chief once explained, "This is not something you put in overhead luggage. We spend thousands of dollars in excess baggage and weight fees whenever we fly someplace."[16] Until recently, a typical flyaway package consisted of seven to twelve cases, with each case weighing up to a hundred pounds.

A related factor is cost. Transporting and supporting the equipment, not to mention the crew, and buying the satellite time to transmit from the field is costly, often reaching tens of thousands of dollars a day. Satellite voice transmissions during the Persian Gulf War were fiscally draining, costing CNN $1 million a week. In 1991 satellite time for video transmission cost as much as $200 a minute. NBC spent $25 million on war coverage and lost another $25 million in revenue when advertisers pulled their spots for fear of being associated with U.S. casualties. In 1991 CBS and ABC experienced declines in first-quarter earnings amounting to 73 per cent and 45 per cent, respectively. Both networks blamed the losses on the expense of covering the war.[17]

In short, although communication satellites ushered in the possibility – and at crucial moments the reality – of global, real-time news coverage, the expense and logistical encumbrances involved have tended to limit the scope of "global" to events that occurred in developed areas. This is beginning to change. As transmission devices shrink in size and power and transmission costs diminish, reporting from remote locations becomes less cumbersome. We will review below several of the technological developments that make this possible.

A NEW GLOBAL TRANSPARENCY

The miniaturization of transmission equipment, the reduction of satellite transmission costs, and the introduction of commercial, high-resolution remote-sensing satellites will create unprecedented levels of global transparency in public (and private) affairs. Though not intended to be comprehensive, the next few pages will review several emerging information technologies. The point here is to provide the reader with an idea of the magnitude of the problems facing the diplomat who "has learned that not only are the best results obtained through confidentiality and privacy, but that often results can be obtained in no other way."[18] We will review the miniaturization of information technology, the deployment of commercial, high-resolution satellite systems, and the launching of a new generation of wireless communication devices.

Miniaturized Flyaway Units and Cameras

Since 1995, significant improvements have been made to the mobility of flyaway units, the equipment carried by television crews working in remote locations and used to transmit video images back to a home base via satellite. Much of the reduction in weight and size of these units has come by way of a switch from analog signals to digitally compressed signals to satellites. Among other benefits, the use of digital signals allows for (1) a reduction in the diameter of the antenna (therefore requiring less space and greater mobility) and (2) a reduction in power requirements. The smaller antennas require between 25 and 30 per cent less power than those used at the beginning of the decade.[19] A digital flyaway unit made in Sweden, for example, fits into two portable flight cases. Once on location, a single person can assemble it in about ten minutes.[20]

Other devices used by the news media have matched the reduction in size and operational complexity of flyaway units. Video cameras, for example, are smaller. In 1997 Eason Jordan, president of CNN International, shot emotionally compelling video images of famine in North Korea with a digital camera he carried in his pocket. In discussing Jordan's report from North Korea, an electronic media trade publication noted, "The increasing use of hand-sized digital video cameras in news gathering may ultimately have much the same impact on television news as did the advent of videotape and communications satellites."[21]

These small camcorders are not only mobile and inconspicuous, they are affordable. Sony sells its DCR-VX1000 for $4,200 and the VX-700 for $3,000, while Panasonic sells its AG-EZ1 model for $4,500. News organizations such as the BBC and CNN are thus turning to smaller cameras because of their relatively low cost and high utility.[22]

Further on the edge of miniaturized video technologies are micro air vehicles. A typical micro air vehicle (MAV) prototype is no more than six inches in length, height, or width, and weighs only a few ounces.[23] Some MAVs look like miniature planes, while other prototypes appear to be more insect than machine. Each unit is expected to cost a few hundred dollars. Their intended purposes are far ranging but include providing "individual soldiers with reconnaissance and surveillance, battle damage assessment, targeting, sensor emplacement, communications relay, and sensing of chemical, nuclear, or biological hazards. The concept calls for real-time imaging at ranges up to six miles and the ability to fly at speeds of up to thirty miles per hour for missions lasting from twenty minutes to two hours."[24]

As with other commercial surveillance systems, however, MAVs have dual-use functions and will be found in the hands of non-military (at least non-U.S. military) users. As one specialty publication noted, "There also is a large prospect for commercial applications, ranging from traffic monitoring to border surveillance, fire and rescue operations, forestry, wildlife surveys, power-line inspection, and real-estate aerial photography, among others."[25] MAVs are just as likely to be used by journalists, humanitarian aid workers, or others to observe areas otherwise too dangerous or too inaccessible to reach. As with smaller cameras and lighter and more mobile flyaway units, MAVs expand the range of the human eye to previously impossible or hard to reach locations.

High-Resolution Satellite Systems

Small and more mobile cameras and transmission equipment here on earth are perhaps not the most revolutionary deployment of new information technology. Of perhaps particular concern to diplomats and military planners will be growth in the capabilities of commercial satellite imaging.[26] In the next five years there will be an explosion of high-resolution, multi-spectral land-imaging satellites. Not long ago, these were the sort of systems available only to a handful of nations. Those who had access to the images produced by these surveillance platforms were limited to the national security elite holding high-level security clearances. Today, anyone with Internet access and a credit card will be able to order one-metre resolution images.

The number of overflight hiatuses had diminished significantly by the year 2000. In a 100-plus-day period, government remote-sensing satellites captured about 30 per cent of the total temporal span. This, of course, is a gross estimate that does not include classified government satellite capabilities. As we more into a more surveillance-saturated environment, less time will be available for unobserved activities. For example, ground operations similar to the famous "left hook" manoeuvre executed by U.S. forces at the start of the ground war in the Persian Gulf in 1991 would be more difficult to conceal in the emerging transparent environment.

Vipan Gupta of the Sandia National Laboratories has demonstrated that even the highly professional and competent 24th Mechanized Division of the U.S. Army failed in its efforts to conceal its presence during the preparation stage of the ground war in the Persian Gulf. Using relatively imprecise ten-metre resolution SPOT satellite images of the area occupied by the 24th Division just prior to the start of the ground war, Gupta was able to detect the presence of the American forces. Now, nearly anyone can have access to imagery far more precise than the ten-metre SPOT imagery used by Gupta in his study.[27] In September 1999 Space Imaging, an American satellite imaging company based in Colorado, launched the world's first one-meter resolution commercial satellite. Another American satellite company, Digital Global, announced plans to launch QuickBird in October 2001. Quickbird will provide two-foot (sixty-one-centimetre) commercial imagery. Space-Imaging plans its own .5-metre resolution imaging satellite, with an expected launch in 2004. These are only a few of the multitude of high-resolution satellite systems that will be available around the world within a few years of the publication of this book.

These systems will have more than sufficient technical capacity to undermine operational security. Governments preparing nuclear test sites, rogue fishing vessels at sea, land developers, timber and mining companies contemplating violations of land-use agreements, or the perpetrators of human rights crimes requiring mass graves will never know whether their activities are observed by government rivals, competing companies, environmental groups, human rights organizations, or anyone with a desktop computer, an Internet service provider, a set of coordinates, and a credit card.

Wireless Communication

The third general technological development challenging diplomats is the expansion of high-bandwidth wireless communication, which will facilitate live coverage of events from distant locations. Two general wireless technologies are involved in this development. The first is the expanding reach and capacity of cellular telephony. The second is satellite-based telephony. Although the cellular system is less expensive than satellite transmission and is more responsive to spontaneous demands, its weakness is its reliance on the cellular phone infrastructure. Just as cellular phone users often find themselves out of range of cellular transmission towers, so, too, do news crews dependent on the availability of those same towers. Forty per cent of the world's population lives in an area with cellular coverage, leaving the remaining 60 per cent dependent on conventional land-line phones or with no phone service at all.[28] That is changing as a variety of communication satellite systems enable digitized communication from anywhere on earth to anywhere on earth.

The use of satellite telephony is revolutionizing remote television broadcasting. A lone reporter carrying a device similar in size and weight to a laptop computer can now replace a two- or three-person television crew and satellite uplink unit. This occurred on several occasions in 2001, most prominently in April when CNN producer Lisa Rose Weaver covered the departure of the U.S. commercial aircraft carrying the crew members of the US EP-3 surveillance aircraft downed in a collision with a Chinese interceptor. As the *Los Angeles Times* noted, "The live images broadcast by CNN as the detained crew members of the U.S. spy plane boarded a civilian airliner to leave China illustrate the innovative capabilities available for broadcast journalism using new satellite technologies."[29]

Weaver's initial coverage ended as she was heard saying that Chinese authorities were taking her into custody. While still in custody, Weaver told the *Washington Post*, "We scouted out [the transmission site] a couple of days before; we anticipated that security would be an issue and that we would not be able to get that close to the American crew members." Weaver continued, "We were lucky [those authorities] showed up after the plane took off. I don't think that was planned. It just took them that long to figure out where we were." This illustrates the challenge facing officials, in this case Chinese officials. Reporters are more mobile and harder to control than previously, as illustrated by Weaver's cellular telephone interview with the *Washington Post* while in custody. It wasn't until the Chinese police realized that Weaver had replaced her satellite phone link with a cellular telephone voice link with the outside world that they made her stop reporting.[30]

News organizations, humanitarian relief organizations, foreign adversaries, and organizations of all types will take advantage of this technology and provide small image-gathering devices to their employees or sympathizers in the field. The entire kit costs under $20,000. We can well imagine individuals in the field operating digital cameras while remote-sensing satellites look down from above. If television networks or on-line news services fail to carry the resulting images, they can be posted on websites, just as cyber-gossipmonger Matt Drudge posts his brand of journalism on his own website. New wireless technologies and imagery collection platforms are moving the locus of news out of briefing rooms and into the field.

CONCLUSION: WHAT MIGHT BE THE CONSEQUENCE OF THE NEW INFORMATION ENVIRONMENT?

Definitive statements concerning the likely consequences of transparency are problematic. Certainly, there will be occasions when the new information technologies just outlined will impede the pursuit of desired policy goals. Commercial high-resolution satellite imagery, for example, will make large military deployments without detection more difficult. On the other hand, rogue states may be less able – and perhaps less inclined – to develop weapons of mass destruction if both regional rivals and a plethora of non-state actors with access to commercial high-resolution surveillance systems can detect their efforts. The effects of new technologies are circumstantial, but generally create a more open, more transparent environment. International actors can never be sure whether their behaviour is under observation. What effect might this have on diplomacy? Let us conclude with a consideration of the systemic and cultural challenges faced by diplomats in this new environment.

An audience's heightened sense of proximity to unfolding events is among the consequences of global real-time television, as we noted above. In the process, the diplomat's relevance as an intermediary is threatened and his or her ability to frame issues is undermined. It would seem self-evident that the new technologies outlined above further undermine the professional diplomat's position. In a study conducted by the Center for Strategic and International Studies (CSIS) in 1998, project director Barry Fulton wrote of the growing irrelevance of traditional modes of diplomacy in a world awash in real-time information: "The world has changed fundamentally. Images and information respect neither time nor borders. Hierarchy is giving way to networking. Openness is crowding out secrecy and exclusivity. The quill pen world in which modern diplomacy was born no longer exists. Ideas and capital move swiftly and unimpeded across a global network of governments, corporations, and NGOs. In this world of instantaneous information, contemporary diplomacy struggles to maintain its relevance."[31] Unless American diplomats embrace the information revolution, Fulton concluded, they will continue their slide into irrelevance.

Although the CSIS study may well be correct, there is another possible result of a "world of instantaneous information." To consider this, one must make an important distinction between data on the one hand and information, knowledge, and even wisdom on the other. The world may indeed be awash in data, but credible information and certainly wisdom will remain in short supply. This offers the professional diplomat a clear opportunity and an equally clear challenge. The diplomat has the opportunity to become – to remain – a trusted source of clarity in a world too given to producing overwhelming complexities.

The avalanche of information may ironically produce an effect similar to no information at all. Or worse still, its results may actually hinder understanding. Humans and human systems can handle only so much input.[32] There is, in short, a key distinction that must be made between the technical capacity to collect data (such as live, unedited television images of distant and perhaps poorly understood wars, famine, and other chaotic events) and the meaning of the data. There is a difference between collecting data and producing meaning. All of the technical hardware described above offers remarkable advances in the technical capacity to collect data.

According to one U.S. State Department chief intelligence analyst, during the first three years of a satellite photograph reconnaissance analyst's career, he is likely to be correct in his interpretations of images only about 10 per cent of the time.[33] If the National Imagery and Mapping Agency (NIMA) is bending under the weight of incoming data, one must wonder where CNN, or Greenpeace, or Amnesty International, or a Matt Drudge–like provocateur will find the expertise to turn data into knowledge. Instead of with knowledge, will they flood the environment with misidentified, misunderstood, or tendentious analyses of raw data? Is there an advantage found in this situation for a professional diplomat and a government foreign policy agency?

In an important article, Robert O. Keohane and Joseph S. Nye, Jr, claim that the "quantity of information available in Cyberspace means little by itself. The quality of information and the distinctions between types of information are probably more important."[34] They continue: "[A] plentitude of information leads to a poverty of attention. Attention becomes the scarce resource, and those who can distinguish valuable signs from white noise gain power." Distinguishing valuable signs from white noise is otherwise known as *sound analysis*.

The voices of diplomats and nation-states that maintain credibility in the cacophony of the new information age are more likely to be heard and heeded. Accuracy is more important than speed. Fact checking and caution have greater value than dramatic but questionable disclosures. "Political struggles," say Keohane and Nye, "focus less on control over the ability to transmit information than over the creation and destruction of credibility." In the end, those who can be trusted lead.

These are the two alternative scenarios. Either diplomats will go the way of the steam engine stokers, or they will take on an importance even greater than before. How is the latter outcome achieved? The 1998 CSIS study counsels the American diplomatic community to, among other measures, end the "culture of secrecy and exclusivity" and instead develop a "collaborative relationship with the public." This includes taking greater account of international and domestic public opinion in the execution of policy.[35]

Overseas, we can already see similar prescriptions put into practice by the British Foreign and Commonwealth Office. The projection of "Cool Britannia" via the "Planet Britannia" CD and website constitutes an attempt to update the international image of Britain and make the foreign ministry appear more in tune with the information age.

The danger in this approach is found in the possibility that diplomats and foreign ministries will become just more voices in the wilderness. Is "Planet Britannia" a government information plan or an advertising theme for the special of the month at a well-known restaurant? Diplomats must be sure to have something more than glitzy appeal. Instead, they must offer careful, sound analysis that is as open as possible and unflinching in its adherence to honesty. If this is done, and if the diplomatic community can maintain a reputation for unflinching honesty at a time when publics everywhere are inundated by yet more undigested data, the diplomatic community will actually improve its position. In the end, the diplomatic community's greatest asset is not better technology; it is an untarnished credibility.

NOTES

1 Although the electronic revolution in diplomacy has picked up momentum since 1980, it began with the invention and installation of the telegraph in the nineteenth century. For an interesting review of the effects of the telegraph and other electronic media on international affairs over the course of the nineteenth and twentieth centuries, see Johanna Neuman, *Lights, Camera, War: Is Media Technology Driving International Politics?* (New York: St Martin's Press, 1996). For an overview of the effects of new media on diplomacy, see Wilson Dizard, Jr, *Digital Diplomacy: US Foreign Policy in the Information Age* (Westport, Conn.: Praeger, 2001).
2 I will usually use the terms *diplomat, diplomatic community,* and *diplomacy* as a shorthand reference to larger institutional structures and processes of foreign affairs and foreign policy decision making.
3 In David D. Pearce, *Wary Partners: Diplomats and the Media* (Washington, D.C.: Congressional Quarterly, 1995), 12.
4 For a now dated but nevertheless classic statement concerning the relationship between official sources and journalists, see Leon Sigal,

Reporters and Officials: The Organization and Politics of News Making (Lexington, Mass.: Heath, 1973).
5 W. Lance Bennett, "An Introduction to Journalism Norms and Representations of Politics," *Political Communication* 13 (1995): 373–89.
6 W. Lance Bennett and Jarol B. Manheim, "Taking the Media by Storm: Information, Cueing, and the Democratic Process in the Persian Gulf Conflict," *Political Communication* 10 (1993): 331–51.
7 The literature on the CNN effect is quite large. Among other publications, see Steven Livingston, *Clarifying the CNN Effect* (Cambridge, Mass: Joan Shorenstein Center on the Press, Politics and Public Policy, Harvard University, 1996). See also Nik Gowing, *Real-Time Television Coverage of Armed Conflicts and Diplomatic Crises: Does It Pressure or Distort Foreign Policy Decisions?* Working Paper 94-1 (Cambridge, Mass.: Joan Shorenstein Center on the Press, Politics and Public Policy, Harvard University, June 1994); Warren P. Strobel, *Late-Breaking Foreign Policy: The News Media's Influence on Peace Operations* (Washington, D.C.: United States Institute of Peace, 1997); and Andrew Natsios, "Illusions of Influence: The CNN Effect in Complex Emergencies," in *From Massacres to Genocide: The Media, Public Policy, and Humanitarian Crises*, Robert I. Rotberg and Thomas G. Weiss, eds (Washington, D.C.: Brookings Institution, 1996).
8 Pearce, *Wary Partners*, 21–2.
9 Bill Carter, "War in the Gulf: The Networks; Giant TV Audience for Bush's Speech," *New York Times*, 18 January 1991: A1. For those who take their cue from Hollywood regarding the methods, capabilities, and technology of intelligence gathering, one might conclude – falsely – that U.S. intelligence agencies can direct imaging satellites to follow fleeing suspects down Washington, D.C., streets (as seen in the film *Enemy of the State*) or provide thermal-imaging video feeds of an attack on a terrorist base camp (as seen in *Patriot Games*). More prudent speculations are in order. During the Persian Gulf War, for example, one of the principal intelligence impediments faced by U.S. policy makers was the lack of accurate image intelligence and bomb-damage assessment (BDA). As *New York Times* writer William Broad concluded at the time, "Bomb-damage assessment, a difficult skill at the mercy of the weather and enemy guile, is proving a frustrating bottleneck in this high-technology war of instant communications and precision-guided arms." At one point an open dispute developed between U.S. Central Command in Saudi Arabia and the Central Intelligence Agency and Defense Intelligence Agency in Washington, with the latter two agencies

unable to confirm the BDAs offered by the former. Part of the dispute resulted from an inability to gather sufficient intelligence data. U.S. intelligence satellites were able to provide photographic coverage of only 20 to 40 per cent of the targets attacked by allied forces. Eventually, only one-third to one-half of the the damage reported to Central Command by returning pilots was counted in official estimates of total destruction. This was the third time the assessment method had been altered during the then thirty-eight-day-old Persian Gulf War. In light of these difficulties with official intelligence operations during the war, one can more easily believe that CNN and other media coverage makes a significant contribution to what officials know and when they know it. See William J. Broad, "The Damage: Assessing Damage Can Be Fettered by the Weather and Pilot Hyperbole," *New York Times*, 24 January 1991: A12; and Bob Woodward, "Command Is Paring Pilot Reports of Damage to Iraqi Armor," *Washington Post*, 24 February 1991: A25.

10 Daniel C. Hallin, *The Uncensored War: The Media and Vietnam* (Berkeley: University of California Press, 1986), 19.
11 Ibid., 20.
12 Robert J. Kurz, "Congress and the Media: Forces in the Struggle over Foreign Policy," in *The Media and Foreign Policy*, Simon Serfaty, ed. (New York: St Martin's Press, 1991), 76.
13 Steven Livingston and Todd Eachus, "Humanitarian Crises and U.S. Foreign Policy: Somalia and the CNN Effect Reconsidered," *Political Communication* 12 (1995): 417. See also the response of Natsios, the head of USAID (U.S. Agency for Internation Development) to the Somalia crisis, noted above, and Strobel's analysis of Somalia, also noted above.
14 Richard Parker, *Mixed Signals: The Prospects for Global Television News* (New York: Twentieth Century Fund, 1995).
15 John Tower, news director, CNN Washington bureau, telephone interview, 12 June 1998.
16 Charles Huff, interview, London, 9 July 1998.
17 Mark Landler, Walecia Konrad, and Chuck Hawkins, "All the News That Can Be Had on the Cheap," *Business Week*, 6 May 1991: 86.
18 Pearce, *Wary Partners*, 12.
19 "Technology Lightening Load for Fly-aways," *Electronic Media*, 12 July 1993: 42.
20 "Faster and Cheaper Outside Broadcast Transmissions with New Mobile Satellite Equipment," M2 Presswire, 4 December 1995.

21 Lee Hall, "Digital Special Report First Steps to the Future: Digital Video Opens News Vistas," *Electronic Media*, 9 March 1998: D6.
22 Ibid., 6.
23 "Unmaned Aerial Vehicles – Drone Wars," *Jane's Defense Weekly* 29, no. 2 (3 June 1998); Mark Hewish and Rupert Pengelley, "Warfare in the Global City," *International Defense Review*, 1 June 1998: 32; Barry Klein, "Micro Planes Designed for Strategic Gains," *St Petersburg Times*, 10 May 1998: B1; "DARPA UAV Technology Budgets Top $500 Million," *Military Robotics* 12, no. 8 (17 April 1998); "U.S. Special Operations Forces Want Robots," *Periscope Daily Defense News Capsules*, 16 April 1998; George I. Seffers, "Special Operations Forces Want to Deploy with Robots," *Defense News*, 13–19 April 1998: 3; Kurt Loft, "On the Fly; Engineers at the Georgia Institute of Technology Are Taking Inspiration from the Insect World to Design a Fleet of Micro-Air Vehicles," *Tampa Tribune*, 30 March 1998: 4; Walter Pincus, "From Tiny Aircraft to Robots and Radars, Pentagon Pursues New Tools," *Washington Post*, 29 March 1998: A2; "Micro Air Vehicles," *Navy News and Undersea Technology* 15, no. 5 (2 February 1998); "The Unmanned Inevitability?" *Defense and Foreign Affairs' Strategic Policy*, February 1998: 7; Barbara Starr, "Six Chosen for Micro-UAV Technology Program," *Jane's Defense Weekly* 29, no. 1 (7 January 1998): 7; Jerome Greer Chandler, "Microplanes; Tiny Spy Planes," *Popular Science* 252, no. 1: 54; J.R. Wilson, "Mini Technologies for Major Impact," *Aerospace America*, May 1998: 36–42.
24 Chandler, "Microplanes; Tiny Spy Planes," 54; Wilson, "Mini Technologies for Major Impact," 42.
25 Wilson, "Mini Technologies for Major Impact," 36.
26 There is a growing literature concerning commercial remote-sensing satellites and their national security policy implications. See John C. Baker, Kevin M. O'Connell, and Ray A. Williamson, eds, *Commercial Observation Satellites: At the Leading Edge of Global Transparency* (Santa Monica, Calif.: Rand, 2001); Steve Brenner, "Proliferation of Satellite Imaging Capabilities: Developments and Implications," in *Fighting Proliferation: New Concerns for the Nineties*, Henry Sokolski, ed. (Washington, D.C.: U.S. Government Printing Office, 1996), 95–129; Stephan E. Doyle, *Civil Space Systems: Implications for International Security* (Geneva: United Nations Institute for Disarmament Research, 1994); Ann M. Florini, "The Opening Skies: Third Party Imaging and U.S. Security," *International Security* 13 (Fall 1988):

91–123; and Michael Krepon, Peter Zimmerman, Leonard Spector, and Mary Umberger, eds, *Commercial Observation Satellites and International Security* (New York: St Martin's Press, 1990).
27 Vipin Gupta, presentation at "Secret No More: The Security Implications of Global Transparency," Washington, D.C., 21–22 May 1998.
28 "Two Cellular Operators Transmitting Videotape over Cellular Frequencies," *Radio Communication Report*, 7 November 1994: 43.
29 Dave Wilson, "Technology Gave CNN Live Images of Departure," *Los Angeles Times*, 12 April 2001: A13.
30 Lisa de Moraes, "Only CNN Gets the Picture," *Washington Post*, 12 April 2001: C1.
31 Barry Fulton, "Reinventing Diplomacy in the Information Age," 34 http://webu6102.ntx.net/ics/dia.
32 For an interesting discussion of the human consequences of information inundation, see David Shenk, *Data Smog: Surviving the Information Glut* (New York: HarperEdge, 1997).
33 This official asked to remain anonymous. I interviewed the official while attending a conference in the United Kingdom in the summer of 1998 concerning diplomacy and new information technology.
34 Robert O. Keohane and Joseph S. Nye, Jr, "Power and Interdependence in the Information Age," *Foreign Affairs* 77, no. 5: 90.
35 Fulton, "Reinventing Diplomacy," 12.

5 Snapshots of an Emergent Cyber-Diplomacy: The Greenpeace Campaign against French Nuclear Testing and the Spain-Canada "Fish War"

ANDREW F. COOPER

This chapter offers two discrete snapshots of the emergent use of cyber-diplomacy as a distinctive component of a technologically oriented diplomacy. The first case focuses on the techniques of new information and communications deployed by Greenpeace in its campaign against French nuclear testing in the South Pacific. As an example of political mobilization around a single issue, in which publicity played a key role, this campaign proved extremely successful. In the absence of an effective information and communication response from the French government, Greenpeace was able to frame the issue essentially on its own terms. Largely through the use of an innovative and multi-dimensional mode of information technology, this non-governmental organization (NGO) fed into a groundswell of citizen activism around the world.

The second case focuses on the public relations battle waged between Canada and Spain during the so-called fish war. Of particular interest is the attempt by the resident Spanish ambassador to Canada to use the Internet as the centrepiece of a campaign of public diplomacy. This dynamic approach was very different from the passive/aggressive response exhibited by the French government towards Greenpeace. While lauded as having been the "first world experiment done in this field by any embassy,"[1] this experiment in cyber-diplomacy cannot be said to have been decisive in the dispute. If interesting as a possible prototype of more mature strategies in the future, this form of public diplomacy was ineffective from a substantive point of view. The ambassador's efforts in the fish war were no match for the high-profile actions (and media sensitivity) of the Canadian government generally and Brian Tobin, the Canadian minister of fisheries and oceans, more specifically.

This chapter's focus on these specific cases is not intended to give undue emphasis to their commonalities as episodes in international relations. Notwithstanding their overlapping time frames (the Greenpeace campaign took place in the later months of 1995 and early 1996, and the Spain-Canada fish war broke out in early 1995), the parallel lines between the cases should not be drawn too finely. Both cases highlight the innovative use of communications in attempts to build on the changing interconnectedness in international relations, but a distinction must be made between the communications campaign undertaken by Greenpeace as an NGO and that conducted in the Spain-Canada case. Greenspeace's campaign centred on a form of non-official information strategy, while the Spain-Canada campaign featured state-sponsored forms of public diplomacy. These differences, in turn, reflect very different contextual frameworks. The Greenpeace campaign against French nuclear testing was part of an ongoing issue-specific struggle dating back to the 1985 French bombing of the *Rainbow Warrior* that killed one of the organization's crew; the campaign by the Spanish ambassador was by comparison far more isolated and ad hoc in nature. At its core the Greenpeace-France case showcased a struggle between a state and societal actors. The fish war, in contrast, was a dispute between states – societal actors, although far from irrelevant, stood on the sidelines. In contrast to its direct participation on the nuclear-testing issue, Greenpeace refused to take sides in the Canada-Spain fish war. To do so, it argued, would play into the tendency to see nation-states as the solution instead of the problem in this type of crisis. As one representative of Greenpeace stated, "fisheries conservation has been held hostage to squabbling over national sovereignty versus international responsibility."[2]

With respect to form, this chapter's showcasing of these changes in diplomacy is not to privilege technological innovation as a sudden break with the past. If we use the 1960s and 1970s as a convenient benchmark, we see that technological change has been altering the practice of diplomacy in a number of ways. *Summit* and/or *personal diplomacy*, for example, was greatly facilitated by the ease with which key personnel could move quickly around the world. We can also think, in this context, of the frequent references made to *Concorde*, *peripatetic*, and *shuttle diplomacy* over the last few decades.

In the same vein, the advent of satellite communication and facsimiles marked a clear departure from the older pattern of communication, which relied on a flow of instructions and reports between headquarters and missions in the field.

It should also be mentioned that the implications of these waves of change have not been entirely missed by academics. Certainly, the impact of technological change was at the heart of James Eayrs's prediction three decades ago that professional diplomatic activity would decline or, as he put it more colourfully, fade into "deliquescence," "melting away into nothingness."[3] Although unaware of the notion of cyber-diplomacy, Eayrs pointed to a future in which technological advances in electronic communication and the easy availability of information would "enable the individual to make his mark upon events by placing at his disposal resources previously monopolized by foreign offices." Forecasting some of the later tactics arising from a variety of societal activists, he went on to say that "[t]he requirements for setting up your own department of external affairs in your basement are remarkably modest. You need only be reasonably literate, fairly persistent, moderately affluent."[4]

The recent innovation of the Internet, along with advances in microchips and fibre optics, of course extends these practices and debates much further. The impact of these technological advances, however, was increased by their coincidence with rapid change in the international political environment, that is, with the release from the "disciplines" of the Cold War, the accelerated pattern of globalization and deregulation, and the extension of civil society. Whether by cause or effect, however, these innovations contributed to an extension of the scope of statecraft and public influence. For one thing, there is now more room for other actors, including smaller states and non-central governments as well as societal activists and NGOs.[5] For another thing, economic and social agendas, along with the security agenda, have broadened appreciably. As Gordon Smith, the former Canadian deputy minister of foreign affairs, has acknowledged, "The number of parties directly involved in international diplomacy is expanding rapidly as complex functional issues such as trade or fisheries or human rights attract a whole new set of public, private and other participants ... [D]iplomacy has now become the domain of an open-ended, well-informed group from outside the traditional foreign affairs departments."[6]

Overall, it may be suggested that the two cases discussed here cast light on a key theme about diplomacy that has recently been brought back to the fore in the literature – the interplay between *newness* and *decline*.[7] One interpretation of all of these changes is that they have confirmed the "world society" view of diplomacy. In accordance with the notion of decline, this line of argument contends that the signs (picked up at an earlier stage by Eayrs) about the retreat of state and professional diplomats have been increasing. As the marketplace of diplomacy is increasingly flooded,[8] the institution of diplomacy can no longer act effectively as an agent that confirms power. Changing modes of information technology, especially via-à-vis cyber-diplomacy, pose an especially formidable challenge. From one perspective, there is an air of inevitability lent to the assumption that the revolution in information technology spells the death-knell of traditional diplomacy.[9] From another, it is thought that this decreasing relevance of the role of professional diplomats specifically and the state more generally is a good thing. Among the many "subversive goals" of an alternative/critical form of cyber-diplomacy is the release of diplomacy from its putative entrapment in an "unauthentic" and rigid condition.[10]

Equally, a view has been put forward that the technological transformation makes the performance of professional diplomats more crucial. This line suggests that, rather than curtailing their activities, the forces of change featuring new instruments of information and communication impel diplomats to widen their expertise and tap "into the information revolution and the growing power of foreign publics."[11] If these changes raise the stakes, they also act as catalysts for successful adaptation. In terms of targeting, the technological changes point to the need of professional diplomats to access a variety of publics to get their own message across. In terms of skill, these changes require diplomats to upgrade their capabilities with respect to information technologies. As Gordon Smith argued, foreign ministries have to catch up with respect to "just in time and place" operational effectiveness, the "the mobility of ... operations," and the "transition to technologically saving diplomatic corps."[12]

ACCESSING THE PUBLIC DOMAIN

The Greenpeace Case

In keeping with the concept that information denotes power, the key for Greenpeace in its campaign against French nuclear testing was to interconnect with as wide an audience as possible. The message emphasized the primacy of international governance over national security. More precisely, Greenpeace took the position that the French government's actions subordinated the good of the international community to a narrow (and outdated) view of national security. In its decision to test nuclear weapons, "France has put at risk the future of the comprehensive test ban treaty and flouted its own commitment made at the Nonproliferation talks."[13]

This message was conveyed through a variety of means. A fax campaign was launched. A petition against nuclear testing was signed by over five million people. Issue-specific networks coalitions were formed. Demonstrations, around the globe, were held. A number of important symbolic dates (the fiftieth anniversary of the bombing of Hiroshama the tenth anniversary of the bombing of the first *Rainbow Warrior*, the UN's fiftieth anniversary) were incorporated into the campaign. Daily press releases were issued through Greenpeace Communications.

At the heart of this information campaign, however, was the use of on-the-spot witnessing. Soon after the announcement by the Chirac government in June 1995 that France was to resume testing after a four-year moratorium, Greenpeace launched a peace flotilla in protest. This flotilla – led by Greenpeace's flagship, the successor *Rainbow Warrior* – sailed to the designated test site at the Moruroa Atoll via Ratonga, Tahiti, and Fiji through June, July, August, and September 1995. This flotilla operated in a highly interactive, multi-technology atmosphere. The Greenpeace personnel aboard the *Rainbow Warrior* encouraged contact by phone, and three of the five campaign vessels had state-of-the-art communication systems, with the ability to send images and colour photos via the latest satellite navigation equipment.[14]

At the same time, the *Rainbow Warrior* used the Internet extensively, carrying detailed "Diaries from aboard the Rainbow Warrior and MV Greenpeace" on the Greenpeace International homepage http://www.greenpeace.org/, which had been established in September 1994.[15] The early messages posted in this diary form, were designed to convey images that juxtaposed the pristine beauty of the South Pacific with the impending disturbance (and contamination) set off by the French actions. Among the diary entries were two entitled "The smell of rich tropical earth and misty mountains (with pictures)" (22 June) and "A swim stop/more and more protests from around the world" (27 June). As the initial phase of the campaign came to an end, this sense of dualism became more acute. On 5 July it was reported that a French naval vessel or "Grey 'friend' had been sighted on the horizon" and on 6 July it was reported that a "French warship refuses contact with Rainbow Warrior (with pictures)."

This witnessing allowed Greenpeace to portray itself as the vanguard of the surge of protest against the French tests; a sharp distinction was made, nonetheless, between the actions of the French government and the attitudes of the French people. References were made throughout the campaign to the support given Greenpeace within French society. A key event that reinforced this distinction was the resignation of French environmentalist Jacques Cousteau from his position as chair of the Council for Future Generations, a body set up by Jacques Chirac to advise the president on the environment. As the president of Greenpeace France noted, "Chirac claims he has listened to the opinions of experts in France but with Jacques Cousteau, who led a mission of experts to Moruroas in 1987, stepping down from a Presidential commission over the testing issue, it is clear that he does not have the support of his own experts."[16]

Equally important, a clear demarcation was made between the attitudes of France as a colonial power and the attitudes of its overseas possessions in French Polynesia and New Caledonia. The obstructionist tactics of the French government were contrasted with the sympathy expressed for the Greenpeace campaign by the local population in the South Pacific. This theme came out in the on-line reports of the *Rainbow Warrior's* attempt to dock in Tahiti on 29 June 1995: "French authorities today refused to allow the Greenpeace ship ... to dock at the main public quay in Papeete as more than 15,000 Tahitian anti-nuclear protestors blocked roads demanding an end to nuclear testing and a berth for the *Rainbow Warrior* at the public quay."

The importance to Greenpeace of getting its message out increased as the momentum built towards direct confrontation with the French military. On the one hand, the opportunities for gaining favourable publicity increased for Greenpeace. France's deployment of state coercion in the defence of older orthodoxies (including national security, sovereignty, a territorial fixation, and a sense of grandeur) could be contrasted with the very different values voiced by Greenpeace (non-territorialism, anti-militarism, and the security of individuals and groups). As a Greenpeace spokesperson put it, "The threat of force and armed surveillance will not deter us from our non-violent protest ... The French military may try to make a show of its military might, but they cannot stop the force of world opinion which is clearly opposed to nuclear testing."[17] This message was repeated, two months later, on the eve of the first test: "Whether in Moruroa, Tahiti or in Paris, the international community's opposition to nuclear testing and its call for an urgent comprehensive test ban treaty cannot be silenced by frigates, helicopters, commandos or bans. France can defend its resumption of nuclear testing only by brute force. It has lost all moral and political credibility by breaking the moratorium on nuclear testing; by going ahead with tests now France will become a pariah of the international community."[18]

The risks increased in this confrontational stage. To be fully effective, the Greenpeace message not only had to be delivered, it had to be got out "just in time" to make an impact as a media event. This meant that the French had considerable incentive to try to impede this process if and when they took action against the Greenpeace flotilla. As the coordinator of Greenpeace's international marine division stated at the outset of the campaign, "In the past, the French have jumped aboard with wire cutters in their hands and have immediately started disabling our communications system. They're not stupid, they know that the story is the important thing."[19]

This threat placed a high premium on both resources and skills. The skill with which Greenpeace used its communication resources was illustrated by the way the organization responded to the boarding of the *Rainbow Warrior* by some 150 black-helmeted and masked French commandos on Sunday, 9 July. Before communications with the ship were cut, Greenpeace managed to send out a final message in the form of a quick-time movie of the French commandos boarding and throwing tear gas canisters. The action was later described in the diary on the Internet: "As the campaigners conducted live interviews to the outside world, describing what is happening, and the radio operator drives his computer to pump out the last moments of video before the cameraman has to drop his video camera and run, the commandos set about the steel door of the radio room with a fire axe."[20]

To add to the effectiveness of this message, Greenpeace had launched five inflatables just prior to the boarding. Four of these reached the lagoon across Atoll, from which they were able to get to the nuclear-testing drilling-rig site. Two of the campaigners scaled the drilling rig and occupied it for more than twenty minutes. Although the other Greenpeace inflatables were eventually boarded by the French after long chases, one (whose crew included veteran campaigner David McTaggart) remained undetected (and in radio contact).

A scenario along these lines was repeated in September as France prepared to carry out its first nuclear test. In an attempt to prevent the testing, Greenpeace sent the *Rainbow Warrior*, ten inflatable boats, and a helicopter into the twelve-mile zone. As in the previous episode, the French authorities boarded the *Rainbow Warrior* and attempted to severe its lines of communication. One campaigner described the event with dramatic flair: "I'm in the radio room talking to Reuters. First the inmarsat [satellite terminal] goes dead ... [the radio operator] tries to get the squisher going, but the line just rings in London. He calls Comms, gets through, shouts at them, tries to squish again. The line is cut, the lights flicker."[21]

At one level, what stands out about the Greenpeace effort is the flexibility and agility utilized in the campaign. This resourcefulness may in part be attributed to the decentralized organizational structures of an NGO such as Greenpeace. As a number of observers have pointed out, the looser process of decision making within NGOs allows them to adapt well to the use of new technologies. In the words of Jessica Mathews, "Technology is fundamental to NGOs' new clout ... In lowering the costs of communications, consultation, and coordination, [information technologies] favor decentralized networks [such as NGOs] ... Governments, on the one hand, are quintessential hierarchies, wedded to an organizational form incompatible with all that the new technologies make possible."[22] At another level, however, the advantages accruing to Greenpeace in the campaign came from the resources it possessed as a large multinational NGO. Greenpeace could claim "a certain authority from the size and international spread of [its] membership."[23] It could mobilize a considerable store of physical and material resources, including an elaborate array of communication devices, unavailable to smaller NGOs. Greenpeace had satellite phones. It also had the helicopter, which after "filming frantically" was able to get all the footage back and "squished," making two tape drops.[24] It had as well the inflatables, which as before were used to drop two divers into the lagoon, where they positioned themselves under the test-monitoring platform.[25]

In terms of collateral targeting, Greenpeace had the sophistication to tailor its message towards different national audiences. In the campaign directed towards Australia, for example, a major effort was made to engage the Australian government more fully in the struggle against the French tests. Greenpeace Australia had urged: "The Australian government must pull out all stops in its protest action."[26]

This targeting exercise was an illustration of the enormously receptive audience Greenpeace found for its campaign in Australia. As exhibited by the number of Internet chat lines on the subject, in addition to the extensive coverage by Australia's mainstream media, the Australian government was increasingly pressured to do more on the issue. Although there were numerous reasons for this type of response, at least one trigger was the contrast which could be drawn between the warrior image of Greenpeace (an image long prized in Australian political culture) and what was interpreted as the equivocal response by the Australian political establishment. One Australian lecturer in cultural studies portrayed the adversaries in this way: "There's absolutely nothing pretentious about Greenpeace members when they're seen on TV; they're hard-working, drably-dressed; there's nothing glamorous about them. And in the face of a politically cynical decision to resume nuclear tests, they begin to look like real crusaders. It contrasts to the slickness of the politicians and their rhetoric telling us that it wasn't such a bad decision."[27]

The Fish War Case

Analogous to the Greenpeace case, the campaign carried out by Spain's resident ambassador in Canada, Dr Jose Luis Pardos, against the Canadian actions on the high seas centred on the salience of global governance. In one of his many messages over the Internet, Ambassador Pardos stated: "The harassment and intimidation against the [Spanish] vessels lasted several months, in an attempt to disrupt their legal fishing activities which were being conducted according to the rules of International Law, the UN Convention on the Law of the Sea, regional agreements such as NAFO and the specific mandate of the Council of Ministers of the European Union."[28]

As a form of public diplomacy, however, the Spanish message was directed in a far more concentrated fashion than the Greenpeace message had been. Instead of being part of a multi-dimensional strategy, deploying a wide variety of information technology, Pardos's campaign made extensive if not exclusive use of the Internet. The core ingredient was the official use of "Si, Spain," the electronic cultural information service of the embassy.

The strengths of this approach rested with Pardos's personal attributes – his intellectual commitment to the application of technology to diplomacy as well as his determination to transform traditional practices. On arriving in Ottawa, Pardos pushed hard for the embassy to embrace rather than fight the information and communication revolution. His immediate goal, in 1994, was to use the embassy's database as a basis for preparing this information in hypertext. His longer-term ambition appears to have been to make the "Si, Spain" site the worldwide information service of the Spanish Ministry of Foreign Affairs and Trade.

The weaknesses of the approach were largely structural and situational in nature. Structurally, in contrast to the richness of Greenpeace's resources, for example, those of the Spanish embassy in Canada were relatively limited. Working with the director of computing and communications services at Carleton University, who was also the president of the National Capital FreeNet (NCF), the embassy originally became involved with this community computer network in the National Capital Region. Considerable time was thus occupied with a number of sensitive but fairly routine technical questions relating to how best to adapt the information produced by the Spanish Foreign Service to the structure of the FreeNet menu, and on procedures for the establishment of guidelines for sponsorship of public access dial-up lines for NCF. After providing NCF with information for almost a year, the embassy sought to extend the scope of its information system through a shift to the World Wide Web. The constraints on this shift were again time-consuming. Technologically, it proved difficult to locate an appropriate provider to convert the NCF files to HTML. Administratively, the embassy was given little encouragement to move in this pioneering direction by headquarters. No budget existed, for instance, for anything like a cultural electronic or computer program. Without any great degree of official support, the embassy had to rely very heavily on private agencies within Spain, such as FUNDESCO (a private body, Foundation for the Development of the Social Function of Communications, based in Madrid), for backing.

Situationally, the fish war occurred at a time when the web server was still under construction. Thus, Ambassador Pardos was at a competitive disadvantage in getting Spain's message out. The seizure of the Spanish fishing vessel, the *Estai*, on 9 March 1995 was given extensive treatment on the website established at the Department of Fisheries and Oceans (DFO) http:/www.ncr.dfo.ca/. Until the "Si, Spain" www server was opened on the Internet, on 12th March, the Spanish embassy had to rely on a "Fisheries Crisis" area on "Si, Spain," back on the FreeNet. It was only well after the fish crisis was past its peak that the embassy undertook technological improvements to give a more up-to-date feel to its public diplomacy (opening home pages for Ambassador Pardos and the embassy's cultural counsellor and building more interactive elements into "Si, Spain").

Equally importantly, the Spanish campaign faced serious questions relating to who the appropriate audience or audiences for its campaign of public diplomacy should be. There were a number of options here. One would be to focus on the inner circle of policy makers. To be sure, this has been the preferred target of most campaigns of public diplomacy. In Canada's application of public diplomacy vis-à-vis the United States, for instance, a concerted attempt has been made to influence or "work" the American political system in a full and ongoing manner. This approach has relied on the ability to gain information about specific issues, to develop strategies on how best to get Canada's point of view across to American decision makers, and to facilitate access to those decision makers. Allan Gotlieb, in his capacity as Canadian ambassador to the U.S., elaborated on this point in a speech in April 1984 at the Brookings Institution: "It is essential for us to bring our message to the principal actors on a particular issue, wherever they may be."[29]

In accordance with this objective, a campaign of Spanish public diplomacy could best work the Canadian political system by trying to gain access to key decision makers. The diffuse nature of the Canadian political/policy system, generally, and the tensions between the hard-liners (in the DFO) and those favouring a more diplomatic means of resolving the fish conflict (clustered in the Department of Foreign Affairs and International Trade [DFAIT], the

Prime Minister's Office [PMO], and the Privy Council Office [PCO]), more specifically, facilitated this approach. Indeed, when Ambassador Pardos tried to implement this type of insider approach, he gained an immediate entrée (albeit not a substantially successful one). This access came about when the fishing net from the *Estai* (or as the ambassador contended, the "alleged" nets) was about to be displayed at the Central Canada Exhibition (CCE) in August 1995. After preliminary meetings with the Privy Council's assistant secretary to the cabinet for foreign and defence policy, Jim Bartleman, and a representative of DFAIT, Pardos set in motion the so-called hotline for emergencies. This was the mechanism to link Gordon Smith, the Canadian deputy minister of foreign affairs, and his Spanish counterpart, Secretary General Javier Conde, by telephone. Pardos then met with Jean Pelletier, Prime Minister Jean Chrétien's chief of staff.

As applied by Pardos, this approach had a number of clear defects. One involved timing. Instead of being an application of public diplomacy in a just-in-time fashion, this intervention was clearly too late to have any real influence on the fish war. The key to any successful deployment of public diplomacy is to work the system at the right time – in this case, from the stage when the *Estai* was boarded to the time when Brian Tobin had the net of the *Estai* sent to New York, where he showed it off with considerable dramatic flair to the world's media to get across his message that Spain was an using an illegal-sized net to catch immature turbot. By the stage at which Pardos intervened – during the net's display at the CCE – the impact of any such action was severely circumscribed. The damage to Spain's reputation had already been inflicted. In any case, the key bureaucratic players were no longer on call. When the ambassador launched his initiative, he had to "drag Mr. Conde from the beach" in Malaysia, where he was on holiday.

Another problem was a consequence of the contradiction between an insider-oriented public diplomacy and the Internet approach that ambassador Pardos used to get Spain's message across. Instead of connecting the two approaches via a campaign that emphasized the "illegality" of Canadian actions on the high seas, Ambassador Pardos played into the hands of Tobin and the hard-liners by resorting to populist tactics of his own. In his final assessment of the fish war, Pardos made much of "the tactless habits and behaviour of the

Hon. Minister of Fisheries and Oceans."[30] He also derided a number of the Canadian civil servants he dealt with, calling them "utterly bureaucratic and useless."

Another choice in the public diplomacy arsenal involves putting the stress less on an insider orientation and more on a populist, bottom-up approach. Once more, the Canadian campaign of public diplomacy directed towards the United States serves as a model for an approach of this type. To a large extent, focusing on mass public opinion has had an image-building, public relations purpose for Canada. Gotlieb said in his Brookings speech, "We need not get too excited about the phenomenon of public disagreement."[31] At a 1982 seminar, Gotlieb mused, "There is nothing wrong with letting our problems hang out ... It is good for the public to understand the differences ... Canada and the US are not always on parallel paths."[32]

In many ways, it may be suggested, this was the second approach followed by Ambassador Pardos in his campaign of public diplomacy. Given some considerable freedom of action, he operated according to the belief that Spain's campaign could be most effective by bringing disagreements with Canada out into the open. Many of his Internet messages served as an explicit attempt to counter what he considered the "manipulation" of public opinion "to the detriment of the average Canadian citizen" on the part of Tobin and the Canadian DFO. For example, on the display of the net at the CCE, the ambassador pronounced:

It is difficult for the average Canadian citizen to understand or perceive the action planned by the DFO – I still think that there was no coordination whatsoever with the DFAIT or even with the PM office – by placing the EU and especially Spain in a desert environment devoid of communications or negotiations with any authorities anywhere ... to manipulate the average Canadian citizen into thinking that the aim was conservation ... to renew a dispute which only benefited Brian Tobin himself in his ambition to preserve and progress in his politically nearsighted glory!

Like the Greenpeace campaign in France, Spain's second option was based on the idea that Canadian public opinion could be mobilized over the head of the Canadian government. However, at least in the case of the fish war, this approach was very difficult to apply. The zeal shown by Canadians for taking on the Spanish fleet was genuine and probably unexpected, since in Canada (unlike in a country such as France) the application of force has been a rarely used aspect of statecraft. Although the extent of force deployed by Canada in the fish war should not be exaggerated, many Canadians applauded these tactics as a positive signal that Canada was no longer content to be confined by its image as a "do gooder" in international politics. One of Canada's leading pollsters attempted to sum up this attitude, saying that Canadians had moved from "the boy scout, Johnny Canuck stage" through to "the adult phase of our development."[33]

The campaign of public diplomacy activated by Pardos also met difficulties in countering a negative image of Spain promulgated by Canadian politicians. In issue-specific terms, the rationale for targeting Spain was readily comprehensible to many Canadians. Canada's experience of attempting to achieve an agreement, or even some basic set of parameters for rule making, with Spain on the fish issue had been acutely frustrating. True, Canada's relationship with the United States has been marred as well by conflict over fish, but while it has been extremely difficult, there has at least existed the possibility of settlement. With Spain, a negotiated settlement never seemed likely. When discussing the fisheries issue, Spain (and Ambassador Pardos) repeatedly affirmed historic Spanish rights (going back four centuries to the time of John Cabot) to unimpeded access to the fishing stocks of the Grand Banks. The issue of stock conservation, in bilateral terms, was non-negotiable. Spain had resisted recognizing Canada's 200-mile offshore zone since 1977, when the measure was implemented. On a number of occasions in the 1980s, moreover, Canadian authorities had gone after the Spanish fleet in "hot pursuit."

A further complicating factor pertained to the technological advances made within the fishing industry. Whereas a decade earlier "rogue" practices could be absorbed because of the still abundant supplies of fish, the Spanish and other fleets' use of increasingly sophisticated equipment (sonar tracking) and unscrupulous methods (including the kind of small meshed nets found on the *Estai*) increased the pressure on these fish stocks. The once rich supplies of northern cod had been exhausted under the weight of overfishing. Other less well known species, including the turbot/Greenland halibut, were in danger of extinction.

To give primacy to the promotion of global governance, paradoxically, lent itself to the argument that Canada was justified in raising the stakes in the fish dispute. Canada's unilateral actions may have transgressed accepted norms of international behaviour (that is to say, Canada's application of armed force in the protection of straddling stocks could be deemed to be illegal in customary form), but its rationale for its actions was not based on a formalized reading of international law. Instead, Canada defended its decision to take its campaign against overfishing beyond the boundaries of its territorial limits as both necessary and right with respect to its global sense of responsibility. Far from being a sharp departure from traditional behaviour, going in an uncharted and potentially risky direction, this action was said to be in close conformity with Canada's established habit of gearing its statecraft towards support for the international order.

In this context, it was exceedingly difficult for Ambassador Pardos to get his message across. Bluntly put, the Canadian public was for the most part unsympathetic to claims based on historical rights and legal obligations. In their eyes, the fish issue had to be dealt with not on the basis of what was technically "right" but on the basis of what was palpably "necessary." Consequently, the Spanish message was easily overshadowed by the message put forward by Brian Tobin: "This issue is not about who gets what share of the fish pie that's out there ... What's at stake here is whether the fish pie itself is going to be sustained. Whether or not there's going to be any fish for anybody in the future ... This wanton destruction of a protein resource that belongs to the world is every bit as irresponsible as the destruction of the rainforest. This is a crime against humanity."[34]

The third and final approach in the Spanish campaign of public diplomacy was to give emphasis (at least implicitly) to some form of symbolic compensation for a more defined audience, that is, the segment of the population in Canada and elsewhere with an interest and/or direct connection with the Spanish language and culture. Buttressing this shift, as Pardos pointed out, was the fact that the most popular area on "Si, Spain" was one offering information for Spanish citizens abroad. From this perspective, public diplomacy is important less as a substantive means to gain access to Canadian decision makers and/or win the hearts and minds of the Canadian public, and more as a form of symbolic compensation and support. What instrumental value existed had less to do with winning favour in Canada and more to do with winning favour in the Spanish foreign ministry in terms of support for a more ambitious form of public/cultural diplomacy.

In terms of these more limited ends, the use of the Internet by Ambassador Pardos was valuable and relatively cost-effective. Not only could the embassy try to validate the Spanish position (by *inter alia* publishing official statements by Spanish cabinet ministers the same day they were issued in Madrid or released in the press), the embassy could use the fish war to help target and even mobilize what amounted to a client group throughout North America. From this angle, it is important to note that the bulk of the visitors to "Si, Spain" in its first year of operation turned out to be neither from Canada (4.1 per cent) nor Spain (5.1 per cent) but from the United States (45.5 per cent).

COMPARING THE IMPACT OF THE TWO CASES

As witnessed in the two cases under review, cyber-diplomacy may be viewed as a symptom of larger changes in the methods of diplomacy currently evolving in the world. In terms of intensity, the two cases reflect the increasing salience of speed and concentration as factors in diplomatic activity. Gilbert Winham has written that an important dimension in the evolving pattern of statecraft is the greater importance attached to issue-specific, mission-oriented diplomacy that cuts across traditional cleavages in the international system. Mission-oriented diplomacy, as described by Winham, is diplomacy "when and where you needed it."[35] From a postmodernist perspective, James Der Derian is even more emphatic on this point, suggesting that *time*, with respect to communications, delivery, and response time, has in many ways replaced *space* as the crucial factor in diplomacy.[36] Der Derian notes that "diplomacy becomes governed as much by the velocity of the events as by the events themselves."[37]

The debate in the academic literature is not about the increasing significance of just-in-time diplomacy for states (although the impact on societal groups is less well researched); rather it is about the cause and effect of this transformation. Some observers, such as Winham and Der Derian in their different ways, privilege the general interaction between system change and the evolution of diplomatic method. Others attribute this process of speeding up primarily to a form of response to an external stimuli (often in the form of a specific situational or institutional demand, but sometimes in the form of a cumulative learning process). Fen Hampson gives pride of place, for instance, to the triggering effect of a particular set of exogenous factors in launching issue-specific initiatives on pollution control and other environmental issues.[38]

The Greenpeace campaign and the fish war give some credence to both of these interpretations. The way these two cases played out was influenced by the fact that they occurred in the post–Cold War context. The shift in the geopolitical environment helped to mobilize opinion on the issue of nuclear testing, as legitimacy was given to the question of why the French needed to take this action when there was no clear enemy against which France needed to be defended. Likewise, in system-specific terms, the targeting by Canada of a fellow member of the Atlantic alliance in a "belligerent" manner was facilitated by the loosening up of the discipline of the Western alliance in the post–Cold War era. The room to disagree on a wide number of issues for the NATO partners was broadened as the common enemy disappeared and the concept of security was extended to include non-military issues. At the same time, both of these cases were hot button episodes in that they were triggered by specific events that raised the stakes and allowed domestic mobilization to take place.

In terms of form, the two cases play into the general theme that muscle can be countered by the use of information as a diplomatic tool. In each case, there were clear discrepancies in the power resources that the actors brought to bear on the issues. As in the past, the French government demonstrated that it was willing and able to direct a considerable degree of state-imposed coercion towards Greenpeace. One of the key elements of Greenpeace's success was its ability to turn that state-imposed violence from a political/military strength into a public relations liability. *Soft power*, directed via a concerted communication and information campaign by an international NGO on a particular issue, proved more than equal to *hard power*, expressed through traditional military means. As one perceptive journalist concluded, "Greenpeace has brilliantly exploited satellite links and the global newsroom hunger for exciting videotape to run rings around flatter-footed opponents."[39]

The resident Spanish ambassador in Canada faced more difficult problems when he introduced his public diplomatic campaign against Canada's actions on the high seas. The Spanish embassy, through its communication strategy, tried to depict Canada in an analogous fashion to Greenpeace's depiction of France as a bully. The difficulty for Spain in making this claim, however, was as much the message as its choice of medium. Operating a website out of the Spanish embassy in Ottawa proved a novelty, but this mechanism by itself could not guarantee winning the hearts and minds of the public in Canada and elsewhere in North America. The image that made an impression was not Ambassador Pardos's plea that Spain be considered a victim in the fish war, but Brian Tobin – in a photograph in the front section of the *New York Times* on 29 March 1995 – standing on a barge moored near the United Nations headquarters in New York with the narrow-mesh net and the undersize fish taken from the *Estai*.

In terms of scope, the two cases demonstrate the extensive range of tactics that can be used in public diplomacy. In the Greenpeace campaign, the significance of the Internet should not be exaggerated. The information war waged by Greenpeace was waged through a comprehensive information and communications–centred approach, utilizing radio broadcasting, the eyewitness accounts of journalists on board the Greenpeace vessels, digital video, satellite links, telephones, and computers. Neither, though, should the use of the Internet be minimized. As a supplementary tool, this method of reaching (and organizing) the public proved to be a valuable component in the strategy. Despite the priority given to getting its message out in real time in order to maximize its news worthiness, Greenpeace did not control the way the media outlets would play the story. From this angle, the Internet offered something very different. Without gatekeepers, Greenpeace could reach the public more directly and with a far more detailed and continuous message. If the diary from the Greenpeace flotilla did not qualify as a news event in itself, it was a place where the stories carried in the mainstream media could be corrected or embellished. As one journalist commented in the context of another dramatic case of cyber-diplomacy, "the Web offers ... a powerful interactive communications tool that bypasses the editorial control of other mass media."[40]

In the case of the fish war, the ambassador's efforts received attention not only in the Spanish media but in the Canadian media as well. Still, this effort was accorded the status of a quirky sideshow. While one might play up its innovative quality, in the sense that it was the sort of thing that "you are going to see more often in the years ahead,"[41] the main theme of the media commentary was as much about the style of the campaign's message as about the medium. In the words of another journalist, "[the] Spanish Ambassador ... has posted on the Internet a vitriolic, sarcastic and humorous package of diaries, policy statements and propaganda that disparages the actions of Brian Tobin and Canada in last year's turbot war. These tales of anger, intrigue, threats of military action and back-room lobbying are written in extraordinarily undiplomatic language."[42]

To downplay the use of the Internet in both of these cases is not to minimize the lessons that can be drawn them about the evolution of cyber-diplomacy. In the Greenpeace case, the central lesson is that societal actors, as well as states, have the capacity to exploit new technology to get their own message across. This is especially true with respect to the Internet, where NGOs do not have the same concerns about security and confidentiality as states have. If communication via the Internet is like an electronic postcard, open to view, NGOs are quite ready to operate in these conditions.[43] Indeed, the NGOs can use the relative fluidity or even anarchy of the system to their advantage. States, especially those with a tradition of top-down control, conversely adapt uneasily and slowly to these ongoing changes. Their instinct is to try to install a Maginot line of defence.

The fish war case offers an example of the attention-grabbing effect of Internet use in a campaign of public diplomacy. Yet, the main lesson from this episode is that the novelty of this instrument will not compensate for the lack of an integrated strategy or a compelling message.

Notwithstanding the Spanish ambassador's entrepreneurial drive and the free hand he was given to operate, little was accomplished in this campaign in substantive terms. The image left from the episode is that of a Don Quixote tilting imaginatively but ineffectively at the windmills of public opinion.

In addition to their intrinsic appeal as interesting case studies, the Greenpeace campaign against the French testing of nuclear weapons and the Spain-Canada fish war tell us a lot about the significance and the constraints of diplomacy. At first glance, they are both cases in which diplomacy appears to have failed. Instead of skilful negotiations gaining the public's attention as these episodes were played out, it was the belligerent components that captured the spotlight. Each case featured some degree of application of military power and state-sanctioned violence. Nonetheless, when one looks at these cases through the lens of information and communications, what stands out is not the *decline* of diplomacy but rather its *newness* in terms of the use of innovative forms of public diplomacy.[44] The Greenpeace case, on the one hand, shows how a resource-rich NGO can grab an edge for itself through the creative and skilful use of the tools of technological change. The campaign mounted by the resident Spanish ambassador in the fish war reveals, on the other hand, not only some of the possibilities but also the limitations of public diplomacy carried on through the Internet. Both cases highlight some of the old methods of resolving disputes, but they also act as harbingers for the evolution of cyber-diplomacy. This evolution will almost certainly move forward in a loose, awkward, and fragmented fashion. Inevitably, however, it will impart on diplomacy a very new and different dimension, one that practitioners and academics will have to take seriously.

NOTES

Author's Note: I would like to thank Evan Potter and Les Pal, who have acted as guides in this subject area. Nigmendra Narain helped by way of research. I also acknowledge the support provided by the Social Sciences and Humanities Research Council of Canada.

1 From an article by Jose A. Lozano, "Si, Spain," *La Verdad* (Murcia), 25 October 1995, taken from http://www.DocuWeb.ca/SiSpain.
2 Matthew Gianni, Greenpeace International, quoted in David E. Pitt, "Pact Eluding Fishing Nations on Talks on Imperilled Species," *New York Times*, 5 April 1993. See also the chapter on the Canada-Spain fish war in Andrew F. Cooper, *Canadian Foreign Policy: Old Habits and New Directions* (Scarborough, Ont.: Prentice Hall, 1997), 142–73.
3 James Eayrs, *Diplomacy and Its Discontents* (Toronto: University of Toronto Press, 1971), 69.
4 Ibid., 78.
5 For one innovative account of these trends see J.N. Rosenau, *Turbulence in World Politics: A Theory of Change and Continuity* (Hemel Hemstead, England: Harvester, 1990).
6 "Cyber-Diplomacy," notes for a speech by Gordon Smith, deputy minister, Foreign Affairs and International Trade, to the Technology in Government Forum, Ottawa, 18 September 1996.

7 Brian Hocking, "Beyond 'Newness' and 'Decline': The Development of Catalytic Diplomacy," *Discussion Papers in Diplomacy*, no. 10 (Centre for the Study of Diplomacy, University of Leicester, 1995): 1.
8 James Der Derian, *On Diplomacy* (Oxford: Basil Blackwell, 1987), 200.
9 See, for example, Tim Zimmermann, "Twilight of the Diplomats," *U.S. News Online*, 27 January 1997, http:/w.w.w.usnews.com/usnews/issue/27dip.htm.
10 For the subversive goals of rebels in Cyberia, see Douglas Rushkoff, *Cyberia: Life in the Trenches of Hyperspace* (London: Flamingo, 1994). For the need to understand the contemporary diplomatic framework as a frame-up, see Costas M. Constantinou, *On the Way to Diplomacy*, Borderlines series, vol. 7 (Minneapolis/London: University of Minnesota Press, 1996), 5.
11 United States Advisory Commission on Public Diplomacy, *A New Diplomacy for the Information Age* (Washington, D.C., November 1996), 4.
12 Gordon S. Smith, "Driving Diplomacy into Cyberspace," *The World Today*, June 1997: 156–7.
13 "International Condemnation of French Tests Welcomed by Greenpeace," 14 July 1995 http:/www.greenpeace.org/.
14 Caroline Milburn, "Return of the Warrior," *The Age* (Melbourne, Australia), 22 June 1995.
15 Sue Lowe, "Word on the Wire," *Sydney Morning Herald*, 11 October 1994.
16 "French President Chirac's Televised Speech Will Increase Opposition to nuclear Tests, Paris," Greenpeace webpage http://www.greenpeace.org, 5 September 1995.
17 "French Warship Turns Tail on Rainbow Warrior," Greenpeace webpage http://www.greenpeace.org, 7 July 1995.
18 "Greenpeace Sends 10 Small Boats into 12-Mile Exclusion Zone as French Prepare to Carry Out First Nuclear Test Moruroa," Greenpeace webpage http://www.greenpeace.org, 1 September 1995.
19 Milburn, "Return of the Warrior."
20 "Greenpeace Vessel sv Rainbow Warrior," 9 July 1995, Greenpeace "Diary Update."
21 Greenpeace diary, Friday, 1 September 1995.
22 Jessica T. Mathews, "Power Shift," *Foreign Affairs* 76 (January/February 1997): 55.
23 John Bray, "A Web of Influence," *The World Today*, August/September 1997: 206.

24 Greenpeace diary, Friday, 1 September 1995.
25 "Greenpeace Divers under Test Monitoring Platform to Stop French Nuclear Test, Mororoa," Greenpeace webpage http://www.greenpeace.org, 1 September 1995.
26 "France Testing New Nuclear Weapons-Australia Must Upgrade Protest, Sydney," Greenpeace webpage http://www.greenpeace.org, 14 July 1995.
27 Milburn, "Return of the Warrior." Foreign Minister Gareth Evans, in particular, was accused of being "too soft over the issue and too entrenched in the champagne diplomatic set." Quoted in Glen St John Barclay, "Problems in Australian Foreign Policy, January–June 1995," *Australian Journal of Politics and History* 41, no. 3 (1995): 352.
28 "Estai's story" http://www.DocuWeb.ca/SiSpain.
29 Allan E. Gotlieb, "Managing Canadian-US Interdependence," in *US-Canadian Economic Relations: Next Steps?* Edward R. Fried and Philip H. Trezise, eds (Washington, D.C.: Brookings Institution, 1984), 133.
30 "A Second Friday's Special ... The Last?" http://www.DocuWeb.ca/Si Spain.
31 Gotlieb, "Managing Canadian-US Interdependence," 134.
32 Quoted in Hyman Solomon, "Old-Style Diplomacy No Longer Rules," *Financial Post*, 21 August 1982: 9.
33 Michael Adams, quoted in Edward Greenspon, "St. Brian among the Turbot," *Globe and Mail*, 18 March 1995.
34 Quoted in "Canada is Ready to Act against Foreign Turbot Ships," *Montreal Gazette*, 6 March 1995.
35 Gilbert R. Winham, "The Impact of Social Change on International Diplomacy," paper delivered to the annual meeting of the Canadian Political Science Association, Ottawa, June 1993: 9.
36 James Der Derian, *On Diplomacy* (Oxford: Basil Blackwell, 1987), 208.
37 Ibid.
38 Fen Osler Hampson, "Climate Change: Building International Coalitions of the Like-minded," *International Journal* 45 (Winter 1989–90): 36–74; Fen Osler Hampson, "Pollution across Borders: Canada's International Environmental Agenda," in *Canada among Nations, 1989: The Challenge of Change*, Maureen Appel Molot and Fen Osler Hampson, eds (Ottawa: Carleton University Press, 1990).
39 Andrew Marr, "Green Power in the World's Saloon Bar," *The Independent* (London), 11 July 1995.

40 Matthew McAllester, "Peruvian Rebels Go to the Web," *New York Newsday*, 8 January 1997 http:/www.newsday.com, quoted in Michael Dartnell, "Insurgency Online" http://burn.ucsd.edu/~ats/mrta.htm, paper presented at the 1998 annual meeting of the Canadian Political Science Association, Ottawa, 2 June 1998: n. 2.
41 Charles Gordon, "Diplomacy Flounders as Turbot War Is Caught in Net," *Ottawa Citizen*, 1 April 1996.
42 Paul Gessell, "Spanish Envoy Tackles Tobin, Canada on Internet," *Ottawa Citizen*, 27 March 1996.
43 Geoff Nairn, "Shoot the E-mail Messenger," *Financial Times*, 23 July 1997.
44 Hocking, "Beyond 'Newness' and 'Decline.'"

6 The New Diplomacy: Real-Time Implications and Applications

GORDON SMITH
AND ALLEN SUTHERLAND

INTRODUCTION

Stripped to its essentials, the art of diplomacy is based on the strategic gathering, assessment, and dissemination of information. Information, whether confidential or public, is the lifeblood of diplomatic negotiation – whatever the medium. Driven by its electronic counterpart, the diplomatic circuit is in the early stages of an important period of change.

Information and communication technologies (ICTs) have far-reaching implications for the practice of diplomacy and the international environment. Written, voice, and visual interactions facilitated through ICTs are changing the way diplomatic organizations gather, assess, and disseminate information. Many time-honoured protocols, reaching back to the medieval era and before, require rethinking in a world where the "death of distance" has increased the pace of the game, and where diplomats are usually not the sole, or primary, interlocutors between citizens of different countries.[1]

That said, it is necessary to be wary of claims founded on technological determinism. Even at a time of accelerated change not everything changes. While ICTs are affecting the environment in which diplomats operate and the tools available to fulfil diplomatic objectives, the leading role of nation-states remains secure. Even as their monopoly on international interactions has been decisively circumscribed by the rise of ICT-enabled non-state actors in a globalized world, nation-states will remain prominent actors on the international scene, and so too will their diplomatic representatives. In fact, diplomats will have important roles in enabling the global information infrastructure, and ICTs are providing them with new instruments and venues to undertake traditional diplomatic functions.

This chapter looks at the implications of ICTs for foreign policy and the practice of diplomacy. The first section will explore the effects of the communication revolution on international relations, as well as its general implications for the practice of diplomacy. The second will examine some of the ways in which Canada's Department of Foreign Affairs and International Trade (DFAIT) has worked to integrate ICTs into its strategies and operating procedures.

Our thesis is that ICTs are promoting an exciting change in the international scene. This change is inevitable, but it does not signal the end of diplomacy. To be effective in this new environment, however, diplomats need to become enthusiastic users of ICT tools. This will require difficult, but necessary, adaptations on the part of foreign service organizations around the world.

REAL-TIME IMPLICATIONS: DIPLOMACY IN A WIRED WORLD

The ICT revolution is one of a number of interrelated developments, such as globalization and multiple centres of power, that are transforming the international scene. As practitioners, we are struck by the growing complexity of the evolving international relations environment not only in terms of the players, but also in terms of the range of issues. Non-state actors include multinational enterprises (MNEs), international organizations, non-governmental organizations (NGOs), civil society organizations, and the media. ICTs have helped each of these groups increase its span of control and ability to function across national borders.

Multinational enterprises have aggressively seized the opportunities made available by international trade liberalization, reduced transportation costs, organizational process innovations, and ICTs. The number of MNEs rose from 7,000 in 1972 to 37,000 in 1992. The world's largest MNEs, such as Exxon and General Motors, have sales in excess of the gross national products (GNPs) of many medium-sized countries, such as Egypt, Indonesia, Nigeria, and Saudi Arabia.[2]

The growing number of NGOs has been no less impressive. Driven by many of the same factors as MNEs, the number of international NGOs rose from 6,000 to 26,000 in the 1990s.[3] If we add to this mix the *civil society organizations* that may periodically have interests in issues with international implications, then the number may be in the hundreds of thousands. Canada alone has some 20,000 civil society organizations.[4] But it isn't just numbers that are important. Some established international NGOs are large and respected players in their areas of interest. For instance, the annual budget of Greenpeace International is twice that of the United Nations Environment Program, and Amnesty International has a larger budget than does the United Nations Center for Human Rights.[5] Both MNEs and NGOs have the means, interest, and also standing to exert influence internationally, at least in specific issue areas.

These facts have led some to suggest that the state and diplomacy are in long-term, irrevocable decline. This argument tends to be based on the concept of *sovereignty leakage*. In a global world, power is said to be shifting down to the local level, up to the international level, and out to the non-state sector. It is certainly true that there is a commingling of interests as the density of connections among people and organizations increases, heedless of borders. The line between domestic and international issues is also blurring, with many issues, such as the environment, having simultaneous local, regional, national, and international implications.

Trying to record and evaluate the influence of the nation-state as it works with non-state partners, or through international organizations, is probably impossible and, more importantly, misses the point. Greater attention should be focused on how the state is adapting to this new environment in order to defend and promote its interests. Fascinating changes are taking place. The nation-state is responding to the growing horizontality of issues, the presence of new players on the international scene, and the distance-destroying impacts of ICTs by developing its own networks and capacities. As Anne-Marie Slaughter has observed, the state is evolving and disaggregating into its own separate, distinct parts in order to address transnational issues.[6] This "government for the information age" includes a dense web of relations among regulatory agencies, courts, line departments, and international bureaus throughout the world.[7] For example, the Global Water Partnership brings together governments, the private sector, and NGOs in the examination of water issues. Some commentators have gone as far as to describe these developments as signalling a nascent transgovernmental order or "world government without the form." If they are right, the building blocks of this new world government remain the nation-state.[8]

A paper by Ron Garson for Canada's Policy Research Initiative "Global Network" describes the impact of these nation-state networks in the following way:

The effect of these new networks is to increase the reach of the state and offer more flexible and functional means of addressing global issues than are possible through more institutionalized international organizations. Trans-governmental networks can expand the regulatory reach of nations and provide states with new channels to spread their views and their society's values. Some of these channels can be non-state actors themselves. Rather than view this as a sign of the state's weakness, it can instead be seen as demonstration of non-state power complementing the power of the state through the sharing of information, working to build support and legitimacy for an issue, and by opening channels to appeal directly to national populations.[9]

Perhaps states have been reactive, even slow, to adapt to their new environment, but despite the inevitable bumps and hiccups along the way, there is little doubt that states are beginning to adjust and that in this new international environment they retain the flexibility and capacity to exert influence in areas of vital interest to them. While it remains to be seen, some believe that this era of "networked" diplomacy may be particularly well suited to middle powers. Middle powers are already well versed in the need to leverage or combine influence through shared sovereignty. As a result, they may be quicker and more creative in seeking out non-traditional partners. Some argue that they may also be naturally more reliant on the power of ideas than are states with a preponderance of economic or military might.

What are the major ICT-related factors that affect the practice of diplomacy? Below, we consider the implications of five of the most significant such factors:

- Many-to-many international communication
- The accelerated pace – coping with the time crunch

- Visibility
- Soft power
- The enabling of a global information infrastructure

Many-to-Many International Communication

There was a time when diplomats were the sole interlocutors among countries. Now, unmediated dialogue and information exchange among citizens from around the world occurs twenty-four hours a day. The international projection of the state is mediated by countless daily interactions over the information highway and by the rapid expansion of foreign travel. At face value, this has led to a dilution of the diplomat's representation function.

However, ICTs also present opportunities by providing additional avenues of communication. Far from rendering diplomats obsolete, these networks or avenues of access offer diplomats new ways to gain information, coordinate national positions, make connections, and exert influence. Most of the international agenda is driven by functional issues, issues that play through different relationships but cannot be contained by them. As issues develop, regress, progress, and transform, their management requires different instruments and strategies. ICTs provide additional options to deal with the increased workload arising from an increasingly interdependent world. More and more, foreign services are adapting by employing a mix of traditional and new instruments to address issues. This new approach will be discussed in greater detail in the second half of this chapter.

To cope, diplomats must be flexible enough to interpret their representation function in new ways, becoming fluent in electronic media and engaging new actors on the international scene (MNEs and NGOs), both of which have substantial virtual presences and are savvy users of ICTs. Moreover, with increased demands for public input into policy making, foreign ministries' efforts to educate their respective publics on international issues and practices will take on greater importance. This will require foreign ministries and their governments to make the transition from the one-to-many "broadcast mode" to the one-to-one "multicast mode." Since the instinct for control is alive and well within bureaucracies, this promises to be a difficult transition.

The Accelerated Pace – Coping with the Time Crunch

Perhaps the most important long-term impact of ICTs relates to pace. Where states could once rely, literally, on sending diplomatic pouches on a "slow boat to China," responses must now be almost instantaneous. Delays could mean loss of international goodwill, loss of political advantage, loss of business opportunities, or loss of life.[10]

There may be concern that this time crunch leads to less consideration of policy options and responses than previously. Certainly, the demand for incisive analysis is as great as ever, and it may be that part of the response will be to allocate a greater portion of a squeezed decision-making process to brainstorming, analysis, and options development. On the one hand, this will be a challenge because the requirements of coalition maintenance and development are also on the rise. On the other hand, when mistakes are costly and difficult to rectify, experience may teach us that the considered approach works best, thus providing a powerful antidote to premature decision making. The analysts in the mid-1990s who suggested that knee-jerk diplomacy would be the norm in the CNN age have not been proven right. Diplomatic nuance, procedures, and traditional conservatism continue to "buy time" when necessary.

Given the stakes, one would think that diplomats would have been among the earliest and most versatile users of these technologies so as to be ahead of the curve, adapt to the faster pace, and reinforce their dwindling information advantage. To date, this has not been the case. With some exceptions, professional diplomats still lag behind their counterparts in both the private and non-governmental sectors, not only in hardware, but also in the creativity with which they apply information technologies.

There are lessons to be learned from the innovative ways in which multinational enterprises have used information technologies to increase corporate spans of control to ensure that there is effective communication among all parts of the organization. In the case of non-governmental organizations, their agile and innovative use of communication technologies as a means of instantaneous, low-cost outreach merits examination. In recent times, foreign affairs units have found themselves outmanoeuvred and in some cases put on the defensive by their more agile NGO counterparts in the battle for domestic and international public opinion. For instance, while their own message may have been unheard or incoherent, the anti-globalization forces at the G8 Summit in Genoa were highly successful in jamming the G8's official messages. This development poses a substantial challenge to the future of summitry.

While instances of conflict between state and non-state players create headlines, the story is not simply one of competition. It is becoming increasingly common to include non-state actors in a nation's delegation; further, working ties between state and non-state actors appear to be growing. Striking examples of this type of cooperation are the 1997 Ottawa Convention banning anti-personnel mines and the 1992 UN Conference on Environment and Development (Rio Summit). In the latter case, non-state representatives served on many national delegations. In total, 4,000 individuals representing 1,400 NGOs were accredited official representation at the conference.[11] In 1999 the official Canadian delegation to the World Trade Organization (WTO) talks in Seattle had representatives from unions and environmental organizations as members. Overall, there is a growing incidence of state and non-state actors working cooperatively to amplify and build on each other's messages. As experience is gained, this may become an increasingly frequent occurrence.

Visibility

Today's citizens have vastly greater access to information than any previous generation. Canadian futurologist Frank Ogden has gone so far as to argue that a daily newspaper contains more information than a person in medieval times would know in his or her entire life. Be that as it may, the point is that citizens have access to information that allows them to understand world affairs.[12] Today's citizens also have a desire to be consulted on governmental directions, including foreign policy.[13] The secrecy that may have been tolerated or have even been the norm in previous eras is unacceptable in an increasing number of countries today (see chapter 4 by Steven Livingston). As Neil Nevitte has noted, many developed countries are experiencing "a decline in deference" marked by a suspicion of elites and an unwillingness to delegate decision-making authority to others. According to pollster Frank Graves, "citizens are no longer feeling deferential. They're no longer feeling that smart people can go out and operate behind closed doors on their behalf and come up with solutions for them. That was designed to deal with a nation of farmers and fishermen a hundred years ago. Today we have a sophisticated citizenry with lots of information."[14]

The "decline of deference" will affect the public communications and directions of foreign policy. Paradoxically, citizens continue to give greater priority to domestic issues and are often unclear or unaware of the links between international and domestic issues that influence their social and economic well-being, even as such links grow in importance. This lack of awareness needs to be remedied, and quickly. At this time when many citizens view foreign policy issues as "luxuries" and of far less priority than domestic – and implicitly more relevant – concerns,[15] foreign service organizations must do a much better job of explaining foreign policy to domestic audiences. In particular, citizens need a better understanding of how international issues affect their daily lives. This is the role of *public diplomacy*, an area that has not been a traditional priority in many foreign service organizations. The function and priority given to public diplomacy needs to be rethought, and ICTs are bound to have a prominent role in future activities.

Soft Power

Conceptually, diplomacy is slowly coming to terms with the implications for the international system of the exponential increase in networks created by ICTs. Much of the early spadework was done by Joseph Nye through his conceptualization of *soft power*.[16] According to Nye, a country possesses soft power if it is able to use information and knowledge to set the terms of debate on issues, subtly shaping them in ways that are advantageous to it. While this type of influence has always existed, its importance has been magnified by ICTs and the breakdown of rigid Cold War alliance structures.

The exercise of soft power is an attempt to occupy the "mind space" of another country through attraction rather than coercion, that is, through appeals and the cultivation of common values, reason, and principles.[17] The principle of attraction turns many diplomatic precepts on their heads, including the prevailing notion that hoarded knowledge is power. Information and knowledge monopolies have long been central features of diplomacy. Nye suggests that knowledge monopolies are of declining value and that disseminated knowledge is a growing source of power in a post–Cold War era. While this view is unlikely to find favour with practitioners of *realpolitik,* diplomats and countries will miss opportunities for influence if they fail to understand the implications of soft power.

Of particular importance may be instances when soft power reaches beyond state-to-state relations to appeal directly to foreign publics. While foreign propaganda has a checkered history, from Tokyo Rose to Radio Free Europe, soft power is not about propaganda; it's about rational argument and common values. On this point, like-minded citizens are expected to be more responsive to the appeals of soft power than are those who have a different world view.

While soft power does not consume as many resources as military power, it nevertheless requires investment. Nations hoping to cultivate soft power must be prepared to make investments in knowledge infrastructures, both within government policy research staffs and throughout their societies. Ideas are the currency of soft power, and nations without them cannot hope to wield soft power effectively. In addition, those using soft power diplomacy must have the courage to challenge the status quo by presenting far-sighted views and risk being "ahead of the curve." Finally, soft power probably requires greater interaction among the various epistemic communities, that is, academics, policy research institutes, NGOs, media leaders, and diplomats. This two-way interaction helps create the environment necessary for innovative foreign policy research, as well as a capacity within government to absorb and use such work in its dealings.

An interesting, and often overlooked, element of soft power diplomacy is that it is usually not a zero-sum proposition, since it is possible to build cooperatively upon the soft power assets of other countries. For example, the fruits of U.S. soft power can sometimes be harvested by Canada because the values Americans promote are often consistent with Canadian values, culture, society, and world view – for example, trade liberalization, democracy, freedom of expression, and pluralism. The opposite is also the case. In this way, over time, the range of common values and interests among countries may grow.

The Enabling of a Global Information Infrastructure

As time goes on, ICT issues will loom larger in their own right as international issues, that is, as subjects requiring diplomacy, negotiation, and, possibly, new institutional infrastructures. Many ICT issues (e.g., privacy, freedom of speech, intellectual property, pornography, and hate literature) will deepen the involvement of international regimes in sensitive areas usually seen as being solely within the purview of the nation-state. Others, such as electronic commerce, could have profound implications for nation-state tax bases and prosperity.

From a commercial perspective, the dazzling prospects offered by the electronic marketplace make up the jewel in the global information infrastructural crown. The intractable issues that may arise from the emergence of a global information infrastructure should not obscure the potential benefits of ICTs. Many aspects of ICTs resonate with people's deeply held democratic values and support the objective of many countries to promote these values internationally.

In order to enable the global information infrastructure, national information infrastructures and societal infrastructures (e.g., marketplaces) will have to connect to a greater degree than in the past. The scope of this formidable challenge is perhaps best understood by analogy. In the virtual world of communication technologies, the genius of interoperability allows different platforms with different operating systems to connect with varying degrees of seamlessness. What is not commonly recognized, being often taken for granted, is the technical genius required to work this marvel. In the real world of nation-states, connectivity depends on the art of diplomacy. Like most things human, it can seem slow-moving, messy, and subject to compromise. As with MS-DOS, diplomacy can seem slow, even archaic, but it still gets the job done.[18]

Diplomacy will be essential if we are to provide connectivity between such diverse operating systems as those that guide us in Canada and those in such countries as China, India, and Brazil. As the global information infrastructure takes on a less English-only and North American hue – and it must if it is to become truly global – diplomacy will be increasingly called on to bridge differences. This will happen despite the libertarian tendencies of the Internet, and most disagreements will benefit from diplomatic intervention. Ironically, early efforts to help enable the global information infrastructure through the World Trade Organization and telecommunications liberalization have relied heavily on traditional diplomacy.

REAL-TIME APPLICATIONS: CREATING A "WIRED" ORGANIZATION AT DFAIT

So far, our focus has been largely abstract. The emphasis has been on considering ICTs as phenomena that have had possibly significant impacts on international relations and diplomacy. In this section, our focus is on the practical. We consider some concrete ways that ICTs can be and are being used in diplomatic organizations. For illustrative purposes, analysis will draw on the experience of Canada's Department of Foreign Affairs and International Trade (DFAIT).

Like other organizations with a global reach, foreign services face considerable challenges in the area of internal communications. All too often, diplomats in the field are "out of sight and out of mind."[19] ICTs enable the organization to increase its corporate breadth of control – possibly a mixed blessing for some diplomats – but they also allow for greater corporate support of diplomats on assignment and better use of an organization's finite human capital. For instance, ICTs allow headquarters to consult their diplomats in the field with greater regularity and enable both groups to keep each other abreast of developments in real time. This has important implications for operational efficiency and effectiveness. Despite lingering concerns over secrecy, diplomatic corps are being driven to adopt ICTs for internal communications in order to cope with the time crunch, just like their MNE and NGO brethren.

There is also pressure – though currently not as much – for foreign affairs departments to adopt innovative ICT strategies in their external communications with other diplomats, national governments, NGOs, and the public. While most diplomatic corps are solidly in broadcast mode, there are also growing pressures for more interactive, many-to-many communication strategies and strategies involving the use of soft power.

Helping Diplomats Do Their Job: The DFAIT Experience

The Canadian government generally and its Department of Foreign Affairs and International Trade (DFAIT) specifically have been working to integrate ICTs into their operating procedures and practices.

Whether it has been to develop the capacity to offer all federal government services on-line by 2004 or to create a more convenient way for Canadian businesses to get foreign market information on-line, like most organizational change, this effort has required experimentation, innovation, and a willingness to take risks.

DFAIT has invested heavily in information technology, so much so that, according to the department's documents, in fiscal year 1999/2000 DFAIT spent more than $100 million on informatics, twice what it had five years previously. At 7.4 per cent of the total budget, this expenditure exceeded personnel costs as well as the combined costs of the department's foreign policy, trade, economic policy, international business development, and public diplomacy operations.

The shift in the organization is more than budgetary. DFAIT's Information Management and Technology Bureau (SXD) is the largest bureau in the department with an official complement of 425 full-time employees and another 100 consultants on-site. Almost unremarked, this group now compares in size with the traditional grouping of political and economic foreign service officers (482) and trade foreign service officers (381). This influx is bound to have long-term impacts on the department's culture and receptivity to technology.

While its efforts are ongoing and incomplete, DFAIT's experience is illustrative of the challenges, prospects, and possible uses of ICTs for diplomats and diplomatic organizations. This section considers the "wiring" of DFAIT from three perspectives:

- Hardware, software, and training
- Managing technological change
- Successful applications

HARDWARE, SOFTWARE, AND TRAINING[20]

To improve contact with posts or "field operations," DFAIT has introduced a highly sophisticated, integrated and dedicated worldwide telecommunications system called MITNET (Multi-user International Telecommunications Network), which handles both voice and data. This is the communications backbone of the department. It provides seven-digit direct dial access to telephones of missions around the world. Such a system is superior to those currently in place in the foreign services of other G7 (Group of Seven) countries. It ensures that, aside from time differences, an exchange over the telephone to any of Canada's posts is really no different than one between Canadian diplomats in the same building. It provides secure voice/data communications at 126 locations in 85 countries. Remarkably, the savings in the cost of voice traffic alone will pay for the upgrade over its lifespan.

DFAIT has also upgraded the mobility of its operations. This permits rapid responses to emergencies and to situations that require temporary communications hook-ups, such as G7 summits or during international crises (e.g., the 1996 crisis in Zaire when Canada responded by forming a "virtual" team with members in Africa, Ottawa, New York, and Washington). Canadian diplomats also possess electronic "call-me" cards that permit them to access MITNET from any telephone booth in the world, a significant advantage during negotiation sessions.

In terms of DFAIT's presence in cyberspace, both department and embassy websites have been developed. The wide variety of information available includes travel advisories, current research, Canadian positions on high-profile issues, as well as links to the constantly growing and already well-developed infrastructure of Canadian government sites. There are ongoing efforts to raise the level of interaction on DFAIT sites, since to be relevant, a website must be an ongoing creative activity. One of the more recent innovations is ExportSource, a web-based service for Canadian exporters that combines expertise and program information from across the federal government in a way that is simple, seamless, and timely.

In terms of desktop applications, over 99 per cent of DFAIT officer-level staff around the globe are connected by a leading edge technology platform called SIGNET (Secure Integrated Global Network), which can support virtually any application or business process that may be needed. It is available in 131 locations and 90 countries.

The simplest application – and the one with the greatest impact both today and in the future – is the provision of e-mail, desk-to-desk around the world, with links to other government departments and to public networks. There are also firewall-mediated links to the Internet, as well as the GTIS x400 Gateway. In 1998 DFAIT handled 30 million e-mail messages on its network.

In addition to the standard word-processing and spreadsheet software, there are a variety of more specialized applications. For instance, DFAIT has WIN Exports, a software package for its 1,200 trade officers that helps link Canadian exporters to foreign consumers. The department receives over 100,000 requests each year from foreign buyers that utilize the software's capabilities.

Another formidable application is the SIGNET/Winframe database system. Winframe provides Canadian foreign service officers throughout the world with an integrated package of international trade and political information. New software applications are continuously being added.

Foreign service officers are highly trained generalists whose human capital must be constantly upgraded. Training, particularly language training, is a difficult task for such a broadly dispersed organization. With predictions of the virtual university and an expansion of distance learning prominent in the thinking of such commentators as Don Tapscott, the Canadian Foreign Service Institute (CFSI), DFAIT's training arm, has been experimenting with ICTs to address training needs. In cooperation with partners elsewhere in the federal government, the institute has developed a number of products, including ORTHO+, a software program on French spelling, and PASAJES LATINOAMERICANOS, a software program that teaches Spanish through the use of video clips, listening-comprehension exercises, and transcription exercises.

The CFSI has also developed a virtual campus that provides universal access to training through text-based self-study modules, network CD-ROMs, and computer programs designed to provide training solutions. The virtual campus is also designed to address the often-ignored training needs of the department's many locally engaged staff at its missions around the world.

MANAGING TECHNOLOGICAL CHANGE

Investment in ICTs can be difficult for managers in diplomatic organizations. It's expensive, outside the realm of many managers' personal experience, and with technology evolving rapidly, it is often difficult to know where and when to place an organization's technological bets. Finally, transitions from one technology platform to another can be very bumpy. The business of diplomacy does not pause simply because one foreign service chooses to adopt a new ICT platform. While some allowances for ICT growing pains may be made as new systems come on-line, they are strictly limited. The decision to switch communications platforms is a stressful one for the entire organization and must be managed with care.

DFAIT's experience with the COSIC technology platform, which was in operation in the early 1990s, offered the lesson that, on balance, it is preferable to buy as much technology off-the-shelf as possible. Besides the obvious cost advantages, there are a couple of other reasons for choosing this route. First, off-the-shelf technology typically is more proven. As technology commentators have observed, most organizations underestimate the maintenance and upkeep costs of technology. Prudent decisions to buy off-the-shelf technologies help to minimize these downstream costs. Second, off-the-shelf ICT products are less likely to have compatibility problems with related applications over time. Put another way, ICT companies may develop new, albeit generic, applications for off-the-shelf products. If your system is highly specialized, it is likely that most related applications will require tailoring, which can be costly in money and time and may deprive the organization of cutting-edge products.

The integration of ICT use within an organization does not move at an even pace. Some parts will move more swiftly than others. Overall, it takes time, and while there have been some hopeful signs of progress, we have yet to see the full impact of ICTs on diplomatic organizations. In terms of operational capacity and efficiency, there are essentially three stages in ICT use. During stage 1, ICTs are used to complete existing tasks with greater efficiency. For example, record keeping is far more efficient in electronic formats. In stage 2, ICTs are fully integrated into existing procedures and protocols. For example, procedures to distribute briefing notes have been revised in many organizations to take advantage of the efficiency of electronic distribution. In stage 3, new protocols and procedures are developed that draw on ICT strengths. At this stage, ICTs are seamlessly melded with traditional instruments, procedures, and practices. The success of the Ottawa Process in producing a landmines treaty by mixing traditional and non-traditional forums is perhaps an example of the path ahead and, hopefully, will provide a boost to accelerate the development of new instruments, processes, and, most importantly, mindsets.

The process of technological change within an organization belies the notion of a technological silver bullet. Initially, new technologies are applied to fulfil existing organizational tasks more effectively. For instance, desktop-to-desktop e-mail coverage has allowed DFAIT to distribute its notes, memos, and telexes with greater efficiency. Even here, the remnants of earlier, once-efficient but now-archaic practices can sometimes be seen. The best examples are the telexes in which pidgin English and French are still used, even as the variable cost of electronic communications falls to zero. This style was once standard practice because of the costly per word technologies of the 1960s. It endures because it takes time for people and organizations to rethink their practices and embrace change. Their persistence is a potent reminder of the time that organizations require to absorb new technologies.

The cultivatation of a sense of adventure about a technology aids organizational learning. DFAIT, for example, found that it was important to provide Internet access throughout the organization and to maintain relatively loose reins on the use of the new technology. This approach allows employees to make the technology "theirs" and to overcome the fear factor. Thus empowered, employees become users capable (and motivated) to apply the technology in an innovative manner. There can be few greater responsibilities for a manager in a knowledge organization than to facilitate this process.

Most importantly, users need to see how the technology benefits them at a very personal level in their day-to-day work. Otherwise, there is little incentive for employees to make the transition to the new operational system, much less to use the new technologies creatively. In situations where benefits are not recognized, organizations can become stuck between the new and old systems, which creates confusion, duplication of effort, and frustration.

Sometimes demonstrations are required. For instance, early in the Peruvian hostage crisis at the Japanese embassy in 1997, DFAIT personnel using traditional diplomatic channels were stymied in their efforts to find information on the demands of the Tupac Amaru. While traditional diplomatic channels were unsuccessful, then under-secretary of foreign affairs Gordon Smith was able to learn what his department could not simply by accessing the Tupac Amaru's website. This provided a poignant demonstration to staff of the usefulness and imperative of learning how to use the Internet.

The strongest impetus for understanding the implications of new technology for any organization must lie with senior management. No one expects senior management to become computer programmers, but it is an abdication of leadership for senior management in any knowledge organization to relegate corporate information investments and decisions to the "techies." For one thing, technology represents too big an operational investment. More importantly, a good manager values the process improvements that can be enabled by prudent information technological investments. Senior managers need to be interested, engaged practitioners who understand and encourage innovative applications.

In our view, only about 15 per cent of the challenge is a technical one; the other 85 per cent lies below the surface in an organization's culture, human resource priorities, and operating procedures.[21] The greatest resistance, in fact, tends to come from the senior levels of the organization. Junior officers take to the technology easily and, if harnessed, can be drivers of technological improvement and innovation. In DFAIT's experience, there is a "leadership from below" acts as a complement to the "leadership from above."

In DFAIT's case, it was decided that a senior-level ICT champion was needed to coordinate existing functions (e.g., data storage, library services, and communications) and to promote ICTs within the organization. The position of chief information officer was created, and the holder of this office has helped to ensure that ICTs have sufficient managerial clout within the organization.

SUCCESSFUL APPLICATIONS

One can perhaps best understand the change at DFAIT by looking at a number of concrete examples of how practices are changing:

Establishing New Embassies and Diplomatic Posts. There was a time when establishing a new embassy or diplomatic post took weeks, even months. Now, it takes a plane ticket, a laptop, a dial tone, and maybe a diplomatic passport. DFAIT can hit the ground running, with huge implications for the mobility of operations and what is being called "just in time and place" operational effectiveness. This approach was used to establish a new embassy in Zagreb, Croatia, at the height of the Bosnian conflict. The embassy was operational within a few hours.[22]

ICTs have been used successfully throughout the world to provide essential support to a growing number of micro-missions. Micro-missions are streamlined Canadian consulates or trade offices that typically are staffed by one or two Canadian foreign service officers and usually no more than three to five locally engaged employees.[23]

Micro-missions are an efficient way to extend Canada's presence and influence to new parts of the world. These "embassies in a suitcase" have been justifiably praised for their cost-effectiveness, particularly for trade promotion. At present, there are some forty Canadian micro-missions, many in regional centres of large countries, such as Russia (St Petersburg), Mexico (Guadalajara), and Japan (Nagoya), or in small states, such as Panama (Panama City) and Lithuania (Vilnius).

Micro-missions have also been used to wave the flag at the earliest possible moment upon the creation of new states. For instance, upon the break-up of the Soviet Union, Canada was able to establish an early presence in many of the new republics – for example, Ukraine.

Effective use of ICTs is essential to the success of micro-missions. ICTs can be a lifeline for the Canadian foreign service officer, providing information and help with such functions as administrative support. To this end, a hub and spoke system in coordination with the nearest full-service embassy is established and nurtured. Ann Collins, a Canadian foreign service officer with extensive experience in Canadian micro-missions, observed in a recent DFAIT newsletter that "with limited human resources at our disposal, mini-missions need a quick, reliable and cost effective connection to our colleagues and clients." In her view, "the introduction of mini-mission e-mail in the fall of 1995 was the single most important contribution to increasing the productivity of our St. Petersburg office."[24]

While one-person embassies date from the earliest days of the Canadian foreign service, ICTs dramatically raise their utility and performance by keeping officers in touch and allowing them to concentrate on their representation function. In times of crisis, they also allow a skilled officer with a laptop and a modem to create a Canadian diplomatic presence anywhere in the world.

Some argue that advanced ICTs may be fine for the embassies of rich countries, but are not relevant for developing countries. Many embassies of developing countries are highly resource-constrained and, in this respect, are akin to micro-missions. Like them, they may gain a large boost to their operational efficiency with the provision of fairly low-cost ICTs, such as electronic mail, a fax machine, or access to the Internet.

Virtual Teams. As issues and/or crises emerge, DFAIT now habitually uses informal and formal virtual teams to develop timely and informed responses. Less human capital is idled or wasted. For instance, during the Great Lakes crisis and the Ottawa Process campaign against landmines, DFAIT officers at national headquarters, the UN, and around the world were in constant communication. In many cases, tasks were assigned regardless of geographic locale. Thus, the department was better able to integrate "at the scene" perspectives to complement expertise drawn from throughout the organization.[25]

The use of such teams is rapidly becoming a standard operating procedure for DFAIT. Indeed, restrictions on the further development of virtual teams are more likely to come from the organizational side of the ledger, that is, from, hierarchy, particularly among departments. The ICT capacity is sound, proven, and already in use.

Establishing Dialogue between Disputants. There was a time when travel always involved passports, visas, medical shots, and punishing itineraries. Now, video conferencing and e-mail provide new opportunities to promote dialogue.

For the price of one return ticket to the Middle East, the UN Refugee Working Group, which is chaired by Canada, has established a list server called FOFOGNET (Friends of the Friends of the Gavel Net) that now includes some 180 select academic and practitioner participants from over 17 countries. This has provided DFAIT and the Canadian International Development Agency with an invaluable window into the international academic community and a means of updating them on recent developments. It has also led to the creation of the Palestinian Refugee Research Net (PRRN – www.arts.mcgill.ca/mepp/mepp.html). The PRRN archives policy papers and provides a directory of issue-relevant sites.

It should be noted that list servers, e-mail, and even video conferencing are not meant to and will not replace the need for face-to-face contact. Instead, they serve to complement face-to-face contact by creating an advanced starting point for discussions. For instance, the virtual community FOFOGNET has begun to meet in person. The first conference, held in December 1997, brought together a wide array of Palestinian, Israeli, Arab, and international researchers to discuss policy research priorities. This gathering proved so successful that a follow-up conference was held in February 1997 and additional workshops and forums are planned.

Electronic Public Diplomacy – A Starting Point. In terms of external applications, DFAIT has gained valuable experience by using information technologies in innovative ways to consult Canadians on foreign policy. In a pilot project, the department invited Canadians to provide insights on the country's foreign policy with regard to Haiti. DFAIT was very pleased with the quality of the feedback, and future consultations are planned.

ICTs and Diplomatic Organizations: Some Emerging Issues

The rapid evolution of ICTs make predictions hazardous. Add to that the cautionary truth that the fact that something is technologically possible does not make it desirable. The waters are muddied still further. Below is our attempt to identify some emerging trends or anticipated developments that seem, from today's imperfect view, to be particularly meaningful for the practice of diplomacy. The reader will note that the key factors associated with the trends vary. Some are technical, but the majority are fundamentally questions of bureaucratic and political will.

THE QUEST FOR THE PERFECT ELECTRONIC DESKTOP
With Bill Gates prophesying that "the computer will become the desk top," the quest for the perfect electronic desktop is likely to occupy governments and foreign service departments for years to come.

A well-organized electronic desktop consists of several elements, including seamless e-mail, word processing, spreadsheets, Internet access, intranet, access to specialized political, economic, and trade information, as well as corporate information and the day's news from a national, country, and international perspective. It will be a tall order to develop a desktop that is able to combine all these functions in a user-friendly and timely way without requiring excessive surfing or swamping the user in excessive detail. In addition to poor functionality, excess complexity and detail are the leading causes of user rejection of electronic interfaces. A key development to overcome this challenge will be the effective use of intelligent search agents and filters. While "perfect information" will forever remain an elusive goal, tomorrow's analyst will have more tools (though possibly even less time) with which to develop policy.[26]

With globalization creating a growing market in international intelligence, we expect that the desktop of the future will draw more extensively on intelligence gathered by the private sector, particularly financial and economic assessments, but also political assessments. Government is both a consumer and a producer of information. In the future, it will be taking a hard look at which types of information are best generated internally and which may be contracted out or left to the market.

TRIPLE-A GOVERNMENT AND THE CITIZEN OF THE WORLD

ICTs are becoming important vehicles for government program delivery. Indeed, the programs themselves are changing as departments throughout government redefine their value added in terms of information and knowledge dissemination. The resulting vision suggests a triple A government, that is, one that uses ICTs to deliver services *anytime*, *anywhere*, and for *anything*. As foreign ministries are often the public face and access point for a growing number of citizens abroad, it will be essential that consular services be integrated with and knowledgable of the broader government's electronic service delivery efforts.

DFAIT has already borrowed from the corporate model, adopting some of the practices of telemarketing. Outside of office hours, telephone calls to Canada's missions abroad are forwarded to Ottawa for responses. Another highly successful application is the posting of travel advisories on the departmental website that can be accessed by travellers throughout the world.

In addition, as part of the Canadian government's Government-on-Line initiative, DFAIT is working to deliver services and connect Canadians to the world by

- putting on-line its key services for Canadians, such as passports, consular services, export/import controls and other export services; and,
- improving access to on-line information for non-Canadian clients of Government of Canada programs (potential immigrants,

foreign visitors, investors, importers, business partners, temporary workers, students, and refugees).

INFORMATION SHARING AMONG FOREIGN SERVICE DEPARTMENTS

It will be interesting to observe the degree to which foreign service organizations introduce an understanding of soft power into their standard operating procedures. Of particular interest will be the attitude of the United States, which, due to its military and technological expertise, has, to quote Joseph Nye, Jr, a substantial "information edge." In the African Great Lakes crisis (1995), for example, the United States held back timely intelligence from the Canadian-led UN team because it disagreed with the mission. This, of course, was their right, but for Canada's purposes, it hampered the mission significantly, since it forced the UN to rely on inferior NGO-provided information on refugee numbers, flows, and status. Is this an example of the limits of information sharing? How will the dynamics change as the private sector becomes a bigger player in the field of intelligence?

There is little doubt that there are substantial benefits to information sharing and getting the facts straight. In many cases, the full sharing of information is a necessary prerequisite to the sharing of perspectives and, ultimately, of views. Nor is there much doubt that considerable economies can be reaped with more information sharing. On the other hand substantial entrenched interests, fears of becoming a "knowledge colony," and the necessity of retaining a capacity for assessment from the national perspective also need to be considered.

HYBRID DIPLOMATIC TEAMS

The Ottawa Process leading to the agreement on landmines represented an innovative partnership between diplomats and members of non-governmental organizations. Similarly, the basis of the success of Team Canada trade missions has been a strong working relationship among the Canadian government, industry associations, and firms. It makes sense that both of these success stories will be built upon in the future. Some have even speculated that this effort will lead to a *new diplomacy*.

The private sector and NGO community have growing presences on the international scene. Their actions will be increasingly subject to scrutiny as potential allies, rivals, or adversaries. While it seems likely that a closer working relationship will be the end result, outstanding questions remain about the motives and capacities of both groups.

In the case of the private sector, the issue surrounds whether the growing power of multinational enterprises will be matched by their growing sense of responsibility. What is the nature of MNEs' obligations in the societies in which they operate? With private sector direct investment in the developing world now at more than three times development assistance (from a rough parity in the early 1990s) and with trade flows outstripping world gross domestic product (GDP) growth by a factor of four, business leaders should not be surprised if this question is raised with increasing regularity and urgency by the public and government.

With respect to NGOs, the barriers to a closer working relationship revolve around the groups' advocacy function. To what extent can NGOs move from advocates to partners in both policy development and program delivery? Where should the lines be drawn? At what point has an NGO sold out? Are there times when advocacy is fundamentally at odds with responsibility?

CONCLUSION: BRINGING KNOWLEDGE MANAGEMENT TO THE CORE OF FOREIGN SERVICE ORGANIZATIONS

Foreign services are knowledge organizations. The timely dissemination, exchange, and even withholding of knowledge is the stock and trade of diplomats. Since foreign services are knowledge organizations operating at the global level, issues related to *knowledge management* must be considered essential to their success. Knowledge management, including the innovative use of ICTs, needs to be systematized and cultivated at the organizational level to a far greater extent than is currently the case in many diplomatic organizations. Knowledge management cannot simply be the responsibility of individual staff members, no matter how talented, as was often the case in the past with the tradition of the gifted generalist. Diplomatic organizations must do more by enabling their staff through accessible ICT applications and infrastructures.

Lou Gerstner, president of IBM, has remarked that knowledge management is the central challenge for organizations in the twenty-first century.[27] It is a challenge that is based more on organizational culture than on technology, and it means promoting horizontality within organizations and reducing knowledge hierarchies. The DFAIT experience confirms the view that the successful introduction of ICTs is primarily a human resource challenge. Diplomatic organizations embarking on this type of organizational change will face steep learning curves and staff scepticism that can only be overcome through careful planning, attention to detail, and making sure that staff receive adequate training and ongoing ICT support, and are made aware of the advantages of the new system from a user's perspective.

ICTs are having a significant impact on the practice of diplomacy and will have an even greater impact in the future. While it will take time for these impacts to be fully absorbed and understood, most foreign ministries need to raise their level of interest and engagement in ICTs and their uses. Failure to keep up with the learning curve will leave them playing catch-up to the disadvantage of their organizations, countries, and the citizens they purport to serve.

NOTES

1 Gordon Smith, "Driving Diplomacy into Cyberspace," *The World Today*, June 1997.
2 ADM Sub-committee, "Canada 2005: Global Challenges and Opportunities," draft interim report, Policy Research Initiative, Ottawa, 25 February 1997, 26–7.
3 See Robert Keohane and Joseph Nye, "Globalization: What's New? What's Not (And So What?)," *Foreign Policy*, Spring 2000: 104–19.
4 Alison Van Rooy, "New Voices in Civil Society," in Rowena Beamish and Clyde Sanger, eds, *Canadian Development Report, 1996–97* (Ottawa: North-South Institute, 1996), 42.
5 Global Opportunities and Challenges Network Research Team Reports, "Understanding How the New Instruments of Influence and New Partnerships (in Particular Non-state Actors) Can Support the Pursuit of Canada's Interests at Home and Abroad," August interim draft, 3.
6 See Anne-Marie Slaughter, "The Real New World Order," *Foreign Affairs* 76, no. 5 (September-October 1997): 183–97.
7 See Global Opportunities and Challenges Network Research Team Reports, "Understanding How the New Instruments of Influence."
8 This expansion of relations means that diplomats, defined narrowly as civil servants working in the foreign service organizations of national

governments, do not have a monopoly on state-to-state relations. Increasingly, the "architecture of relations," particularly among countries with close ties, will include civil servants whose primary responsibilities are not "diplomatic." While it is possible that the handling of a large amount of fairly routine administrative relations by non-diplomats could create problems, this has not been the case to date. In fact, the growing density of ties would seem to confer significant benefits that outweigh possible disruptions. In this case, familiarity appears to breed content and greater understanding. This development does, however, point to the need for foreign services to inform their civil servant colleagues of the state of play in bilateral relations.

9 Quoted from Ron Garson, paper for the Global Opportunities and Challenges Network Research Team Reports. See note 7 above. See also Gordon Smith and Moisés Naim, *Altered States: Globalization, Sovereignty and Governance* (Ottawa: International Development Research Centre, 2000), and also the website globalpublicpolicy.net.
10 Smith, "Driving Diplomacy into Cyberspace."
11 Ron Garson, paper.
12 For a contrary view, see Benjamin Barber, *A Place for Us: How to Make Society Civil and Democracy Strong* (New York: Hill and Wang, 1998).
13 Citizens want to be consulted, despite the fact that, relative to domestic issues, foreign policy issues barely register in polling on priority issues, in the absence of a crisis.
14 Frank Graves (Ekos Research), speech to Search Conference, "Improving Relationships within the Policy Research Community," Policy Research Initiative, May 1998, 44.
15 John E. Reilly, *American Public Opinion and U.S. Foreign Policy 1995* (Chicago: Council of Foreign Relations, 1995), 10.
16 Joseph S. Nye, Jr, *Bound to Lead: The Changing Nature of American Power* (New York: Basic Books, 1990).
17 ADM Sub-committee, "Canada 2005."
18 Gordon Smith, "Policy-Making on Cyberspace's Frontier: An International Perspective," speech to ITAC/ITAA Washington Summit, Combined Board of Governors dinner, 30 April 1997.
19 Smith, "Driving Diplomacy into Cyberspace," 156.
20 The authors are indebted to Rick Kohler, the chief information officer at DFAIT, for his assistance in developing this section.
21 Smith, "Driving Diplomacy into Cyberspace," 156.
22 Ibid.
23 The authors are indebted to Sigi Johnson, a foreign service officer from DFAIT, for her observations on micro-missions.

24 Ann Collins, "Being There on the Banks of the Neva," *Bout de Papier* 14, no. 4: 13.
25 For a more detailed discussion of how the Canadian foreign service has used "new instruments" in the pursuit of foreign policy objectives, see Policy Research Initiative, *Global Challenges and Opportunities*, vol. 3: *Case Studies* (Ottawa, September 1997).
26 "ICTs and Policy Research: The Quest for the Perfect Desk Top," *Horizons* (Policy Research Secretariat) 1, no. 2 (August 1998): 12.
27 Alan Nymark and Jim Lahey, "Executive Brief: Understanding the Knowledge-Based Economy and Society," *Horizons* (Policy Research Secretariat) 1, no. 2 (August 1998): 2.

7 Information Technology and Canada's Public Diplomacy

EVAN H. POTTER

INTRODUCTION

By the early 1990s a number of related forces – globalization, the information revolution, the end of the Cold War, and the growing democratization of international relations – together challenged traditional notions of diplomatic conduct, perhaps none more so than public diplomacy. This new world privileged persuasion, openness, engagement, and coalition building rather than the brute use of force. The objective was attraction, the creation of willing followers, rather than coercion. Around this time, the term *soft power* was coined by American political scientist Joseph Nye, to describe the use of ideas and knowledge to confer international influence: In the wired world this influence was power – an "information edge."[1]

Never before have borders been as open to the flow of ideas and images. With the increased availability of, access to, and speed of delivery of information, the ability of the state to promote its views to foreign publics has become a central feature of diplomacy. This public dimension of the information age includes not only sensitivity to public opinion, a long-standing concern, but also public engagement – consultation, outreach, and feedback.[2] From the mobilization of opposition to the Multilateral Agreement on Investment (MAI) to protests against human rights abuses in Chiapas and the anti-globalization protests on the streets of Seattle, Prague, and Quebec City, ordinary citizens, using both traditional and new information technologies, are developing new competencies and confidence for global engagement. As the former Canadian ambassador to the United States has put it, "The new diplomacy, as I call it, is, to a large extent, public diplomacy and requires different skills, techniques, and attitudes than those found in traditional diplomacy."[3] Advances in information technologies offer an opportunity to redefine public diplomacy, to move it from the sidelines to the core of diplomacy.

Canada, both as a middle power with limited military might but possessing a highly educated population and an international reputation as a coalition builder, and as a leader in the development of communication technology, would appear to be ideally suited to exercising soft power in support of its foreign policy goals and, in so doing, to redefining the conduct of its public diplomacy. The purpose of this chapter is to examine a paradox, namely, that despite these favourable conditions, Canada is at risk of being drowned out amid a cacophony of competing voices in the international arena because the public dimension has not yet been accorded primacy in its diplomacy. Over the past decade of declining foreign affairs' budgets, the potentials of new and old communications technologies to advance Canada's interests to foreign audiences have not been fully exploited. Ottawa has not identified international broadcasting and, in particular, the use of short-wave radio as a key element in its public diplomacy. Indeed, Canada has never had a truly coordinated and adequately resourced international information strategy to make its national presence felt in global communications. This sets the Canadian approach to public diplomacy apart from the public diplomacies adopted by many of its Group of Seven (G7) counterparts as well as those adopted by other middle powers to which it is frequently compared.

The first section of the chapter defines public diplomacy and explains how four major trends brought about by advances in information technology are affecting the public dimension of foreign policy making. The second section highlights the paradox of Canada's public diplomacy efforts in an information age. To provide a measure of comparison, the discussion outlines the investment in international broadcasting as a tool of public diplomacy by some of Canada's closest allies. The third section describes the role and extent of Canada's participation in international broadcasting (television, short-wave radio, and the new media). The fourth focuses on how governments' foreign ministries are responding to a twenty-four-hour news cycle, a global media, and an increasingly interconnected global civil society. The final section describes the initial Canadian response in the late 1990s to the new environment in the form of a proposed Canadian International Information Strategy.

THE CHANGING CONTEXT

Public diplomacy is the effort by the government of one nation to influence public or elite opinion of another nation for the purpose of turning the policy of the target nation to advantage (see www.publicdiplomacy.org//.htm for a variety of related definitions). National goals and interests are communicated to foreign publics through a variety of means, including international broadcasting, cultivation of foreign journalists and academics, cultural activities, exchanges, programmed visits, speakers, conferences, and publications. It is not just a one-way street, however. As Gifford Malone points out, the ability to understand others is indispensable to success: "If we strive to be successful in our efforts to create understanding for our society and for our policies, we must first understand the motives, culture, history, and psychology of the people with whom we wish to communicate, and certainly their language."[4] (Public diplomacy is distinct from a foreign ministry's public affairs role, which often uses similar activities and techniques but directs them at its own citizens to help them interpret the outside world from a national perspective and to raise their awareness of the diplomatic service's functions.)[5]

Revolutionary advancements in communication technologies, such as the convergence of data, audio, and video transmissions on a single pathway, the exponential increase in the use of the Internet, and the emergence of global television networks, in combination with more active civil societies around the world, are having four major impacts on the conduct of public diplomacy.

First, the rapid growth in access to telephones, radios, televisions, and the Internet means that countries can bypass the increasingly ineffective controls exercised by those target countries in which they wish to project their views.

Second, the reach of the traditional information media is being expanded by an unprecedented growth in global distribution systems. However, these media face competition and diffusion of impact owing to the deployment of electronic multimedia technologies such as the Internet. This is so because not only are the sources of information multiplying, but access by individuals to those sources is expanding exponentially.

Third, the ability of government to control, shape, or even influence information and its distribution has been dramatically altered. As we move from the long-standing few-to-many relationship of broadcast media to the population towards a many-to-many model that will allow individuals to interact with multiple information sources, government is being compelled to change its approaches to public diplomacy. It is true that as the number and scope of information media increase, government has the advantage of multiple outlets for information distribution; however, at the same time, government's traditional levers of influence on media content are becoming less effective. With government no longer having a monopoly over information, the hierarchical model of the past is evolving into a distributed decision-making model that privileges collaboration between officials and civil society.

Lastly, the information "noise" resulting from competing media is forcing individuals, corporations, and governments to make ever greater efforts to stand out from the pack. Expanding choices mean that individuals will gravitate to those information sources that are of the highest quality and credibility. Branding has become key: the same conglomerates that dominate the world of the television, movie, and publishing industries have come to dominate the Internet. With a multibillion-dollar electronic commerce market opening up, this branding is sure to intensify. It has been estimated that as few as a thousand large sites attract up to half the worldwide traffic on the Internet and, tellingly, that the majority are created from an American perspective. This will put additional pressure on other governments to ensure that their information outlets are attractive, compelling, updated regularly, and accurate.

THE IMAGE PROBLEM IN CANADA'S PUBLIC DIPLOMACY

How will the above trends affect Canada's pursuit of its public diplomacy objectives? It is conjectured that Canada's ability to influence other states will depend increasingly on factors that transcend raw economic or military power and that appeal to public perceptions abroad. This is what scholarly observers in the early 1990s, such as Andrew Cooper et al., referred to as Canada's ability to demonstrate intellectual leadership and be a "good dancer" on the international policy stage.[6] A more recent variant has been former foreign minister Lloyd Axworthy's promotion of Canada's *soft power*.[7] For both, public diplomacy is destined to become more and more central to the success of Canadian diplomacy in the decades ahead.

Canada's success, for example, in promoting a human security agenda, which includes protection of human rights, good governance, economic rights, environmental sustainability, support of the rule of law, will depend on how convincingly Ottawa advocates its positions to the citizens and leaders of other countries. On the trade side, having over 40 per cent of its gross domestic product (GDP) dependent on exports means that Canada's international reputation and image are fundamental to Canadians' well-being. The strategic use of information technology and electronic communications – whether through the establishment of an international television presence, the more strategic use of short-wave radio, the creation of an innovative national Internet site, or an aggressive strategy to use electronic networks to pitch Canadian ideas to global media and civil societies – will thus be a *force multiplier* for Canadian foreign policy. It will enable Canada to act as a knowledge broker, to influence others, and to ensure that the world views Canada as an attractive and sophisticated business partner.[8] The benefits of using information technologies in support of Canadian diplomatic initiatives were amply demonstrated by the Canadian government's alliance with a diverse group of NGOs that led to the ratification of the landmines treaty (known as the Ottawa Convention).

But there are some daunting challenges and paradoxes. One is the huge gap between how Canadians view themselves and how others perceive them. In the eyes of the world, Canada remains largely what it was a century ago – a resource economy – and it is therefore routinely passed over when foreign governments and businesses are contemplating investment or partnerships. To wit, Canada's share of world investment has dropped precipitously from 9 to 4 per cent over the 1990s. An international poll conducted in 1997 by the Angus Reid research organization found that fewer than 1 per cent of Germans and Japanese associate Canada with telecommunications or other technologically based products.

More than 50 per cent associated Canada with lumber, pulp and paper, and food.[9] In short, Canada has an image problem, with "image" being defined as one part presence and one part promotion.[10] A digital world thus presents multiple avenues through which Canada can gradually provide foreign audiences with a more balanced and accurate view of Canada by increasing both increased its presence and self-promotion.

It is ironic that Canada finds itself with this image problem for a number of reasons. The Department of Foreign Affairs and International Trade, as the eyes and ears of Canada abroad, has invested heavily in information technology over the last decade. Indeed, DFAIT is probably the most advanced foreign ministry from a technological standpoint, with a global communications infrastructure that is the envy of its G8 counterparts. The introduction of a global infrastructure, starting in 1993 with a universal e-mail system, SIGNET, and a telephone service, MITNET, created a transformation in the work of employees abroad and at headquarters. DFAIT spearheaded the use of virtual missions and virtual teams to deal with crises from the former Yugoslavia to the African Great Lakes in the mid-1990s. The new information technologies also facilitated coordination with non-governmental organizations and other government departments to build an international network of supporters for such high-profile initiatives as the campaign to ban landmines, leading to the Ottawa Convention.

As pointed out in the chapter by Smith and Sutherland (chapter 6), it is instructive that by 2000 the department had spent in excess of $100 million on informatics, twice what it did five years earlier. This was 7.4 per cent of the total budget in the fiscal year of 1999/2000 and was more than personnel costs (6.9 per cent), and more than the annual combined costs of all the department's foreign policy, trade, economic policy, international business development, and public diplomacy operations. The point is that although Canada has one of the most advanced communications systems of any foreign ministry, much of the improvements are internal – allowing officers to work with each other across the globe "almost as if people were down the hall," as one internal report put it. But until the Government-on-Line initiative (GOL) initiative started in 1999, the focus had been more on using information technology to serve the needs of internal audiences than on using it to promote Canada's image to external ones.

A second irony is that Canada is the world's second-largest producer of television programming for children; it is a leading producer of computer software; and it has among the highest per capita producers and users of information on the Internet (especially in the French language).[11] However, much of this activity is invisible to the rest of the world. Canadian television programming, in particular, is often absorbed into local broadcasting around the world, or, increasingly, into the program schedule of U.S.-based specialty channels. With the partial exception of TV-5, which broadcasts only in French, and Newsworld International/TRIO (a partnership between CBC and Power Corporation), which are not overtly branded as Canadian services, a Canadian television identity is more or less absent from international broadcasting.

Indeed, it could be said that Canada is practically invisible for all intents and purposes in government-financed international broadcasting. As will be shown below, the $15.52-million (FY 1999–2000) annual federal appropriation for Radio Canada International (RCI) and the contributions by the federal and Quebec governments of $9.1 million (including $500,000 channelled through the Canadian International Development Agency) and $5.2 million respectively to the international French-language broadcaster, TV-5, are but small fractions of what is being spent not only by the first tier of international broadcasters (mostly Canada's G7 counterparts), but also by other so-called middle powers. These amounts are even low compared to investments being made by some developing countries. Many other national broadcasters, in addition to expanding their international television coverage, continue to invest heavily in "old" radio technology to reach foreign publics, using satellites to improve audio quality, for example. James Woods states that the growth in "propaganda broadcasting" – led by the U.S., the former Soviet Union, China, Germany, and the U.K. – has been three-dimensional: that is, in numbers of countries, numbers of broadcasters per country, and numbers of transmitters.[12]

To put Canada's investment in international broadcasting into perspective, the following are the dollar values of the investments of some of its G7 counterparts: the extensive U.S. government network of overseas broadcasting organizations (Voice of America [VOA], Radio Free Europe/Radio Liberty, Radio and TV Marti, Radio Free Asia, Radio Democracy for Africa, and Worldnet), U.S.$386 million plus $40 million appropriation for transmitter construction;[13]

Deutsche Welle, $574 million, radio and TV; the BBC World Service, an estimated $455 million in public funds for radio and television; Radio France International, $204 million, radio only; and NHK Japan, $130 million, radio and TV. While it may be intuited that, given new communication technologies, there would be a decrease in the need to use short-wave radio, in fact quite the opposite appears to be true. The BBC World Service, whose costs are met mostly through a grant in aid from the Foreign and Commonwealth Office (FCO), is broadcasting more program hours than at any other time since the 1950s.[14] A good indication of the importance attached to political information broadcasting by the U.K. is that the FCO, obviously feeling that the World Service by itself was insufficient to promote Britain's interests to the world, had by the late 1990s expended an additional estimated £2 million on a commercial service, British Satellite News. This service produced a daily newsfeed (including text) that could be downlinked to television stations around the world at no charge (except for satellite time). In addition, the FCO finances the London Radio Service, which provides news programs that are distributed to over eight thousand radio stations in the United States. The United States, meanwhile, has been adding to its short-wave facilities in recent years (e.g., Radio Free Asia and Radio Democracy for Africa) and has inaugurated the use of Direct Broadcast Satellite to China and Iran.[15] In addition, the "control" of the airwaves by the private satellite Arab news network, Al-Jazeera, in the early stages of the war against terrorism in Afghanistan prompted the Bush administration to strengthen the VOA's Asian and Middle East programming.

Below this first tier of broadcasters are a number of medium-sized players, to which Canada usually compares itself, such as Radio Netherlands and Swiss Radio International with budgets of over $60 million, followed by smaller niche broadcasters such as Radio Australia and Vatican Radio; even less-developed countries – Brazil, Poland, Portugal – are now using television to present themselves abroad. The greatest expansion of state broadcasting capability is occurring in the Middle East, where a multi-frequency, global broadcasting capability is allowing Arab voices to be heard around the world.[16] All these state-supported broadcasters are striving to make their national voices heard in increasingly crowded airspace.

To the above public broadcasters must be added private and para-public enterprises such as CNN, which broadcasts in English around the world twenty-four hours a day and in Spanish in Latin America. Thanks to satellite technology, American media giants are able to launch global specialty channels almost overnight, reaching into every continent with local-language versions of popular programs. Through Eutelsat, the programming of many European nations is available to the Mediterranean basin, the Near East, and Latin America in Spanish and English. To these Western broadcasters must be added regional satellite channels. Brown notes that the Middle East Stations "with an explicit transnational remit such as Al-Jazeera, Arab News Network, Middle East Broadcasting Centre compete with nationally-based satellite services like Egypt's Nile News for the attention of audiences across the region."[17]

CANADA'S APPROACH TO INTERNATIONAL BROADCASTING

For most countries, the three core pillars of public diplomacy consist of state-supported international broadcasting, the media relations offices of their foreign ministries, and international cultural relations offices (e.g., the U.K.'s British Council, Germany's Goethe Institute, France's Alliance Française). The following section will provide a more detailed examination of state-supported broadcasting.

Short-Wave Broadcasting

The most experienced player in Canada's international broadcasting is Radio Canada International, which started broadcasting in 1945 as the CBC [Canadian Broadcasting Corporation] International Service (CBC-IS). RCI has also had the most problematic internal history, lacking adequate domestic governmental support at crucial periods of its evolution, even during the Cold War. In the words of Keith Spicer, the former chairman of the Canadian Radio-television and Telecommunications Commission (CRTC), "The history of RCI has been a series of intermittent terrors with reprieves at the last minute for a few years and then it starts all over again with a new breed of politicians who again do not know about it."[18] A thumbnail sketch of RCI's history will give the reader a flavour of the challenges that it has faced.

The establishment of the Iron Curtain around the former Soviet Union fostered the need for a new phase of operational policy development in Canada, one that involved "participation in the war of ideas."[19] As a result, in its early wartime broadcasting, CBC-IS was involved in "psychological warfare."[20] Prime Minister Lester B. Pearson ensured that differences existed between those broadcasts beamed to Western Europe, particularly NATO member states, and those sent to the Soviet bloc.[21] Although RCI's "country plan" priority listing was confirmed by the Department of External Affairs and reflected Canadian foreign policy, trade, tourism, immigration, and aid interests, the extent of the federal government's involvement it its operations was minimal. As early as 1963, with the Treasury Board having already decreased appropriations for RCI in 1955 and 1961, rumours floated around Ottawa that the government would sharply downsize, if not completely abolish, RCI.[22] Among the many perennial problems undermining RCI's organizational mandate were its own management's concern about the level of control External Affairs could exercise over it, the level of the CBC's commitment to short-wave broadcasting, and the question of whether one of the RCI's core functions was to broadcast in French and English to Canadians serving in the military or living abroad (this would become policy in the next decade).[23]

By the 1970s RCI's main operational policy continued to be to convey Canadian identity through the use of short-wave broadcasting, complemented by relays, transcriptions, and sound and visual recordings. With Canada's growing interest in the Pacific Rim, RCI lobbied for new resources that would allow Japan and China to be included within its target zones.[24] Despite such attempts to remain relevant to Canada's foreign policy needs, RCI continued to be hit by hard times in the 1980s and again between 1989 and 1996.

Perhaps the biggest problem was the lack of affinity between RCI and its parent, the CBC. By late 1989, RCI was no longer considered part of the CBC's core service, a decision stemming from decades of estrangement between the two organizations combined with the severity of cuts to the national broadcaster's budget. The CBC put the ball in the government's court and said it could no longer pay for RCI. A deal was arranged whereby half of RCI's budget was paid by the CBC and half by the federal government. However, this would not forestall the next crisis, in December 1996, when the CBC announced that it was closing RCI. Just a week prior to RCI having to turn off its transmitters and after employees had received their termination notices, DFAIT and Heritage Canada (as major shareholders), along with the Canadian International Development Agency (CIDA) and the Department of National Defence, rescued the service through a three-year shared-funding arrangement.

A decade of uncertainty had taken its toll. By the time of the reprieve, services in Polish, Czech, Slovak, Hungarian, German, Japanese, and Portuguese had ceased to exist; Canada had discontinued all broadcasting to foreign audiences in its own official languages except for a small number of newscasts. The shutting down of the Japanese service even led to a letter-writing campaign urging Canada to sustain the RCI service, the fourth most popular foreign short-wave service in Japan.[25]

By the end of 1998, with a new management team in place, the weekly audience for the broadcaster was approximately six million (not including China, India, and Southeast Asia, for which reliable figures are not available). Its broadcasts were in seven languages, generating approximately 153 hours of programming a week: a third CBC English-language, a third Radio-Canada (CBC French-language), and third RCI programming (14 hours in Russian and Ukrainian, 14 hours in Spanish, 10.5 hours in Mandarin, and 8 hours in Arabic). There was a concerted attempt by RCI management to reposition the broadcaster as a programmer (it placed its programs through FM and CD distribution to sixty-two countries, and it had real-audio availability on the Internet) and to distance itself from its antiquated image as a short-wave broadcaster. A $5-million investment in capital spending meant a 100 per cent change in RCI's infrastructure and reflected a desire that by the year 2000 the broadcaster would distribute digital radio programming. The only area of operations that, for reasons of cost, could not be dealt with immediately was the tailoring of programming to local conditions. It was of course recognized that, in an information universe exploding with new media sites every day, quality – measured in availability, attractiveness, ease of use, feedback, and reliability – would be a key factor in Canada's voice being heard abroad.

International Television

As mentioned, Canadian-branded television is virtually invisible in international broadcasting. TV-5, which reaches 66 million households on five continents and which was launched into the United

States in January 1998, is financed by leading members of La Francophonie. Although the bulk of this broadcaster's budget and programming is furnished by France, the Canadian federal government, through Canadian Heritage and the government of Quebec, acting as partners, together make the second-highest contribution. TV-5 has 15 per cent Canadian content in Europe, 13 per cent in Asia, 12 per cent in Africa, and 28 per cent in the United States and Latin America (where it is positioned as a specialty channel for French speakers). Although it is an important international projection of Canada's francophone character and a valuable showcase for Canadian French-language programming, the fact remains that it does not broadcast in languages other than French and its identity for viewers is influenced by the predominance of programming from France. And, as if to underscore the somewhat precarious nature of Canadian influence in international television, as of 1 August 2001, TV-5 Monde (based in Paris) has taken over the management of programming for the U.S. and Latin America, a function that had been based in Montreal.

There are a handful of other examples of Canadian broadcasters testing foreign markets. The problem is that they suffer from a lack of clear branding; that is, they do not necessarily identify themselves as Canadian networks. The Newsworld/TRIO joint venture broadcasts a mixture of Canadian news, drama, and documentary programming by satellite (DirecTV) to three million subscribers in the United States. WETV, a Canadian-developed block of programming – two hours a week – on sustainable development and cultural diversity, is sent to a network of broadcasters in Latin America, the Caribbean, Sub-Saharan Africa, and Western Europe. Canada Live News plans to provide a daily package of Canadian news (drawn from the private sector English-language Canadian network CTV, and the French-language, Quebec-based network TVA) for television broadcasters and a small number of other clients in Asia.

The New Media

The discussion thus far has focused on the increased use of traditional media in support of public diplomacy objectives; what then of the new media? One of the advantages of the new media is its greater ability to bypass traditional state controls (although, as China has demonstrated, the Internet can also be "jammed"). The challenge by the mid-1990s was to establish a credible presence in cyberspace. The existing "Canada sites" undermined public diplomacy objectives by portraying a drab and/or outdated image of Canada, conveying mostly government information. By the end of the decade the federal government's Government-on-Line (GOL) initiative sought to address this problem with a portal designed for non-Canadians.

Although many individual Canadian companies, individuals, and governments were represented on the Internet, there was no one site that drew these together and presented them in a coherent fashion to Internet users in other countries. The best Canadian private sector sites were confined to promoting individual companies; they did not propound the advantages of Canada as a business partner. Until GOL, existing Canadian Internet directories did not provide a single window on Canada from abroad; key sites were missing and many of those listed lack relevance.

Many Canadian government sites, while attractive and easy to navigate, were aimed largely at Canadians and did not reflect the richness of Canada for a foreign audience. DFAIT's website, when it was first constructed in 1995, provided an international benchmark for how to project a foreign ministry on the Internet and won plaudits from other foreign ministries for its high standards in editorial selection and technical presentation. That being said, by seeking to provide information on Canadian foreign policy (rather than on Canada writ large) to both foreign and domestic audiences (through speeches, policy papers, etc.), the site blurred the line between public diplomacy and public affairs.[26] In fact, it was conceived as a tool to "engage" Canadians.

The lack of an authoritative presence for Canada on the Internet created a vacuum that other countries had no trouble filling. The consequences were rather startling: with the exception of websites run by Canadian embassies in Latin America and Spain and RCI's Spanish-language broadcasts, in the mid to late 1990s the major source of information provided by Canadian governments in Spanish was that provided by the provincial government of Quebec. Canada.com, a commercial site operated by Southam News featured a sophisticated search-by-category function based on an American search engine that led users to Disney and other American sources but not to Canada's SchoolNet initiative, which provides Internet programming to Canadian schools. A search for government listed the U.S. Congress and the U.S. military; for culture, events from Broadway and London's West End. This did not mean that there were not many outstanding Canadian Internet sites (government departments, National Film Board, CBC), just that they required much browsing to reach.

As in the international television and radio media, Canada was falling behind its mid-sized competitors. Sweden, for example, boasted a well-organized site (managed by the publicly funded Svenska Institute) with information in Spanish, German, Japanese, Chinese, Korean, Spanish, French, and English. International broadcasters such as Deutsche Welle and the BBC were projecting national cultures and outlooks in expanded Internet sites that were examples of the convergence of media (having audio and video-streaming).

Starting in 1999, GOL began to address the problem of creating a definitive national presence for Canada on the World Wide Web. Its main purpose was to enable Canadians to interact more effectively and efficiently in the international environment, while at the same time reducing the cost of doing so and stimulating electronic commerce. GOL's principle of citizen-centric on-line service delivery aimed to brand Canada internationally as a best-practice model for good governance in the digital age. In fact, in 2001, Canada was ranked number one among twenty-two nations in e-government – ahead of the U.S., U.K., and Australia.

The Department of Foreign Affairs and International Trade, for its part, worked to connect Canadians with the world and the world to Canadians through its leadership of the international component of GOL, first by starting to put its key services for Canadians on-line, such as passports, consular services, export/import controls, export services, etc., and second by improving the access of non-Canadian clients to Government of Canada programs targeted at potential immigrants/newcomers to Canada, foreign visitors, investors, importers, business partners, temporary workers, students, refugees, and so on.

In summary, taken from a global perspective, Canada's international broadcasting has, in general, been uncoordinated and sporadic, responding to narrow market opportunities, or limited thematically or linguistically. With the exception of RCI, which is limited due to its small size, there has been no international broadcaster strongly identified with Canada. Although it could not be expected that Canada would produce an equivalent to the major broadcasters from the United States, there continues to be no systematic attempt to pursue an international branding strategy. The absence of a well-marketed international focal point for Canada on the Internet or on television is striking, given the number of Canadians developing communications technology and programming. It seems that Canada's capacity has been closer to that of the Nordics (Sweden, Denmark, and Norway), countries of significantly smaller size.

Short-wave radio as a means for communication has been framed as an open question. Now that the Cold War is over, much of the political uses of international short-wave radio broadcasting have ostensibly become dated. But a closer examination reveals that radio has also been affected by technological change, with audio programs being carried by cable and satellite and now increasingly over the Internet as well. And even though CNN may be observed worldwide through satellite transmission, in the Third World only the urban centres have access to television sets. The majority of the rural, uneducated, and broadly spread out world populations will continue to rely on short-wave radio broadcasting for news, information, and entertainment programming. Canada's radio broadcasting presence among the community of nations is thus pivotal.

THE GROWTH OF GLOBAL MEDIA AND CITIZEN ACTIVISM

The rise of mass communications over the last two decades represents a full-scale assault on the culture of diplomacy. As others have observed, the ubiquity of global media makes it increasingly difficult (though certainly not impossible as the chapter by Gilboa shows) for foreign ministries to maintain a culture of secrecy and exclusivity. Certainly, there will be a greater incentive to develop more collaborative relationships with the public. The static practice of cable reporting by foreign ministries will have to be supplemented by a dynamic network of information exchange. Epistemic communities, as have arisen around issues such as the environment or landmines, will increasingly include practising diplomats.

The vast majority of citizens form their opinions on the basis of information received from the mass media, in particular television and radio. The electronic media (both state and private), by acting either as propagandists or as filters, have the ability to legitimate government policy decisions before the widest audience. It is primarily through the media that governments receive immediate feedback from domestic and foreign audiences on the level of support for their policies. Thus, the monitoring of media and the cultivation of journalists, whether at home or in target countries, are key means for allowing foreign ministries to check the effectiveness of their messages and campaigns and to assess the images held by foreigners of their countries.

Despite public diplomacy having always needed the press and the press having always required open diplomacy, it can be said that diplomats have traditionally held ambivalent views on the fourth estate, viewing journalists as both enemy, particularly when in the midst of negotiations, and ally, when the government wished to garner public support for certain initiatives. However, it is increasingly being recognized that the media is not the enemy. The advent of 24-hour news cycles, the rise of global news organizations, and the proliferation of news and information outlets brought about by the Internet have challenged foreign ministries to adapt to a media-saturated age.

As their governments' windows to the world, foreign ministries are on the front lines in an environment in which the public feels an urgency to engage leaders and also demands feedback. There are growing demands on diplomacy to be more proactive, to educate and to inform, and for diplomats to step out of the shadows of anonymity and to engage the public through both the traditional and new media.[27] It has been easier in countries such as the United States for certain high-profile professional diplomats (e.g., Lawrence Eagleburger and Richard Hollbrooke) to become, in effect, public diplomats. However, in Westminster systems such as Canada's and the United Kingdom's, there has been a greater reluctance to have officials participate directly in on-the-record briefings, although this is gradually changing.

Another major challenge for public diplomacy relates to how the rise of the Internet has enabled the NGO community to marshal its resources. The active participation of well-informed NGOs at the UN women's conference in Beijing (1995), the Kyoto conference on climate change (1997), and the Seattle meeting of trade ministers in 1999 illustrates the new and complex environments in which diplomacy now operates. The rich connectivity afforded by the Internet has allowed interest groups far more direct influence on foreign policy development than at any other time in the history of Canadian diplomacy.[28] Certainly, the success of the Ottawa Convention on the elimination of landmines was in part due to the ability of different networks of activists to form connections – a testimony to the power of technology. The route of the Organization for Economic Co-operation and Development's (OECD's) Multilateral Agreement on Investment (MAI) is another example of how the influence of NGOs can be amplified by the Internet. A diplomat involved in the negotiations admitted to a reporter, "This is the first successful Internet campaign by non-governmental organizations. It's been very effective."[29] OECD secretary-general Donald Johnson, explaining the diplomatic setback, said, "It's clear we needed a strategy on information, communication, and explication." Hundreds of advocacy groups – from the Council of Canadians to the Third World Network – galvanized the opposition that led to its defeat. Canada's trade minister, Sergio Marchi, said that he had learned the lesson that "civil society should be engaged much sooner in a negotiating process, instead of governments trying to negotiate around them."[30]

THE CANADIAN INTERNATIONAL INFORMATION STRATEGY

How has the Canadian government responded to the expansion of global communications? The development of GOL has already been mentioned, but were there any grand plans that sought to address the roles and functions of both the traditional broadcasting instruments and the new media for the purposes of strengthening Canada's public diplomacy?

In December 1996, Canadian foreign minister Lloyd Axworthy, following a series of regional meetings on Canada's international relations, announced his intention to launch the development of a Canadian International Information Strategy (CIIS). "What we need," the minister told an audience from the Canadian high technology sector,

is a strategy that puts our domestic capacity to work to address the international and domestic challenges of the information age. A strategy that allows us to reach foreign markets more effectively and influence international audiences. A strategy that puts new information technology to work for Canada as it pursues its internationalist vocation, and as it seeks to advance our interests and values internationally. And a strategy that provides a sharp national focus, and is horizontally integrated, across both government and the private sector.[31]

This approach was amplified six months later, when the Liberal government's platform (*Red Book II*) stated that the CIIS would "focus on the strategies of information, through international broadcasting and electronic networks for trade, education, and development." In a nutshell, the idea was that the CIIS, by providing an integrated approach to presenting Canada's image abroad, would strengthen economic competitiveness, attracting investment, tourists, and students. This would in turn advance Canadian culture and values and, through the promotion of Canada's achievements on a world stage, serve as a unifying force at home. The CIIS obviously arose out of a desire to resolve the paradoxes and deficiencies, as discussed in this chapter, in Canada's approach to its public diplomacy. It was clear to the minister that the status quo was not good enough and that Canada risked falling irretrievably behind as some countries, a number of them not in the G7, aggressively exploited new and old technologies to enhance their international images.

It was left to DFAIT officials over the course of the following year, in a temporary CIIS secretariat, to put some flesh on the minister's proposal. Consultations on the CIIS clarified the need for a private-public partnership, including the strategic combination of Internet, radio, and television. The resulting Canadian International Information Network would provide a sustained electronic presence for Canada in the world. DFAIT proposed the creation of a "premier Internet presence" for Canada designed specifically for, and marketed to, foreign audiences; such a presence would provide an international window for the promotion of Canadian innovations. The duly named "Canada Internet Channel" would act as a gateway to information and investment opportunities, Canadian exporters, and Canada's cultural, tourism, education, and NGO sectors. In addition, it would lead foreign audiences to the wide variety of existing high-quality Canadian sites. Under the CIIS, Canada's neglected international broadcasting capacity was due for the greatest change. Radio Canada International, given its fifty years of experience in reaching foreign audiences, would receive new funding for its infrastructure; it would be asked to expand its digital broadcasting capacity; and it would be asked to introduce additional languages (e.g., Brazilian, Portuguese) of relevance to Canada as well as to produce more market-driven programming for specially targeted audiences of decision makers. In terms of an international television presence, there appeared to be no appetite, for reasons of cost and public perceptions, for a wholly government-owned and -run operation (as in the case of radio). Instead, inspired by the Australian government's decision to transfer its international television to the private sector in 1997, the Canadian government raised the idea of a joint public-private partnership to create a Canada Television Channel that would begin by broadcasting in the Caribbean, Mexico, and Brazil. The options for delivering programming included the use of regional direct-to-home satellite services, cable operators in urban centres, or individual over-the-air stations. The reason for starting in the Western hemisphere was low knowledge of Canada in Latin America, the prevalence and influence of television in the region, and the support that such exposure would give to Canada's foreign policy priorities in the hemisphere, running the gamut from human security issues to Canada's efforts to promote trade liberalization (e.g., NAFTA and FTAA). This new television presence would complement Canada's participation in TV-5.

Great Idea, Bad Timing

Innovative public diplomacy is not cheap public diplomacy, however. It was estimated that the cost of investing in all three media (radio, television, Internet), taking into account the synergies and private sector partnerships, would be about $100 million dollars, a considerable amount by Canadian standards and equivalent to about 9 per cent of the entire DFAIT budget. There were a number of hurdles for such an initiative. The timing for a major new investment to make Canada's voice heard around the world was not propitious. The announcement of the new strategy came three years into Program Review (1994–98), the largest-ever downsizing of the federal public service, which had as its goal the elimination of the federal deficit. There were no policy reserve funds anymore. The only way new initiatives could be funded was for departments to reallocate the funding of existing programs. "Good idea, but come back next year," was the message to DFAIT from central agencies. Second, and often overlooked in an examination of Canada's public diplomacy approach, was the difficulty in coordinating Canada's international broadcasting strategy when its major components – RCI and TV-5 – were not controlled by one department. It has not been easy for DFAIT to achieve interdepartmental momentum for a change in Canada's international information strategy. The closest form of coordination has come about through GOL, an expression of the Internet channel idea.

In sum, after an initial surge of interest, in part brought about by the funding crisis experienced by RCI in 1996, the issue of a concerted international information strategy slipped from the foreign policy agenda. It would take another three years for such a strategy to emerge again, this time in the form of a branding strategy driven by Investment Partnership Canada, a joint DFAIT and Industry Canada initiative. This branding strategy, targeted at specific regions in the United States (Boston and Dallas), was to help to increase the flows of investment into Canada. There were also notable Canadian public diplomacy successes in countries such as Taiwan and Japan, where Canadian diplomats launched innovative public relations programs to alert host populations to Canada and its interests. That said, DFAIT was never asked to lead a government-wide effort to brand Canada abroad, nor were there any major developments in rethinking Canada's international broadcasting strategy.

CONCLUSION

There is an old Cornish proverb that says, "the tongueless man gets his land took." In the information age, the absence of an international television, radio, and Internet "tongue" that states, "This is Canada," could prompt a disturbing question, "What is Canada?"[32]

A small, open economy such as Canada's is vulnerable by definition, meaning that it lives and dies by its reputation. Despite its failure to update the image it conveys to the rest of the world, a tremendous amount of goodwill is directed towards Canada by citizens around the world. For this reason, there is an urgent need to create a vibrant public diplomacy, using all the communication and technological tools at Ottawa's disposal, both to defend Canada's sovereignty and to promote its values and economic development. A renewed international information strategy, one that emphasizes international broadcasting, can play a pivotal role in projecting an informed, sophisticated image of Canadian views and concerns in a knowledge-based environment.

The following precepts will underlie any such strategy. First, credibility is key in a universe awash in information. The proliferation of new information outlets risks having the louder and louder soundbites smother dialogue. For this reason, government will be obliged to remain active in the marketplace of ideas. DFAIT will have to be the site of record across a host of issue areas. This will not mean a passive presence such as the simple loading of official documents on departmental sites on the World Wide Web or diplomats "lurking" in Internet chat rooms. There must be an attempt by government officials to engage civil society using the new technology. Furthermore, the price of admission in this new communications environment is not measured in kilowattage or broadcast hours, but in the quality and presentation of information. The Canadian government's websites must therefore reflect the most current technology while at the same time maintaining its ease of use, to cater to the most sophisticated foreign publics (many members of which will be future decision makers) as well as to the least adept users.

Second, DFAIT should establish additional surge capacity for crisis broadcasting to support Canadian diplomatic initiatives. Such broadcasts might be short-lived, as during a crisis or for a major conference or diplomatic or trade initiative. It has been suggested that this capacity could also be employed to counter a rogue regime's use of the media as a weapon of death. It will certainly be needed in the current context of the "war on terrorism" and the difficulty the United States and its allies have had in getting out their messages to broad publics in the Middle East and Pakistan.

Third, given the investment being made in short-wave radio by other countries, it would seem that old and new broadcasting technologies need to be developed in tandem. The question for the Canadian government is how to make a successful transition to the new technologies – to direct satellite broadcasting, to language services on the Internet, to enlarging its networks of affiliates – without abandoning the benefits of the old technologies.

Fourth, in the absence of significant core funding since the early 1980s in Canada's international broadcasting organizations, it will be difficult for Canada to launch an ambitious international information strategy, since it is starting from a relatively low baseline. To bring Canada in line with the capacities of some of its G7 counterparts would require considerable political will. However, it may not be realistic to compare Canada to other members of the G7, and Ottawa should perhaps aim for parity with other smaller countries. It may be necessary to start small, perhaps with a Canada Internet site, before addressing the more complex issues of an international television presence.

Finally, government departments – but especially foreign ministries with their disparate domestic and foreign audiences – find themselves (as do corporations) on a virtual treadmill, under constant pressure to meet the latest standards for technological development (e.g., websites, CD-ROMS, video links). Since the new technology costs as much as the traditional paper-based medium, the effort to keep pace effectively duplicates the costs and staff for public diplomacy. However, if public diplomacy is to be a key pillar of foreign policy in the next century, then these additional costs will have to be reflected in departmental appropriations.

NOTES

Author's Note: I am grateful to Gaston Barban and Daryl Copeland of the Department of Foreign Affairs and International Trade for their helpful comments. I would also like to thank Robert O'Reilly (former executive director, Radio Canada International) for favouring me with interviews. I have also benefited from a number of discussions with officials from DFAIT on the theme of "connecting Canadians with the world" as part of a broader exercise undertaken in the summer of 2001 to update Canada's foreign policy. Finally, the views expressed are those of the author only and should not be considered to represent the views of the department. This chapter is a revised version of a paper that was originally presented at the International Studies Association Annual Conference, Chicago, 2001.

1 See Joseph S. Nye, Jr, and William A. Owens, "America's Information Edge," *Foreign Affairs* 75, no. 2 (March/April 1996): 20–36; and an elaboration on the thesis of information technology and soft power in Robert O. Keohane and Joseph S. Nye, Jr, "Power and Interdependence in the Information Age," *Foreign Affairs*, 77, no. 5 (1998): 81–94.
2 Centre for Strategic and International Studies (Washington, D.C.), "Reinventing Diplomacy in the Information Age," draft report, 9 October 1998, 9, www.csis.org/ics/dia.
3 Allan Gotlieb, *"I'll Be with You in a Minute, Mr. Ambassador": The Education of a Canadian Diplomat in Washington* (Toronto: University of Toronto Press, 1991), vii.

4 Gifford D. Malone, *Political Advocacy and Cultural Communication: Organising the Nation's Public Diplomacy* (Lanheim, Md: University Press of America, 1988), 12.
5 Some countries make a clear distinction between the two functions. The U.S. Information Agency's mandate is to communicate U.S. interests to foreign audiences, while the State Department engages in public affairs activities within the United States. In the U.K.'s case, the Foreign and Commonwealth Office makes no provision for public affairs activities in its information department's budget; all its informational/communications activities (with the exception of a separate media relations office) are directed explicitly at foreign audiences.
6 See Andrew F. Cooper, Richard Higgott, and Kim R. Nossal, *Relocating Middle Powers: Australia and Canada in a Changing World Order* (Vancouver: University of British Columbia University Press, 1993).
7 DFAIT, Statements and Speeches, "Notes for an Address by the Honourable Lloyd Axworthy Minister of Foreign Affairs to the National Forum," 22 January 1999, 99/4; and Joseph S. Nye, Jr, "The Challenge of Soft Power," *Time*, 22 February 1999: 30.
8 See "Connecting with the World: Priorities for Canadian Internationalism in the 21st Century" (International Development Research Centre, 1997). This taskforce report can be found on the IDRC website at http://www.idrc.ca. The report emphasized the potential for information-based networks to link Canada with the developing world.
9 Angus Reid Group, *Canada and World, 1997*. This is the last major survey of foreign attitudes towards Canada. The survey sample consisted of 5,700 adults in twenty countries.
10 I am indebted to my colleague Gaston Barban for this observation.
11 A seminal treatise on the importance of culture in the projection of Canada's image abroad remains John Ralston Saul's essay on "Culture and Foreign Policy," which originally had been commissioned for the 1994 parliamentary review of Canadian foreign policy. It is reprinted at http://www.media-awareness.ca/eng/issues/cultural/resource/articles.htmJohn Ralston Saul.
12 James Wood, *History of International Broadcasting* (London: Peter Peregrinus, 1997), 130.
13 U.S. figures are drawn from CSIS "Reinventing Diplomacy," 45.
14 Wood explains that the expansion of the BBC World Service owes much to satellite technology (Wood, *History*, 169).
15 Ibid.

16 Wood attributes this expansion to the recognition by Arab governments of the strategic value of radio since the spoken word dominates the written in the Middle East (ibid., 4).
17 Robin Brown, "Power and the New Public Diplomacy" (paper presented at the British International Studies Association Annual Conference, Edinburgh, 17–19 December 2002).
18 Quoted in Arthur Siegel, *Radio Canada International: History and Development* (Oakville, Ont.: Mosaic Press, 1996), 175.
19 James L. Hall, *Radio Canada International: Voice of a Middle Power* (East Lansing, Mich.: Michigan State University Press, 1997), 70.
20 Ibid., 182.
21 Ibid., 70.
22 Ibid., 102.
23 Ibid., 157.
24 Ibid., 163.
25 Siegel, *Radio Canada International*, 180.
26 A DFAIT-related site that is more conspicuous by its focus on a domestic audience is that of the Canadian Centre for Foreign Policy Development (housed within DFAIT headquarters in Ottawa).
27 CSIS, "Reinventing Diplomacy," 66.
28 One of the earliest examinations of the relationship between information technology and interest groups can be found in William Stanbury and Ilan Vertinsky, "Information Technologies and Transnational Interest Groups: The Challenge for Diplomacy," *Canadian Foreign Policy* 2, no. 3 (winter 1995).
29 Quoted by Madelaine Drohan, "How the Net Killed the MAI," *Globe and Mail*, 29 April 1998.
30 Ibid.
31 DFAIT, "Notes for an Address by the Honourable Lloyd Axworthy Minister of Foreign Affairs, 'Foreign Policy in the Information Age,'" 96/53, Ottawa, 6 December 1996.
32 Hall, *Radio Canada International*, 188.

Index

African Great Lakes Crisis, 19, 169, 172, 182
Al-Jazeera, 184–5
al-Shara, Farouq, 99
Amnesty International, 18, 37, 41, 122, 153. *See also* human rights issues
anarchy, 13, 30, 32, 147; websites and Battle of Seattle, 67
Arab-Israeli relations, 18, 95, 98–9, 101
Arab News Network, 185
Arafat, Yasser, 97–8
Argentina, 59
Asia-Pacific Economic Co-operation Forum, 33
Assad, Hafez-al, 99
Australia, 57, 59, 190
Austria, 58–9
authoritarian regimes/dictatorships, 10, 33–4, 76, 113, 119, 188

Baker, James, 89
Barak, Ehud, 98
Begin, Menachem, 96
Bennett, W. Lance, 89, 112
Beschloss, Michael, 92
Blue Planet Project, 72
Bosnia, 11, 87, 102–3; Alija Izetbegovic, 96; Canadian embassy in Zagreb, 167
Boutros-Ghali, Boutros, 88
branding: national, 6, 21, 123, 180, 188, 190, 191, 196. *See also* Canada; image
Brazil, 59, 184, 195
British Broadcasting Corporation (BBC) World Service, 184, 190. *See also* broadcasting; television
British Satellite News, 184
broadcasting (short-wave): Canadian, 178, 181, 183, 185–91; in crisis situations, 197; funding shortfall (Canada), 197–8; live, 84; peace, 23; Radio Canada International (RCI), 183, 185–7, 190, 194, 196; second-tier short-wave broadcasters, 184; web-based, 67. *See also* television; France; Germany; Japan; United Kingdom; United States
Burns, Nicholas, 97
Bush, George, Sr, 90–1, 100, 103

Cable News Network (CNN), 99, 122, 184, 191. *See also* CNN effect
Camp David Accords, 96–7, 101
Canada, 10, 13, 14–15; coalition building, 14,

178; human security agenda of, 181, 195; image problem of, 182, 189; initiate consultation process, 10; knowledge broker, 181; as middle power, 178; soft power re U.S., 159, 172, 196. *See also* Department of Fisheries and Oceans; Department of Foreign Affairs and International Trade
Carleton University, 137
Carter, Jimmy, 96
Castells, Manuel, 50–1
Center for Strategic and International Studies (CSIS), 3, 6, 121
Cheney, Dick, 112
Chile, 59
Chirac, Jacques, 133
Chomsky, Noam, 35–6, 37
Christopher, Warren, 97
citizen activism, 8, 128; global citizenship, 71; related to global media, 191–3; and technology, 16, 34, 52, 62
Clarke, Tony, 71
Claude, I., Jr, 94
Clinton, Bill, 99, 103; Camp David, 98; re television, 89, 96–7
CNN effect (curve), 11, 83, 102–3; Bosnia, 88; definition of, 85; effect on diplomats, 111–15; humanitarian crises, 86–7; level of determinism of, 88–9; perceived constraints of, 93; reforms needed, 104. *See also* television
Cold War, 8, 14, 21, 23, 42, 113, 130, 185; post–Cold War, 34, 54, 87, 89, 100–1, 102, 144, 158–9, 177, 191
Comor, Edward, 36
consular services, 14, 171, 190
convergence, 4, 190
Cooper, Andrew, 181
Council of Canadians, 61, 72, 78; anti-MAI campaign, 57, 193; Maude Barlow, 71
Cousteau, Jacques, 133
Cuban missile crisis, 92, 114

Denmark, 191
Department of Fisheries and Oceans (Canada), 138, 140
Department of Foreign Affairs and International Trade (Canada), 8, 182; adaptation of staffing and operations, 20, 166–8; Canadian International Information Strategy, 179, 193–6; consultation and dialogue with civil society, 10, 14, 17, 75, 169–70; ExportSource as web-based service, 163; fish war with Spain, 138; Government-on-Line, 171–2, 182, 189–90, 193, 196; integration of information and communications technologies in, 14, 152, 161–70; language training software, 164, 197; micro-missions, 14, 167–8, 172; MITNET, SIGNET/Winframe internal communications systems, 162–4, 182; mobility of operations upgraded, 163, 167; Ottawa Process (landmines), 14, 157, 165, 169, 181–2; short-wave broadcasting strategy, 186; websites, 163, 189. *See also* foreign ministries
Derian, James Der, 143
Deutsch, Karl, 32
Deutsche Welle, 184, 190. *See also* broadcasting
Dickie, John, 99
Digital Global, 118
diplomacy: closed door, 11, 96–8; cooperative security agenda (drug trafficking, infectious diseases), 7, 14, 21; defined, 7, 83; economic, 18, 181; just-in-time, 143; media, 11, 85–6, 102; mission-oriented, 23, 143; networked, 154; open, 94; shuttle/travelling, 98–9, 129; summit, 99–101, 129; traditional, 84, 90, 152, 166; world society view, 131. *See also*

Foreign ministries;
new diplomacy; public diplomacy;
Drudge, Matt, 120, 122

Earth First, 37
Eayrs, James, 15, 130–1
Eban, Abba, 84–5, 94, 102
Ebo, Bosah, 98
Egypt, 185
Eisenstein, Elizabeth, 38
electronic commerce (e-commerce), 180, 190
electronic mail (e-mail), 34, 60, 163, 168; anti-MAI campaign, 61; Battle of Seattle, 64–6. *See also* Department of Foreign Affairs and International Trade
elites, 18, 76, 79, 179; media, 36, 90; political, 112; public suspicion of, 157–8
European Union (EU), 33, 74

Fitzwater, Marlin, 90–2
Foreign and Commonwealth Office (FCO, U.K.), 17, 123; broadcasting, 184; and London Radio Service, 184
foreign ministries: broadcasting, 185; connectivity of, 160–1, 191; consultation with civil society, 21, 75, 122, 131, 157; environmental issues, 144; generational and cultural divide in, 17–18, 20; interactive protocols, 79; as knowledge organizations, 19, 120–3, 173; public relations/diplomacy, 17, 154, 177; relevance of, 7, 8, 22–3, 100, 102–4, 111, 122, 130–1, 155; time pressures affecting, 156–7. *See also* Department of Foreign Affairs and International Trade; diplomacy
Foucault, Michel, 51
France, 12–13, 16, 185; Greenpeace, 131–6; and MAI, 57, 59; Radio France, 184; TV-5 and, 188
Fransworth, D., 83
Free Trade Agreement of the Americas (FTAA), 73, 75, 195
Friends of the Earth (FOE), 60, 64
Fukuyama, Francis, 34
Fulton, Barry, 121

Garson, Ron, 154
Gergen, David, 85, 93
Germany, 59, 183, 185
Gerstner, Lou, 173
Geser, Hans, 52
Gill, Stephen, 36,
Gilpin, Robert, 30
globalization: economic, 41, 43, 50–1, 54–5, 77; environmental, 71; intelligence and, 171; information technology as related force, 177; media and, 73, 84; politics and, 50, 76, 78; protests against, 54, 63, 71, 157, 177; technology and, 50–1, 65, 67, 70, 152
global society: emergence of, 9; government control in, 19; market forces and, 37, 40, 72
Global Trade Watch, 64
Global Water Partnership, 153
Gonzalez, Elian, 73
Gorbachev, Mikhail, 91; summits with Reagan, Bush, 100–1
Gore, Al, 33
Gotlieb, Allan, 138, 140
Government-on-Line (GOL, Canada). *See* Department of Foreign Affairs and International Trade
Gowing, Nik, 19; on CNN, 88–9
Gramsci, Antonio, 36
Graves, Frank, 157
Greenpeace, 12–13, 16, 37, 41, 122, 153; campaign vs. French nuclear testing, 128–36; decentralized, 135; use of satellite technology to allow witnessing, 41, 132–3
Group of Seven (G7), 36, 178
Gupta, Vipan, 118

Haiti, 89, 170
Hallin, Daniel C., 113
Ham, Peter van, 6
Hampson, Fen, 144

hard power, 30, 42
horizontality, 173–4;
corporations, 51;
Internet and, 51; of
issues, 153; of networks, 77; resistance
networks and, 54
humanitarian crises, 12,
85–8, 101, 103; CNN
effect, 93; HIV/AIDS,
73. See also CNN
effect; human rights
issues; Rwanda;
Somalia
human rights issues, 7,
11, 73, 76, 102, 153,
177, 181; websites,
15, 16, 52. See also
Amnesty International
Hurd, Douglas, 88, 91,
94, 102
Hussein, Saddam, 87,
92
hypermedia environment, 6, 8, 9, 22, 27
hyper-realities, 27, 44
hypertextuality, 5

image, 6, 103, 140, 177;
Australia, 136; Canada, 180–5, 188, 194,
196; Iran, 99; national, 85, 93, 192;
Spain, 141, 146; symbolic power, 114. See
also branding
information: accelerated pace of, 5, 89,
92, 102, 122, 154;
accuracy and credibility of, 19, 121–3, 134,
156–7, 197; as data,
122; decentralization,
5; gatekeepers to control, 5, 145; glut of,
12, 19, 121–2; as
noise, 180
information and communication technologies
(ICTs): in Battle of
Seattle, 65; costs of, 5,
12, 115–17, 120, 135,
162, 182, 195; dislocation, 5; driver of
change, 5, 16; facilitate horizontal organizational networks, 77;
hardware in Canadian
foreign ministry,
162–3, 170–1; impact
of, 10, 77–8; as international issues, 160;
and new balance of
power between state
and non-state actors,
22–3, 155; organizational support for,
161; Ottawa Process
and, 4, 17; program
delivery, 14, 171–2;
revolution in, 3–4;
social capital, 77; time
vs. space, 143. See also
Department of Foreign
Affairs and International Trade; electronic mail; Internet;
non-governmental organizations; websites
Innis, Harold, 3, 9, 29,
38
interest groups, 5, 7, 34,
192
intergovernmental organizations (IGOs), 54,
67, 70–1, 76
International Monetary
Fund (IMF)/World
Bank, 53, 60, 67; campaign, 73; Fifty Years
Is Enough Campaign,
53; Jubilee 2000, 54.
See also Multilateral
Agreement on Investment; World Trade
Organization
international relations
(IR) theory, 8; ignoring communications,
28. See also liberalism; Marxism; realism; postmodernism
Internet, 98, 130, 180,
187, 189, 191–2;
anti-MAI campaign,
55–62; Battle of Seattle, 62–73; BBC, 190;
democracy and, 33,
160; digital divides,
70; diplomacy, 79;
drawbacks of, 61; foreign ministries underutilizing of, 20, 24;
exponential growth
of, 4, 6, 10, 35; and
government, 23, 180;
intellectual property
and, 58; jamming of,
188; libertarian tendencies of, 160; and
media, 66, 145; mobilization of resistance
through, 66–9, 70,
73; public education,
67, 70, 73; role in
Canada-Spain fish
war, 13, 15, 128, 132,
134, 136–43, 145;
sharing of information through closed
lists, 65; Svenska
Institute (Sweden),
190; transnational
social movements, 37,
50. See also Depart-

Index

ment of Foreign Affairs and International Trade; electronic mail; non-governmental organizations; websites; World Wide Web
Iraq, 87, 89
Islam, 23

Jakobsen, Peter, 89
Japan, 184, 186–7, 190, 196
Johnson, Lyndon, 114
journalism, 19, 23: indexing re government, 89, 112; in summit diplomacy, 101. *See also* media; public diplomacy

Kalb, Marvin, 86
Kennan, George, 87
Keohane, Robert O., 122
Khatami, Mohammed (Iran), 99
Kissinger, Henry, 93, 95, 98–9
Koppel, Ted, 103
Kosovo, 87, 102, 113
Kropotkin, Petr, 28
Kurz, Robert J., 114

Lake, David, 36
landmines, 14, 191, 193; campaign to ban, 48, 157, 165. *See also* Department of Foreign Affairs and International Trade (Ottawa Process)
Law, David, 36
leadership, 104, 122, 166–7, 190
leaks, 98–9; anti-MAI campaign, 56, 65;

Free Trade Agreement of the Americas, 75; World Trade Organization, 65; Wye conference, 98
Ledeen, Michael, 94
liberalism, 9, 31–5, 43
lobbying, 21, 60, 65; and information and communications technologies, 78
London Radio Service, 184
Luger, Richard, 85

McLuhan, Marshall, 3, 9, 28, 29, 38
Macomber, William, 111
McTaggart, David, 135
Malone, Gifford, 179
Manheim, Jarol, 112
Marchi, Sergio, 193
Marxism/neo-Marxism, 9, 35–8, 43
Matthews, Jessica, 135
media, 7, 18, 52–3; alternative (net-based), 67; anti-MAI campaign, 55–7, 60, 62; Battle of Seattle, 67; censorship, 114; conglomerates, 43; controls on, 114, 180; democratization of, 27; and diplomacy, 84–5, 95, 98, 101, 102–3; in diplomatic negotiations, 94–101; events, 100–1, 134; foreign ministries dependent on, 20; and government (medialism, teledemocracy), 85, 113; news structure of, 36; new technologies, 110, 115–20;

ownership, 35, 37; print, 16, 35, 90; radio, 4, 16, 23, 35, 145, 178, 183; rise of, 4, 23, 179; sensationalism, 67, 73. *See also* broadcasting; CNN effect; elites; Internet; journalism; new media; satellites; television
Médecins sans Frontières, 73
medium theory of communications, 9, 29, 38–43
Mermin, Jonathan, 89
Mexico, 195
Middle East Broadcasting Centre, 185
Milosevic, Slobodan, 96
Multilateral Agreement on Investment (MAI), 10, 17, 48, 177; anti-MAI campaign, 55–62; Internet, 56–7, 193; mailing lists, 60; multinational enterprises, 152, 156; responsibility of, 173

Netanyahu, Benjamin, 97
Neuman, Joanna, 85, 103
Nevitt, Neil, 157
new diplomacy: defined, 84, 99; media events, 100–1; and Team Canada trade missions, 172
new media, 4, 23, 119–20; and Canada, 178, 188–91
new politics, 77–9

non-governmental organizations (NGOs), 10, 12, 13, 17–18, 19, 43, 110; alternative values, 77; authenticity, 75; and Battle of Seattle, 62–73; coalition building, 22; as conduits, 70; government consultation with, 74–5; imbalance between, 72; impact on politics, 77; impact on public and international agendas, 54, 62, 73–6, 130; and Internet, 52, 57; journalists, 66; proliferation of, 53, 153; representation, 75, 173; and resistance, 48–79; transnational business, 76. *See also* Greenpeace; Internet; media; Multilateral Agreement on Investment; transnational coalitions/constituencies; transnational social movements; websites; World Trade Organization

North American Free Trade Agreement (NAFTA), 33, 48, 53, 56, 60, 195

Norway, 191

nuclear testing, 13, 132, 134–5, 144

Nye, Joseph S., Jr, 84, 122, 158, 172, 177

Ogden, Frank, 157
O'Heffernan, Patrick, 103

Ohmae, Kenichi, 33
Organization for Economic Co-operation and Development (OECD), 55, 60; anti-MAI campaign, 55–62; relations with non-government organizations, 56
Owens, William, 84

Pal, Leslie A., 10, 15, 16, 18, 52, 76; on calibrating information and communications technologies, 20
Palestinian Refugee Research Net, 169
Panopticon, 51
Pardos, Jose Luis, 136–43
Pearce, David D., 112
Pearson, Lester B., 186
Perot, Ross, 90
Persian Gulf War, 12, 87, 89–90, 92, 103, 112, 115, 118
Poland, 184
Portugal, 184
postmodernism, 42, 143
Powell, Colin, 89, 91, 112
Powell, Jody, 97
Powlick, Philip, 93
propaganda, 35, 159; disinformation, 18; propaganda broadcasting, 183, 192
Public Citizen, 57, 64; Lori Wallach, 64; Ralph Nader, 64
public diplomacy, 13, 14, 21, 23; Canada-U.S., 140, 154–5; Canadian broadcasting and, 187, 194; Canadian International Information Strategy and, 195; defined, 179; at Department of Foreign Affairs and International Trade (Canada), 170–1, 190; educational role, 158, 192; ethnic minorities, 20; in fish war, 129, 137, 144, 147; and journalists, 192; and non-governmental organizations, 192; as passive, 17; vs. public affairs, 179, 189; redefined by information and communications technologies, 178–9

public opinion: demands to participate in foreign policy making, 7, 192; fragmentation of, 6–8, 10, 13; IMF/World Bank campaign, 73; polling research (Canada), 73, 181; and pressure on foreign policy decision-making, 85, 92–3; shaped by media, 88, 94, 100–2, 112–13; Spain's failure to mobilize in fish dispute with Canada, 140, 146
public trust, 7, 122–3

Quebec, 183, 188–9

Radio Australia, 184
Radio Netherlands, 184

Rainbow Warrior, 132, 133–4
realism theory, 8–9, 29–31, 43
real-time news and information, 4, 19, 89, 110–11, 115, 145; re ambassadors, 90; re government, 5; levelling effect of, 113. *See also* diplomacy
Ridgway, Rozanne, 87
rogue states, 12, 120, 197
Rosenau, James, 6, 51
Rubin, James, 97
Rwanda, 11

Sadat, Anwar, 96, 101
Sandia National Laboratories, 12, 118
satellite technology, 4, 11, 12, 19, 34, 110, 116, 130, 185, 191; commercial, 117–18; expense of, 115, 116; low-level private spy satellites, 18, 110; micro air vehicles, 12, 19, 117; National Imagery and Mapping Agency (NIMA), 122; radar satellites, 43; radio, 183; remote-sensing satellites, 110, 113, 116; SPOT, 12, 118
Schlesinger, James, 103
secrecy, 11, 16–17, 102; Arab-Israeli peace process, 18, 95; re diplomacy, 84, 86, 90, 94, 122, 157; MAI talks and, 56; media, 85, 96, 97–8; military, 118, 121; re non-governmental organizations, 13; talks re Northern Ireland, 95; venues to ensure, 95–7
Singapore, 59
Slaughter, Anne-Marie, 153
Smith, Gordon, 130–1, 139
social movements, 8, 14, 17, 50; global governance, 136, 141; global responsibility, 71
soft power, 15, 21, 30, 144; Canada and, 178; defined, 84, 158–9, 177; emotional persuasion in, 20; investment in, 159; vs. propaganda, 159. *See also* public diplomacy
Somalia, 11, 87, 88, 89, 101, 103, 115
Spain, 13, 15, 189; Canada-Spain fish war, 136–47
Spicer, Keith, 185
Stephanopoulos, George, 87
Stop GATS Attack, 74
surveillance and intelligence, 12, 18, 22–3, 27, 42–3, 51, 134; democratic surveillance, 51; electronic-eavesdropping, 43; U.S. EP-3 (China), 119; via satellite, 110. *See also* satellites; secrecy
Sweden, 190–1

Swiss Radio International, 184

Taiwan, 196
Tapscott, Don, 164
telegraph, 6, 28
telephony, 119; secure lines, 84, 98; via satellite, 119, 135. *See also* Greenpeace; satellites; surveillance
television, 4, 12, 16, 18, 35; Canadian (international), 183, 187–8, 195; crisis, 11, 101; re diplomacy, 11, 85, 86, 87–9, 90, 101, 102–3, 121; flyaway units, 115–16; global networks, 83; Kurdistan, 41; re new actors in foreign policy, 11; Persian Gulf War, 92; re public diplomacy, 23; re public opinion, 88, 112; satellite telephony, 119; Soviet Union, 90–1; Tiananmen Square, 91; and transparency, 11, 116–23; TV-5 (Canada), 183, 187–8, 195–6; U.S. networks, 37, 103, 115. *See also* broadcasting; CNN effect; Department of Foreign Affairs and International Trade; media; public diplomacy
terrorism, 14, 102, 197; 11 September attacks, 23; info-terrorism, 13, 22

Thailand, 5
Tiananmen Square, 87, 91, 103
Tobin, Brian, 129, 139, 140, 142, 145, 146
transnational social movement organizations (TSMOs), 10, 41–2, 48–9; alternative values, 77; civil society organizations, 153; and environmental issues, 72, 141, 191
transparency, 5, 10–11, 17, 18, 21, 34, 44, 67, 75; new global level of, 12, 116–20; post-CNN effect, 11; and WTO members, 74
Trilateral Commission, 36
Tudjman, Franjo (Serbia), 96
Tupac Amaru hostage crisis, 166
TV-5 (Canada), 183, 187–8, 195–6. See also broadcasting; television

United Nations (UN), 132; environmental issues, 53, 87, 153; Global Compact, 76
United States: China, 91, 95; EU, 74; French-language broadcasting directed to, 188; MAI and, 56, 59; overseas broadcasting of, 36, 183–4, 191; public diplomats,

192; State Department, 17. See also broadcasting; diplomacy; public diplomacy; soft power
United Kingdom (U.K.), 59, 183–5, 190, 192
Uruguay, 59

Vatican Radio, 184
video technologies, 66, 116–17; re Canada-Spain fish war, 145; flyaway units, 115–16; micro air vehicles, 117. See also satellites, television
Vietnam, 11, 89, 101; Gulf of Tonkin incident, 113–14
virtual teams, 163, 169–70
Voice of America, 183–4

Weaver, Lisa Rose, 119
websites: anti-MAI campaign, 55, 57–62, 64–70; Battle of Seattle, 65; Canada website needed, 181, 189–90, 196; cost of for Canada, 198; foreign ministry sites, 75; quality of content, 24, 61, 197. See also Internet; World Wide Web
Whitaker, Reg, 51
Wilson, Woodrow, 84, 85
Winham, Gilbert, 14
Wired magazine, 33

Woods, James, 183
World Economic Forum, 76
World Social Forum, 71
World Trade Organization (WTO), 10, 33, 48, 50, 157, 161; Battle of Seattle, 62–73; consultation with NGOs, 74–5; greater transparency through website, 74; *WTO Observer* as online newspaper, 66. See also Internet; non-governmental organizations
World Wide Fund for Nature (WWFN), 60
World Wide Web, 5, 10, 16, 18, 27, 37, 41, 110; collaboration through linking, 68; searchable archives, 67; Southern perspective on, 68; WTO official sites, 67. See also Department of Foreign Affairs and International Trade; Internet
Wright-Patterson Air Force Base, 96–7
Wye Plantation, 96–7

Yeltsin, Boris, 91
Yugoslavia, 23, 182

Zaire, 163
Zapatista rebellion, 48–9